SUICIDE –
THE BIBLICAL VIEW

SUICIDE –
THE BIBLICAL VIEW

*How to Biblically Handle
Disappointment,
Discouragement,
Defeat, Depression,
and Despair*

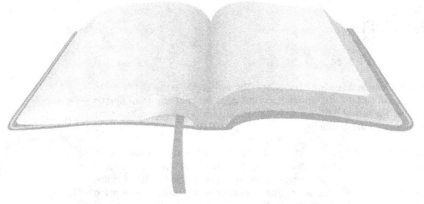

"Out of my distress I called on the Lord; the Lord answered me and set me free."
Psalm 118:5 (ESV)

Marti Scott

XULON ELITE

Xulon Press
555 Winderley Pl, Suite 225
Maitland, FL 32751
407.339.4217
www.xulonpress.com

© 2023 by Marti Scott

All rights reserved solely by the author. The author guarantees all contents are original and do not infringe upon the legal rights of any other person or work. No part of this book may be reproduced in any form without the permission of the author.

Due to the changing nature of the Internet, if there are any web addresses, links, or URLs included in this manuscript, these may have been altered and may no longer be accessible. The views and opinions shared in this book belong solely to the author and do not necessarily reflect those of the publisher. The publisher therefore disclaims responsibility for the views or opinions expressed within the work.

Unless otherwise indicated, Scripture quotations taken from the King James Version (KJV) – *public domain*.

Unless otherwise indicated, Scripture quotations taken from the English Standard Version (ESV). Copyright © 2001 by Crossway, a publishing ministry of Good News Publishers. Used by permission. All rights reserved.

Unless otherwise indicated, Scripture quotations taken from the Holy Bible, New International Version (NIV). Copyright © 1973, 1978, 1984, 2011 by Biblica, Inc.™. Used by permission. All rights reserved.

Paperback ISBN-13: 978-1-6628-8522-8
Ebook ISBN-13: 978-1-6628-8524-2

Dedication

This book is dedicated to the memory of my parents, Ken and Shirley Moore, who brought me into this world, gave me a Christian upbringing, and modeled the Christian life before me. Though assuredly not perfect, they were the greatest human influence in my becoming a follower of Jesus Christ. May Jesus Christ be praised!

It is dedicated also to the memory of my brother, David Moore, who took his own life in 2005, thereby starting this book in process. May Jesus Christ be praised!

It is dedicated to the memory of my sister, Nancy Heldt, who died in 2021 of complications from COVID -19. I miss our conversations about spiritual matters, and I am disappointed that she will not be able to read my book. However, I am glad that she has already reached Heaven – her final destination and her ultimate goal – due to her faith in the sacrificial death of Jesus Christ on the cross on her behalf. May Jesus Christ be praised!

My only remaining immediate family – my twin sister, Lynnie Klingler, and my younger sister, Kendra Ro – both traveled the road of our brother's suicide with me. In addition, we have often talked together about our profound gratitude for the influence our parents have had on our lives. It is fitting that I complete the honor of our family by listing their names as well. May Jesus Christ be praised!

Lastly, and most importantly, I dedicate this book to my Lord and Savior, Jesus Christ, and to His kingdom. He is the source of every good thing. He is the Author and Finisher of my faith. He is the great Comforter. He has guided my life, bringing me to the place where I have the desire and the wherewithal to write this book. Praise God from whom all blessings flow!

Table of Contents

Dedication vii
Forward xi

Part 1
Suicide – The Biblical View

Chapter One: The Suicide 1
Chapter Two: The Unbiblical Nature of Suicide 8
Chapter Three: The Implications of Suicide. 25
Chapter Four: A Foiled Plan 35
Chapter Five: A Mother's Rescue 40
Chapter Six: A Wife and Child's Aftermath. 44
Chapter Seven: A Father's Cry 47
Chapter Eight: A Husband's Healing 50
Chapter Nine: Practical Help for the Desperate 55
Chapter Ten: An Outcome Worse than a Difficult Life 66
Chapter Eleven: Conclusion 71

Part 2
How to Biblically Handle Disappointment, Discouragement, Defeat, Depression, and Despair

Chapter Twelve: Introduction 75
Chapter Thirteen: The Study of Hagar 84
Chapter Fourteen: The Study of Job 91

Chapter Fifteen: The Study of Ruth............................110
Chapter Sixteen: The Study of Joseph........................125
Chapter Seventeen: The Study of Saul 167
Chapter Eighteen: The Study of David........................183
Chapter Nineteen: The Study of Solomon 198
Chapter Twenty: The Study of Elijah 207
Chapter Twenty-One: The Study of Jonah....................221
Chapter Twenty-Two: The Study of Jeremiah 233
Chapter Twenty-Three: The Study of Esther 247
Chapter Twenty-Four: The Study of Nehemiah 265
Chapter Twenty-Five: The Study of Jehoshaphat 279
Chapter Twenty-Six: Word of Encouragement................288
Chapter Twenty-Seven: The Study of Psalm 73 and Psalm 37 ...298
Chapter Twenty-Eight: The Study of Peter 314
Chapter Twenty-Nine: The Study of Paul.....................320
Chapter Thirty: The Study of Jesus............................328
Chapter Thirty-One: The Study of Psalm 42 and Psalm 43......343
Chapter Thirty-Two: Truths about the True and Living God and the Christian Life...................................346
Chapter Thirty-Three: Final Conclusion 359

Forward

God's Word says, "And we know that in all things God works for the good of those who love him, who have been called according to his purpose" (Romans 8:28 NIV). In Chapter One of her book, the author, Marti Scott, shares her own painful story of the tragic suicide of her brother. This book is a masterful example of how God has used Marti's heart-wrenching family event to inspire her to write for the purpose of glorifying Him through providing Biblical guidance and encouragement to others who find themselves in similar painful situations.

But this is not a one-topic book about successfully dealing with the fact of suicide or thoughts about suicide. In her book, Marti has gone well beyond giving advice to those who might be contemplating suicide. Marti also provides excellent counsel on how suffering people can successfully deal with many other spiritual, mental, and emotional issues such as disappointment, discouragement, defeat, depression, and despair.

Marti demonstrates a clear understanding that many issues we all face are not due to clearly-defined medical and/or organic causes, but rather are often spiritual and emotional issues that are addressed in the Holy Scriptures. Therefore, Marti's book is filled with examples of Bible characters who experienced many of the same struggles that Christians face today, and Marti shares how these Bible characters coped with their struggles and rose above them.

This book communicates the author's conviction that the Bible is the Word of God! As such, the Word of God is both authoritative because it is His Word, and it is practical for daily living, because as our Creator and Redeemer, He knows our needs and the answers to our needs!

Those who ponder the contents of this book will also discover that it is filled with love and compassion. Marti's style of writing and the contents demonstrate that her heart breaks for all who are hurting.

Pastors and church staff members who counsel will find excellent, practical help for their counselees through this book. Bible college and seminary professors who are preparing young adults for life-long ministry will find this book to be a simple-to-understand, yet theologically-rich resource for training their students for practical, successful ministry.

I have been a student of God's Word for more than forty-five years. Yet, as I read through the pages of *Suicide – The Biblical View: How to Biblically Handle Disappointment, Discouragement, Defeat, Depression, and Despair*, I discovered that I was gaining fresh insight into God's Word. I was rejoicing in His grace and power that God offers to all of us in our struggles in a fallen world. The examples from Scripture were so compelling that I did not want to put the book down. I found myself crying out to God to continue to grow me in Christlikeness, and I thought of so many others with whom I could share the contents of this book.

I feel highly honored that Marti Scott asked me to write the forward to her book. I have known Marti (and her husband Jeff) for over thirty-five years. In 1988, my wife and I planted a church with Marti and Jeff. Jesus grew His church to a large congregation of committed Christians. For twenty-two years, I was Marti's pastor at that church! Up close, I observed her daily walk with Christ and found it to be genuine and consistent. This book is written by a godly woman who has walked faithfully with her Lord and Savior, Jesus Christ. I encourage you to read it for your own spiritual growth but also so that you can use this handy resource to help others who are under the onslaught of Satan through disappointment, discouragement, defeat, depression or despair.

This book has the potential to be greatly used by the Spirit of God as we absorb it ourselves and then boldly share it with others. May God put His blessing upon this book, and may He see that it gets into the hands of all who so desperately need encouragement from God in their daily struggles.

Wesley Rowe
Master of Divinity
Doctor of Ministry
Grand Rapids Baptist Seminary

Introduction

I do not remember exactly when the idea of writing a book about suicide first occurred to me, though I do know that it was after my brother's own suicide in 2005. I have done so much analyzing about how suicide is unbiblical that it makes sense to put it all into a book to share with others. Now after COVID-19 and other ills have ravaged the world, causing suicide and assisted suicide to skyrocket, it seems that a timely book on such a dark topic is needed and warranted.

This book started out merely as a commentary on suicide from the biblical perspective. Some of it was written well before 2011. Then in 2011, I wrote most of the lessons on how to biblically handle disappointment, discouragement, defeat, depression, and despair. Therefore, much about my personal life and experiences recorded in the book happened several years ago. Nevertheless, I think it is all still relevant to the topic.

A friend suggested that I merge these two related topics together in one book. Obviously, I thought she had a great idea! So this book, as it turns out, is not only about suicide from the biblical perspective; it is also about handling difficulties biblically so that one does not resort to suicide as the solution to these difficulties. God has much better remedies to our struggles and negative emotions than taking our own lives!

It is my belief that the Bible is God's communication to us for our benefit. We are exceedingly unwise to ignore or disregard it. In part, it is a handbook on how to deal with life in a way that is eminently helpful to those who apply its principles and in a way that appropriately honors God. "All Scripture is breathed out by God and profitable for teaching, for reproof, for correction, and for training in righteousness, that the man of God may be complete, equipped for every good work" (2 Timothy 3:16 & 17 ESV). When we pick and choose which verses and passages we will allow to rule our minds and our behavior, we do so to our own detriment, ultimately affecting others. Therefore, throughout this book I admonish and encourage readers to think and act biblically. To do otherwise is to be disobedient to God but also to complicate our difficulties with the far-inferior thinking of fallen humans. How foolish it is to settle for something so inferior to the revealed will of God! How absurd it is to think we know better than our Creator God what is best!

While I unapologetically maintain that the taking of one's own life is sinful in many ways, it is not my intention in any way to disparage the name, reputation, or memory of anyone who has chosen to take this path to deal with the problems of life. Some were, no doubt, true believers and followers of Jesus Christ who made a desperate and faulty choice. And that is the crux of the matter. People who commit suicide, as godly as they may have been, did so despite the fact that it is not biblical to do so. We can deeply sympathize with their struggles and their feelings from which they sought to escape and yet acknowledge that their choice to end their own lives was not in line with Scripture. In this book, I seek to show this. I ask that you objectively study the Scriptures to which I refer and see if this is not so.

I do not believe Scripture teaches that the act of suicide in and of itself condemns a person to Hell. Though I do not downplay the sinfulness of taking one's own life, suicide is not a line one can cross which will automatically condemn his soul to Hell. What sends anyone to Hell is not trusting in Jesus Christ as Lord and Savior. John 3:16-18 says, "For God so loved the world, that he gave his only begotten Son, that whosoever believeth in him should not perish, but have everlasting life. For God sent not his Son into the world to condemn the world; but that the world through him might be saved. **He that believeth on him is not condemned: but he that believeth not is condemned already, because he hath not believed in the name of the only begotten Son of God"** [emphasis added] (KJV). (In Chapter Ten, I explain what it means to believe in the name of Jesus Christ.) I hold that there will be people in Heaven who took their own lives. I do not base this conclusion on my own wishful thinking, which would be so foolhardy to do. Rather, this conclusion is based on the authoritative Word of God.

My hope is that this book will be helpful to those who read it. It was written with the premise that Christians often have not thought through the implications of their decision to take their own lives. I earnestly hope that this book will assist readers in thinking biblically about suicide so that those who are contemplating taking their own lives will avert this devastating, unbiblical decision. Also, it is written with the understanding that people who lose a loved one due to suicide could use a big dose of help and encouragement. Perhaps, some day in the future, some of you will be able to share these truths with friends or family members who are tempted to take their own lives. Or maybe you have already experienced the suicide of a loved one and are still reeling in disbelief and agony. This book offers you encouragement from others who have experienced that same storyline. Or it could be that you have given up on life and are close to that point yourself. To any and all of you, I pray that God uses this book to bring you conviction and hope!

Whether or not my urgent pleas can or will actually prevent anyone from committing suicide is, of course, totally unknown to me. I question whether or not my words, as passionate, logical, and biblical as I deem them to be, could cause someone bent on ending his own life to change his mind. I have frequently heard people who are that close to killing themselves described by others as "not in their right minds." However, I write with the hope and prayer that the Holy Spirit will work in the hearts and minds of those believers who are tempted to resort to suicide as the solution to their troubles. If this book helps just one person, it will have been well worth the effort. The outcome is in God's hands. I know that God's Word is powerful and without a doubt has the potential to change hearts and lives!

The thought that perhaps God would choose to use this book to encourage someone else is extremely thrilling and humbling. I am stepping out, trusting that God wants me to use my experience of losing my brother to suicide to in some way help someone who is struggling with this issue. That would be a very gratifying end to a very painful experience. The results of this book are up to Him. May He be forever praised!

I have chosen to utilize the traditional and grammatically correct use of pronouns in this book. Therefore, I frequently use "he" when meaning "he and/or she."

When referring to one person, a singular pronoun is called for. For example, in my statement, "I question whether or not my words, as passionate, logical, and biblical as I deem them to be, could cause **someone** bent on ending his own life to change his mind," "someone" is singular and requires a singular pronoun. It would be grammatically incorrect to say, "I question whether or not my words, as passionate, logical, and biblical as I deem them to be, could cause someone bent on ending their life to change their mind," since "their" is plural. In addition, to continually use "he and she" or "he or she" is awkward. Therefore, I decided the best solution is to simply use "he," meaning "he and/or she." It is not my opinion that males are superior to females. Neither do I think that males need to hear biblical instruction more than females do; I apply my conclusions equally to both males and females.

There are several instances in my book where I quote a verse which needs clarification because I have not quoted the complete text. On those occasions, I have put the clarification in [brackets].

For example:

Luke 22:31:

> "Simon, Simon, [Peter] behold, Satan demanded to have you, that he might sift you like wheat, but I have prayed for you that your faith might not fail" (ESV).

Luke 22:54:

> "Then seizing him [Jesus], they led him away and took him into the house of the high priest. Peter followed at a distance" (NIV).

1 Peter 1:7:

> "These [trials] have come so that the proven genuineness of your faith—of greater worth than gold, which perishes even though refined by fire—may result in praise, glory and honor when Jesus Christ is revealed" (NIV).

Hebrews 12:5-15:

> **5** And have you completely forgotten this word of encouragement that addresses you as a father addresses his son? It says,
>
> "My son, do not make light of the Lord's discipline,

and do not lose heart when he rebukes you,
6 because the Lord disciplines the one he loves,
and he chastens everyone he accepts as his son." [Proverbs 3:11 & 12] (NIV)

(Here I provide the reference to the Old Testament verses which are quoted in Hebrews 12:5 & 6.)

The words in brackets are my words inserted for clarification. They are not words found in the biblical text.

I have emphasized in bold certain verses within some of the Bible passages I quoted. The purpose is to pinpoint the exact part of the passage that corresponds to the point I am making at that particular part of my book. I indicate my emphasis with [emphasis added]. The function of the brackets is to denote that the verses in bold are bolded by me and do not appear in bold in the biblical text.

Part 1
Suicide - The Biblical View

"Or do you not know that your body is a temple of the
Holy Spirit within you, whom you have from God?
You are not your own, for you were bought with a price.
So glorify God in your body."
(1 Corinthians 6:19 & 20 ESV)

Chapter One

The Suicide

T he phone rang that bitter January morning.

"This is the coroner of Dakota County, Apple Valley, Minnesota…" And I knew.

The reality and finality of it cut like a sharp knife thrust deep into my gut, and I choked and gasped to breathe. "No! No!" I wailed. My husband reached his hand over to comfort me as our grandchildren looked wide-eyed at the scene. But there was no comfort at that moment, for I had just witnessed a drowning!

It was not a literal drowning but a man going under after being thrown out a life preserver, nonetheless. After precariously holding onto the life preserver for several days, he deliberately and hopelessly let loose and went under, never to come up again.

That man was my brother David, and the coroner had just confirmed that the police had found him hanging in his apartment in Minnesota. I was in Michigan, hearing the news that I would have to pass on to my family: my dying mother, her caretaker-husband (my father), and my three sisters. Wheezing from suffocating pain, I clumsily started making the phone calls that would inflict that same pain on them when they heard the news from me.

I thought about my parents in Florida. They should not have to hear the news by phone but in person, to soften the blow. They were relatively strong emotionally, I knew, but my mother was physically frail from her disease and Dad was worn out from taking care of her, the house, the shopping. And he was worn out from concern about my brother, his only son.

I called my brother-in-law in Florida and asked him to go over to Dad and Mom's house with my sister and tell them that what they had feared **might** happen **had** happened! It was the best way — or the least harmful way – I reasoned, of hearing the news. He was their pastor anyway, so difficult tasks like this came with his calling as pastor.

So, I reluctantly set in motion the necessary calls that I dreaded, my heart crumbling as I dialed. God's grace empowered me as I did what needed to be done. My husband called **our** pastor. We needed him!

As the days passed, we dealt with funeral arrangements. I can only imagine the agony my dad experienced as he made the arrangements for David's body to be flown to Michigan for burial, as he settled David's estate, and he paid off debts and all. It should not have ended this way!

David had not yet reached his fortieth birthday. So much life never to be lived. The final chapter of his life was already written. It should not have ended this way! He should have died as an old man with his wife, loving children, and grandchildren around him. Instead, he died alone in his apartment in frigid Minnesota far away from those who were trying to help him. And somebody had the gruesome task of taking down his body. (Thank you, whoever you are!)

David saw no way out, no solution to the tangles of his life. The problems were too big, too complicated, too overwhelming, he believed. Relationships, finances, employment, and obligations were too heavy a load to carry and too fearful a future to contemplate facing. And everyone would be better off without him, he thought. This was the final chapter of my brother's life. It shouldn't have ended this way!

An incident when he was twelve years old set into motion the events that would lead up to his suicide. And nobody knew about it until years after it happened. Only David knew. David and his predator.

David was delivering newspapers one day when one of his customers invited him into his house and sexually abused him. He threatened to harm David's family if he ever told them, so David told no one until around 2002, twenty-five years later.

My heart stung as my brother told me about the abuse, and some of his behavior started to make sense that never did before. Thinking about David as a helpless twelve-year-old boy experiencing this traumatizing abuse at the hands of this perverted, licentious adult male (I will not even call him a man) made me feel sorry for David and angry toward that monster.

Now, three years after telling his family about this mortifying experience he had endured twenty-five years earlier, David is dead. Dead by his own hands. There is no way to go back in time and make different choices. The final chapter of his life has already been written. No more time to make things right. No more time to work on that which needed to be fixed. No more time to enjoy the results of the hard work it would take to fix those things. No more time to positively influence other people in his life. It shouldn't have ended this way!

Many people in the world today eventually do make the same choice to end their own lives. To them, death seems to be the answer to the struggles in their lives. They desire to get away from the pain, to rest in peace where the problems, the worries, and the heartaches are gone. The earthly problems are gone for the one escaping life by choosing death, but what about the people left behind?

Some have expressed the belief that their loved ones would be better off without them – that they were a burden to their families and friends. I think Satan has deluded these people into believing this lie! Satan reigns over the culture of death. He has come to steal, kill, and destroy (John 10:10). He has convinced some people that the solution to their problems is death.

I can certainly understand the desire to escape the hard things in life. I have often tried to escape the ugliness by pulling the covers over my head and drifting into the soothing world of sleep. Delicious at the time, that escape is nauseating later and only a temporary fix. The same ugliness is there to be faced when I inevitably wake up. And I am no further ahead in working to overcome my problems.

I had sympathy for David's feelings about his complicated life. Where does he start to untangle the mess, to confront and conquer the formidable problems that are the result of choices made earlier in life and the problems that are a result of the sin of other people? There were so many problems and no easy solutions. Escaping is tempting, I know! But it shouldn't have ended this way!

When I hear about the suicide of Christians, some of whom are even church and ministry leaders, I can identify with the desire to escape this world of economic meltdown, terrorists who want to wipe out America, a society that wants to do away with the true and living God and His guiding principles. (I wrote this in 2005, long before the pandemic outbreak of COVID-19, which has made life even more difficult and scary!) In Heaven, there is no more pain, no more problems – only bliss and perfect peace!

Still, it shouldn't end this way. Family and friends are left behind to grieve and mourn, to pick up the pieces, and to adjust to life without their loved one. Compounding the pain are the gruesome, haunting, recurring visions of the deceased hanging or shot, leaving family and friends agonizing over what might have been.

I sensed the utter despair of a Christian man as he informed his Facebook friends that his wife had killed herself. He cried out to God for help as he thought about raising his little girls on his own. Every day, he misses his wife, his only true love. Life is now much more complicated for him as he chooses to live and face the hardships of life. Now he faces more than just the "normal" hardships that we all face; he faces the heavy burden of living life without his mate and raising his little girls without their mother. It shouldn't have ended this way!

Because the pain and problems of life can sometimes seem so unbearable and impossible to solve, we often focus so much on the pain and problems that we do not make full use of the resources that God has provided. I gently but urgently remind us all that God's Word tells us that He has given us believers everything we need for life and godliness (2 Peter 1:3). Praise God! We all need to make use of His resources!

I do not at all minimize the feelings of those in despair. I know that the torment is very real and that the burden of it can become so great that in time, one can lose hope of ever finding relief. The one in despair must acknowledge and grapple with those feelings and that pain.

Though I have experienced feelings of despair at times myself, I do not know what it is like to carry the burdens that others have to carry. I do not have a special needs child, for example. I have never lost a child. I have never been sexually abused or robbed at gunpoint. I have not had to live with chronic pain. My husband has not left me. My house has not burned down or gone into foreclosure. I have not had to battle cancer or other life-threatening diseases. But I have had other problems, and the pain and anguish are very real. The problems can seem so overwhelming and exasperating that escaping is extremely tempting. I have temporarily escaped under my covers many times. However, I can testify that, with God's help, I came through some trials that I didn't think I could survive. But I did survive, facing one day at a time, one step at a time.

None of this monologue helps the deceased – those who have already taken their own lives. Regrettably, the final chapter has already been written for them. But I hope my analysis is a help to someone who is currently considering the ultimate escape – suicide. If you are a believer and follower of Jesus Christ, please open your mind to what I am saying. This is written especially for you, believer!

Even though it seems like there is no hope, there is. There is hope for your pain. There is hope for your problems. There is hope for you, for your life. That does not mean that you can ever live life without pain or problems, of course. But there is hope and help for you to live **despite** the pain and **despite** the problems. You can live a vibrant, rewarding, victorious life, even in a prison cell or without your family or with a severe handicap or with little of this world's goods or whatever your circumstances!

Please cling to hope. **There is always hope because there is God!**

"May the God of hope fill you with all joy and peace in believing, so that by the power of the Holy Spirit you may abound in hope" (Romans 15:13 KJV).

Chapter Two

The Unbiblical Nature of Suicide

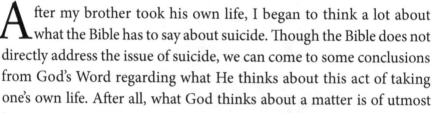

After my brother took his own life, I began to think a lot about what the Bible has to say about suicide. Though the Bible does not directly address the issue of suicide, we can come to some conclusions from God's Word regarding what He thinks about this act of taking one's own life. After all, what God thinks about a matter is of utmost importance, or at least it should be to all professing Christians. My mind began to assess the act of suicide in light of what God says in His revelation to us. Thinking about how the act of self-murder is sinful in the eyes of God occupied my mind for several months. Those times of assessment prompted me to write down the thoughts to possibly share with others some day.

    To anyone thinking about ending his own life, this evaluation might seem overwhelming and harsh. I do not intend for it to be. My goal is to help you, not condemn or burden you! I do not want to push anyone further in the direction of hopelessness! However, truth must be told in order to bring hope and help. It does no long-term good for anyone to live in a world of delusion, denying the truth. Truth is truth, despite one's feelings. I write these things with utmost compassion and concern for the weary who are seeking to end it all. My motive is to try to lure you away from the precipice of a final, faulty decision which is really not the answer to your despair. This

is not just my opinion; more importantly, it is *God's* opinion. Please consider the things I am communicating despite how uncomfortable it is to read it. Do not let your heart be overwhelmed by the weight of these objections to suicide. Take the time to consider what God, whose commands and guidelines are given from His heart of concern for the welfare of all people, thinks about the issue. One little step at a time can lead you in the right direction. Your situation does not have to improve drastically overnight in order for your small steps at change to be very helpful.

Several reasons why suicide is wrong have occurred to me as I thought about the whole counsel of God in the Bible (Acts 20:27).

1. **Suicide is a violation of one of the Ten Commandments:** "You shall not murder" (Exodus 20:13 NIV).

The most obvious, basic reason why suicide is wrong is because God prohibits murder, which, of course, is the taking of a human life. Do you think that murder is only the killing of another person? What about taking your own life? That is also murder. As a Christian, your life is not your own; you were bought with the precious blood of Jesus Christ. 1 Corinthians 6:19 & 20 says, "Or do you not know that your body is a temple of the Holy Spirit within you, whom you have from God? **You are not your own, for you were bought with a price. So glorify God in your body**" [emphasis added] (ESV).

Does a person glorify God with his body when he kills the body that God intends to be used for His glory?

Further, you are not the master of your own fate. When you called upon Jesus Christ to save you, you relinquished control of your life to Him. He is now the Lord of your life rather than you yourself. Only God has the right to decide when you should leave this life and enter into the next. We tend to think that we own ourselves – that we own our own bodies. But that is really a secular concept, not a biblical one. No one has the right to take his own life. Even unbelievers do not own themselves. They were created **by** God and **for** God and are therefore His! They are not His in the same way believers are – as in God's family – but they still belong to God. God is the Creator and the sovereign Lord of this universe, and He owns everything in it. "Everything under heaven belongs to me," God declares (Job 41:11 NIV). Psalm 24:1 says, "The earth is the LORD's, and the fullness thereof; the world, and they that dwell therein" (KJV).

Suicide is disobedience to God's prohibition against the taking of a human life.

2. **Suicide argues with God about trials.**

He said that we would have trials, and they are designed by a loving, all-knowing God for our good.

> "Consider it pure joy, my brothers and sisters, whenever you face trials of many kinds, because you know that the testing of your faith produces perseverance. **Let perseverance finish its work so that you may be mature and complete, not lacking anything**" [emphasis added] (James 1:2-4 NIV).

Do you see what God says about perseverance? He says that we must allow perseverance to finish its work. The fulfillment of that work will make us mature and complete. And that is God's ultimate goal. **Suicide does not allow perseverance to finish its work, and therefore, it is cutting short the work that God wants to do within a believer. It is interfering with God's work, and that is very serious!** Philippians 1:6 says, "And I am sure of this, that he who began a good work in you will bring it to completion at the day of Jesus Christ" (ESV). He began the good work in you by saving you from the penalty of your sins and adopting you as His child. Until the day of Jesus Christ when His work in you is complete, He wants to work in you to conform you more and more to be like Jesus Christ. Taking your own life would put a premature end to the work that God wants to do in your life on Earth.

3. Suicide displays an idol in your heart and life — that your comfort, your ease of pain, your escape from problems, is more important than God's glory.

We all have to guard our hearts from idolatry. Anything we cherish more than God and His glory is an idol. Idols can be obvious, tangible things such as money, status, experiences, and pleasure, for example; but they can also be subtle, intangible things like comfort and ease.

God's glory can be displayed in our lives when we allow Him to work in and through us – even in the midst of great pain and loss!

Several godly Bible characters expressed a desire to die. As Job grappled with the pain of losing all of his children and his earthly possessions, he cursed the day he was born. He lamented that he had been born. If he had never been born, he reasoned, he would not have had to suffer so much. Listen to Job's own words:

"Why did I not perish at birth, and die as I came from the womb? Why were there knees to receive me and breasts that I might be nursed? For now I would be lying down in peace; I would be asleep and at rest with kings and rulers of the earth, who built for themselves places now lying in ruins, with princes who had gold, who filled their houses with silver. Or why was I not hidden away in the ground like a stillborn child, like an infant who never saw the light of day? There the wicked cease from turmoil, and there the weary are at rest. Captives also enjoy their ease; they no longer hear the slave driver's shout. The small and the great are there, and the slaves are freed from their owners. Why is light given to those in misery, and life to the bitter of soul, to those who long for death that does not come, who search for it more than for hidden treasure, who are filled with gladness and rejoice when they reach the grave? Why is life given to a man whose way is hidden, whom God has hedged in? For sighing has become my daily food; my groans pour out like water. What I feared has come upon me; what I dreaded has happened to me. I have no peace, no quietness; I have no rest, but only turmoil" (Job 3:11-26 NIV).

Have you ever felt this way? Have you ever felt the seeming senselessness of living with such pain?

Job's pain is poignant in his description of his suffering:

"If only my anguish could be weighed and all my misery be placed on the scales! It would surely outweigh the sand of the seas – no wonder my words have been impetuous. The arrows of the Almighty are in me, my spirit drinks in their poison; God's terrors are marshaled against me" (Job 6:1-4 NIV).

"Do not mortals have hard service on earth? Are not their days like those of hired laborers? Like a slave longing for the evening shadows, or a hired laborer waiting to be paid, so I have been allotted months of futility, and nights of misery have been assigned to me. When I lie down I think, 'How long before I get up?' The night drags on, and I toss and turn until dawn. My body is clothed with worms and scabs, my skin is broken and festering. My days are swifter than a weaver's shuttle, and they come to an end without hope. Remember, O God, that my life is but a breath; my eyes will never see happiness again" (Job 7:1-7 NIV).

Though Job refused to listen to his wife's advice to curse God and die, he did long for refuge in death. Dying would bring relief!

We know from the first two chapters of the book of Job that the reason he suffered so much was because he was being tested by God. Despite all of Job's groaning and complaints, he says, "But he knows the way that I take; when he has tested me, I will come forth as gold" (Job 23:10 NIV). And I ask, what earthly element is more precious than gold? Once his trial was over, "The LORD blessed the latter part of Job's life more than the former part" (Job 42:12 NIV). The very last verse of the book of Job resounds with triumph and peace: "And so Job died, an old man and full of years" (Job 42:17 NIV). Though Job at one point wanted to die, and he had some misconceptions about the Almighty, he passed the test! **He got through that time of deep despair alive and still praising God**. Not only did he live to see even more prosperous days than before his trial, but he also came to know the true and living God more intimately than he had known Him before, which brought him to his knees in repentance.

The Old Testament prophet Jeremiah echoes Job's regret about having been born. Jeremiah, like Job, cursed the day he was born. Here are Jeremiah's own words:

> "Cursed be the day I was born! May the day my mother bore me not be blessed! Cursed be the man who brought my father the news, who made him very glad, saying, 'A child is born to you – a son!' May that man be like the towns the LORD overthrew without pity. May he hear wailing in the morning, a battle cry at noon. For he did not kill me in the womb, with my mother as my grave, her womb enlarged forever. Why did I ever come

out of the womb to see trouble and sorrow and to end my days in shame?" (Jeremiah 20:14-18 NIV).

It is easy to understand why both of these men wished that they had never been born, for their lives were not easy. Jeremiah had the unenviable task of proclaiming to the wayward people of Judah for forty years the impending judgment of God, barring their repentance. The people, of course, treated him with utter contempt. They threatened his life. Jeremiah was mocked and scorned by the people when he delivered God's message of warning to them. He was beaten and imprisoned in a dungeon where he was held captive for a long time. He was later thrown into a cistern without water where he sank into the mud. God used Jeremiah as a living object lesson.

Jeremiah's feelings about this mistreatment drip with anguish and frustration:

> "You deceived me, LORD, and I was deceived; you overpowered me and prevailed. I am ridiculed all day long; everyone mocks me. Whenever I speak, I cry out proclaiming violence and destruction. So the word of the LORD has brought me insult and reproach all day long. But if I say, 'I will not mention his word or speak anymore in his name,' his word is in my heart like a fire, a fire shut up in my bones. I am weary of holding it in; indeed, I cannot. I hear many whispering, 'Terror on every side! Denounce him! Let's denounce him!' All my friends are waiting for me to slip, saying, 'Perhaps he will be deceived; then we will prevail over him and take our revenge on him'" (Jeremiah 20:7-10 NIV).

Another Old Testament prophet, Elijah, whose life was threatened by the brazenly wicked Jezebel, wife of King Ahab, prayed to the Lord to take his life.

But all of these men, though apparently wanting to die, continued to put their trust in the God they knew to be sovereign over all things and able to meet their needs. They kept on living – probably struggling as they did – but they kept living! None of them took his own life, though each one asked God to take his life. God did not do so until much later – after His purposes for them had been completed.

What an example these men are to us! Despite their strong feelings of wanting to escape their difficult lives through death, they continued to do what God wanted them to do. And that is the greatest achievement in life – the thing that makes life so worth living: completing what God has called me to do, despite the difficulties and my own insecure feelings.

4. When a person takes his own life, he plays the role of God. This is a form of rebellion.

This is closely related to objections #1 and #2. Only God has the right to decide when someone's life should end, and He has the right to use trials in our lives, for He alone is God. The taking of one's own life figuratively shoves God out of the way and puts oneself on the throne. It declares that the self-murderer does not want God to rule over this area of his life. Such an attitude is a form of rebellion, whether intentional or not.

5. Suicide is often a selfish act that hurts other people.

Often, the real reason someone takes his own life is due to selfishness. He is really thinking about his own interests above the interests of others. Do you really think that you can kill yourself and it will not hurt anyone else? Heed the words in Romans 14:7: "For none of us liveth to himself, and no man dieth to himself" (KJV). Putting one's own life in danger to help someone else is one thing, but the willful taking of one's own life because he no longer wishes to live is another. The former is a

selfless, admirable, praiseworthy thing. The latter – the taking of one's own life to escape reality – is often a **selfish** act, and it leaves loved ones hurting more deeply than a natural death. It is a horrifying thought that one would lose a cherished family member, friend, or associate by the hands of another person, and it is almost as horrifying to lose a loved one at his own hands. Suicide is a savage, cruel act that brings pain to others. Unless you are a hermit with no human contact, you affect the lives of other people. Someone is probably depending upon you in some way or another. You probably have some family and friends. If you are a true believer in Jesus Christ, you value His bride, the church, and you are probably involved in a local church, as you should be. Do you think you can end your own life and it will not bother anybody else? Are your needs more important than the needs of those around you? If you are involved in a church, you might well be involved in some ministry, which every believer should be. Do you think that people in your ministry will carry on without you as if you never belonged to that ministry? And what about your spiritual gifts which God gave to you for the benefit of the body of Christ? In taking your own life, you would also be taking away your spiritual gifts from your church. And that would hurt your church! If you are a husband, you are supposed to love your wife enough to lay down your life for her. How can you do that if you are not around? Do her needs mean so little to you that you can dismiss them by taking your own life? You may protest that you do care about the needs of your wife. Well, you may care to some extent, but if you take your own life, it is likely that **you** mean more to yourself than your wife does! Do not think that your wife does not need you! Are you a wife? Do you think that your husband does not need you? Why did God create marriage? In part, He created marriage for the benefit of the husband and the benefit of the wife. He also created marriage to picture His love relationship with His bride, the church! If you are not around, you fail to mirror that love relationship that Christ has with the church. If you take your own life, you may very well be declaring that your first allegiance is to yourself, not to others!

Suicide places a heavy burden on family and friends whom you leave behind.

6. Suicide sets a bad example for other people.

Several years ago, I was involved in a ministry at a women's prison. I learned that often when a woman at the prison takes her own life, it incites other women at the prison to do the same – to take their own lives. We are responsible for the kind of example that we set for other people around us. It would seem that if someone takes his own life because of my example of taking my own life, that I am somewhat culpable for that person's suicide. Are you a parent? If you take your own life, what kind of an example are you leaving for your child? Will he learn from you that the answer to life's difficulties is to take his own life? If your suicide incites your child to take his own life, are you culpable before God for your child's self-murder?

If you are a blood-bought Christian, all of your sins have been forgiven – past, present, and future. There is no condemnation for those who are in Christ Jesus (Romans 8:1). So, when you stand before God, you will not be punished for causing someone else to sin. However, you will forfeit rewards that you could have had for being a good, positive example to others.

7. Suicide gives God's enemy and your enemy, the devil, some victory in your life, for he has come to steal, kill, and destroy (John 10:10).

Do you, as a follower of Jesus Christ, the Lover of your soul, the One who redeemed your life from Hell, and the One who gives abundant life – do you really want to glorify Jesus' enemy Satan by doing what Satan wants rather than what God wants? All of our thoughts, words, and actions glorify either God or Satan. Do you want your last action on Earth to glorify the one who hates you and wants to destroy you? You may protest, "All I want to do is stop living so that I can be relieved of this pain in my heart. I don't want to hurt anyone else. I just don't want to live anymore!" But all of our actions have consequences. We cannot escape that law. Your self-murder would glorify the evil one, not God!

8. Suicide robs God of the opportunity to salvage or redeem your life from difficulty, for His glory. It also robs you of the joy of seeing God help you.

A marvelous example of God redeeming a bitter situation and bringing beauty instead, is the life of a woman who lived during Old Testament times – probably more than three thousand years ago.

Naomi was a Jew who fled Judah with her husband and two sons to Moab because of a famine in their land. While they were in Moab, Naomi's husband died, and both of her sons married Moabite women. Then both of her sons died, leaving her daughters-in-law as widows. Once the famine was over in Judah and there was plenty of food to eat there, Naomi decided to return to her native land. One of her daughters-in-law, Ruth, insisted upon going to Judah with Naomi to start a new life with her there. Naomi was an obviously bitter woman. She had lost her husband and her two sons after leaving her homeland. Upon arriving in Judah, Ruth began working in the field that belonged to Boaz, and he watched over her as she attempted to glean pieces of grain for herself and her mother-in-law. She ended up marrying Boaz, and they had a son who is in the lineage of Jesus Christ! Naomi not only had a faithful daughter-in-law; she now also had a grandson to hold and love. The story is a picture of God's redemption of our souls, but it is also a story of His redemption of a destitute family.

God can take your shattered life and make something beautiful out of it. **Your life is not over because of your problems.** Maybe you lost your home, or your health, or your job, or your family, or even your reputation. That does not mean that your life is over. **Just because you can see no resolution to your problems does not mean that there is none and that God cannot help you.** His resources are limitless! You are finite, but He is infinite! Do you suppose that the Israelites ever imagined that their means of escaping the Egyptian soldiers who were hotly pursuing them would be the parting of the Red Sea? Yet that is the means that God used to save His people. God can take your broken life and make it whole again in a way you never dreamed. He can make beauty out of ashes. And He will be with you as you pick up the pieces while your heart is breaking. He can redeem your life and restore your soul. But you have to stick around and give Him the chance to do that!

9. **Suicide denies you many things.**

Suicide not only denies you the joy of having God help you through the trials; it also denies you encouragement from Him and closeness with Him in this life. Suicide also denies you future joys such as accomplishing goals like finishing school, getting a job, getting married and having children. Or you would miss out on other blessings such as becoming sober, being the parent your child needs you to be, getting released from prison, reconciling with your family, acquiring new friendships, or getting your own place to live, for example. These are all some of the blessings you could miss out on in this life.

There are, however, blessings far more lasting than those: eternal blessings. Suicide denies you opportunity for future fruit in God's kingdom; there is now no more time to work in the harvest field. There is no more opportunity to help and influence others. There is no more time to store up treasures in Heaven (Matthew 6:19-21).

10. **A person who takes his own life deals with his problems in a fleshly way rather than in a Spirit-filled way.**

That person is being driven by his feelings rather than faith. This is, as all of the above, dishonoring to God.

"The flesh" refers to the natural mind, which is human thinking that is the result of the fall of mankind. The flesh is at odds with God. Fleshly thinking and behaving are contrary to biblical or godly thinking and behaving. It is dead to God.

Notice how the flesh and the Spirit are contrasted in the following verses:

> "For those who live according to the flesh set their minds on the things of the flesh, but those who live according to the Spirit set their minds on the things of the Spirit. For to set the mind on the flesh is death, but to set the mind on the Spirit is life and peace. For the mind that is set on the flesh is hostile to God, for it does not submit to God's law; indeed, it cannot. **Those who are in the flesh cannot please God**" [emphasis added] (Romans 8:5-8 ESV).

Just look at the list of the fruit of the flesh:

> "The acts of the flesh are obvious: sexual immorality, impurity and debauchery; idolatry and witchcraft; hatred, discord, jealousy, fits of rage, selfish ambition, dissensions, factions and envy; drunkenness, orgies, and the like. I warn you, as I did before, that those who live like this will not inherit the kingdom of God" (Galatians 5:19-21 NIV).

Contrast that list with the list of fruit of the Spirit:

"But the fruit of the Spirit is love, joy, peace, forbearance, kindness, goodness, faithfulness, gentleness and self-control. Against such things there is no law" (Galatians 5:22 & 23 NIV).

Here is the contrast: The flesh produces death. It is hostile to God. It does not and cannot submit to God's laws. It cannot please God. Obviously, then, it is sinful. Conversely, the Spirit produces life and peace; it submits to God's laws and pleases God. We are commanded to live to please the Spirit of God rather than our flesh. Consider the following verses:

"But put on the Lord Jesus Christ, and make no provision for the flesh, to gratify its desires" (Romans 13:14 ESV).

"But I say, walk by the Spirit, and you will not gratify the desires of the flesh. For the desires of the flesh are against the Spirit, and the desires of the Spirit are against the flesh, for these are opposed to each other, to keep you from doing the things you want to do" (Galatians 5:16 & 17 ESV).

"The flesh," then, is an unbiblical, ungodly way of thinking and behaving. It is sinful and does not glorify God.

The patriarch Abraham and King David both dealt with some of their problems in a fleshly way rather than being led by the Spirit of God.

God had promised Abram (Abraham) that he would have a son, even though he and his wife Sarai (Sarah) were old, and Sarai was past child-bearing age. So Sarai, taking matters into her own hands, convinced Abram to sleep with her handmaid, Hagar, so as to fulfill God's promise of having a son. Hagar did bear a son for Abraham, but this was not the son that God had promised. Later, God allowed Sarah to bear Isaac from her union with Abraham, and this was the son that God had promised. The fleshly solution to barrenness brought all kinds of problems for Abraham and Sarah!

King David tried to cover up his sin of impregnating Bathsheba, another man's wife, by having Bathsheba's husband killed in battle. Then he took Bathsheba to be his wife. See how he dealt with his problem in a fleshly way rather than being controlled by the Spirit of God? Not only did he commit adultery, stemming from covetousness; he also committed murder. All of this is against God's explicit commands.

Whenever we choose to sin rather than doing things God's way, we are resorting to the flesh, rather than being led by the Holy Spirit. Suicide is an act that is the result of resorting to the flesh to solve problems, rather than submitting to God's revealed will.

11. Suicide denies the world the opportunity to see the power of God working through your trials.

As others around you observe you living life through God's power despite great difficulty, it can be a powerful testimony to what God can do!

How encouraging and convicting are the words of Psalm 40:1-3:

> "I waited patiently for the LORD; he turned to me and heard my cry. He lifted me out of the slimy pit, out of the mud and mire; he set my feet on a rock and gave me a firm place to stand. He put a new song in my mouth, a hymn of praise to our God. **Many will see and fear the LORD and put their trust in him**" [emphasis added] (NIV).

I urge you to keep on living, to cry out to God for help, and to patiently wait for Him, so that others can see God lifting you out of the pit and placing you on firm ground. Let them see this so that they will fear God and put their trust in Him!

12. Suicide sends a false message to the world about who you are in Christ. Suicide mischaracterizes who you are as a believer in Christ, a child of God.

Reflect upon this passage in Romans 8:

"What shall we then say to these things? If God be for us, who can be against us? He that spared not his own Son, but delivered him up for us all, how shall he not with him also freely give us all things? Who shall lay any thing to the charge of God's elect? It is God that justifieth. Who is he that condemneth? It is Christ that died, yea rather, that is risen again, who is even at the right hand of God, who also maketh intercession for us. Who shall separate us from the love of Christ? shall tribulation, or distress, or persecution, or famine, or nakedness, or peril, or sword? As it is written, For thy sake we are killed all the day long; we are accounted as sheep for the slaughter. **Nay, in all these things we are more than conquerors through him that loved us** [emphasis added]. For I am persuaded, that neither death, nor life, nor angels, nor principalities, nor powers, nor things present, nor things to come, nor height, nor depth, nor any other creature, shall be able to separate us from the love of God, which is in Christ Jesus our Lord" (Romans 8:31-39 KJV).

God says, through the writings of the Apostle Paul, that we are **more than conquerors**. We may not feel like conquerors, but God declares that we are. We do not conquer through our own strength, wisdom or willpower. We are conquerors through Christ because Christ has conquered. Does a believer who takes his own life appear to be a conqueror? No, he appears to be a defeated victim. If we are more than conquerors, should any trouble in this life ultimately defeat us?

13. Suicide cuts short the race that we are commanded to run.

Hebrews 12 tells believers that life is a race to be run with endurance. Those who take their own lives fail to complete the race.

> "Wherefore seeing we also are compassed about with so great a cloud of witnesses, let us lay aside every weight, and the sin which doth so easily beset us, and let us run with patience the race that is set before us, Looking unto Jesus the author and finisher of our faith; who for the joy that was set before him endured the cross, despising the shame, and is set down at the right hand of the throne of God" (Hebrews 12:1 & 2 KJV).

As believers in Christ, we are meant to complete the "race" of life. We are meant to continue living for Christ until He calls us home.

In conclusion, there are several reasons why suicide is wrong, unbiblical, and sinful. It is never condoned in Scripture and creates more problems than it solves. It is not the answer to life's difficulties.

I hope that you read the rest of this book for solutions to your difficulties other than taking your own life.

Chapter Three

The Implications of Suicide

Think about the implications of the act of suicide. A person who takes his own life, especially a Christian, a true follower of Jesus Christ, sends messages to the world without even trying to or perhaps without even realizing it. These messages might not be at all what that person is thinking, but the observing world probably does not know that. What are some of those possible messages?

1. My pain and my problems are bigger than God.

When a believer takes his own life, he ceases trusting in God's grace to see him through his problems. Relying on God's grace in our weakness is one of the most important things in life that we believers can do. God's power is manifested most gloriously and greatly in the midst of our weakness, in our suffering.

Reflect on what God said to the Apostle Paul when he asked God three times to take away a difficulty in his life, which he described as "a thorn in my flesh, a messenger of Satan to torment me." God said, "My grace is sufficient for you, for my power is made perfect in weakness" (2 Corinthians 12:9 NIV). We do not know with certainty what that difficulty was. Even after Paul pleaded with God three times to take away the difficulty, God did not take it out of Paul's life. Instead, God gave him the grace to live with it.

Paul then concluded paradoxically, "Therefore I will boast all the more gladly about my weaknesses, so that Christ's power may rest on me. That is why, for Christ's sake, I delight in weaknesses, in insults, in hardships, in persecutions, in difficulties. For when I am weak, then I am strong" (2 Corinthians 12:9 & 10 NIV).

Suicide says that God's grace is not sufficient for my life of difficulties, but that is contrary to what God says through the Apostle Paul, who says that God's grace **is** sufficient for our difficulties and that His power is manifested in our weaknesses. Paul chose therefore to be glad about his hardships and difficulties. He apparently did not argue with God or resist God's work in his life. Instead, he accepted God's will for his life and learned to glory in this difficulty because God's power could be displayed through it. He went on to accomplish what God called him to do!

What or who is bigger, your problems or the sovereign God of the universe? I do not think any true Christian would actually say that his problems are bigger than God. He surely knows that this is an unbiblical perspective. But the believer who takes his own life is belying what Scripture says about God's ability and willingness to help us solve our problems.

The God who created the universe and sustains it every second of every day, who created our bodies and minds and knows what we need, who knows when a little bird falls to the ground and knows the very number of the hairs on your head, is able to help you in your situation, no matter what it is. Many things are too difficult for us, but nothing is too difficult for God! Genesis 18:14 says, "Is anything too hard for the LORD?" (ESV). God can either take away any of your problems or help you live through them. "And my God will meet all your needs according to the riches of his glory in Christ Jesus" (Philippians 4:19 NIV).

How vast are the riches of God? If you are a true believer, I think you know the answer. His riches are limitless!

"Therefore I tell you, do not worry about your life, what you will eat or drink; or about your body, what you will wear. Is not life more than food, and the body more than clothes? Look at the birds of the air; they do not sow or reap or store away in barns, and yet your heavenly Father feeds them. Are you not much more valuable than they?" (Matthew 6:25 & 26 NIV).

How big is your God? The true and living God, the God of the Bible, is much bigger than any problem. Nothing is too difficult for Him. But if you take your own life, what does it say to the world about your God? Does it not give the world the false impression that your God is not big enough for your problems – that He must not be all that great? Is this the impression you really want to leave to a skeptical, cynical world? If you are a true believer, you would not knowingly want to leave the world with this false view of God!

Suicide denies the world the opportunity to see a Christian living in the midst of a trial and God's grace abounding in his life, enabling him to continue to live a meaningful life. It denies the world the opportunity to witness the greatness of the true and living God.

2. Christianity does not work.

Christianity is viewed by many today as mere superstition – a fairy tale religion that does not have real answers for real problems that real people face in this real world. This world is a rather frightening and complicated place. When a believer takes his own life, he discredits the relevance of God and His Word in this current world. Doubters see Christianity as an archaic religion which offers no realistic hope for the world in which we live. Is this message one that you really want to leave with the world that has rejected Jesus Christ and His Gospel?

3. I live in obedience to God's Word only to a certain extent. There are some areas in life where the Bible cannot be trusted to guide me.

All Scripture is given by the true and living all-wise God. Therefore, we can trust every part of the Bible. Among the Ten Commandments is the command to not kill. No one has the right to decide when someone else's life should end. God has not granted us the right to decide when our own lives should end. Our perspective is so very limited. We tend to dwell on our own feelings and our own welfare and minimize the consequences of our actions on other people. We want to act independently – to not have to make choices based on how our actions affect others. We feel that we have rights! "I shouldn't have to give up my rights for somebody else!" That perspective is not Christian, however. Christians are to love their neighbors as themselves. They are to lay down their lives for others.

4. Life is not worth living.

This has been my sentiment at various times in my life. Life is sometimes hard, and eventually the pain seems to outweigh the joy of living. I have caught myself momentarily believing the lie that life is not worth living. Yes, it is a lie! Life is worth living, even while going through difficult times. It is not the amount of riches, honor, pleasure, experiences, or ease one has that determines the value of his life. Your life has value because you were created by God.

If it were true that life is not worth living, then God would not continue to give me life to live on this Earth, for He does nothing without purpose. You believe that God is good, don't you? Does He ever cease being good? Can God ever misjudge something? Can He ever come to a wrong conclusion because He does not view things from our perspective? Maybe He just does not know how difficult and painful life can be. But wait a minute! Consider Jesus' life. Hebrews 4:14 & 15 says, "Therefore, since we have a great high priest who has ascended into heaven, Jesus the Son of God, let us hold firmly to the faith we profess. **For we do not have a high priest who is unable to empathize with our weaknesses, but we have one who has been tempted in every way, just as we are – yet he did not sin**" [emphasis added] (NIV). Jesus understands every one of your struggles because He lived as a man upon this Earth and confronted the very same temptations that we face. He faced unbelief and lack of support from the disciples, attempts to entrap Him by religious leaders, an unjust trial which condemned Him to a horrible death on a cross, and much more.

Jesus was fully God, but He was also fully human. He got hungry, thirsty, and tired. His sweat was like drops of blood at the thought of dying on the cross (Luke 22:44). He knows what it is like to live life here on Earth. He can identify with everything about being human except for sin. He can understand your struggles and your pain, and He sympathizes with them.

Maybe sometimes, from my own fallen perspective, life does not seem worth living; however, to God, my life is worth living. He has created me to glorify Him, so He wants me to live to fulfill that glorious purpose!

5. My trials and problems are more than I can bear.

In a sense, this is true, but what this is saying is that I am the only resource that I have. I cannot bear my trials and problems, so therefore, I cannot go on living. But Christian, you are not meant to bear life on your own! When you trusted in Christ, you gave your life to Him, so it is not your life anyway. And **He wants to bear those burdens for you,**

to come alongside you and help you with them. The glorious Holy Spirit was given, in part, to comfort and sustain us.

Isaiah 41:10 says:

> "Fear not, for I am with you; be not dismayed, for I am your God; I will strengthen you, I will help you, I will uphold you with my righteous right hand" (ESV).

Psalm 46:1-3 says:

> "God is our refuge and strength, an ever-present help in trouble. Therefore we will not fear, though the earth give way and the mountains fall into the heart of the sea, though its waters roar and foam and the mountains quake with their surging" (NIV).

6. God's provisions are not adequate for my needs.

> "Is anything too hard for the LORD?" (Genesis 18:14 ESV).

I remind you of a verse quoted earlier: "And my God will meet all your needs according to the riches of his glory in Christ Jesus" (Philippians 4:19 NIV). These verses refute what you would be telling the world if you take your own life; it is clear from these two verses that God is able to provide everything you need – even hope and encouragement and a renewed purpose for living.

Consider another powerful verse:

> "His divine power has given us everything we need for a godly life through our knowledge of him who called us by his own glory and goodness" (2 Peter 1:3 NIV).

What more needs to be said? We must make use of the sufficient resources that God has provided.

7. Getting relief from my pain and my problems is more important than God's plans.

God has some purpose for your life – something for you to accomplish, a purpose to fulfill. He has a good purpose, even in your trials, struggles, troubles, and problems. God's plans are always greater than our own plans. He is far wiser, and He has information that we lack. **Is fulfilling His plans for your life not more important to you than escaping your problems?**

By taking your own life, you would be opting out of the greatest opportunity in life. It is sort of like the person who completes only so much of high school or college and then drops out. He never realizes the ultimate result of completing the requirements: a diploma or a degree. The same is true for the person who begins a worthy project but abandons it before it is completed. **Please do not throw away your life as you would a half-finished research paper or painting or building project with which you have become frustrated! Your life has value, even though it is flawed!**

The completion of God's plan for my life is important to God, and it is therefore important to me. I do not want to cut that short!

Think for a minute about how differently the story of the Apostle Paul's life would read had he decided to escape the pain and problems of his life by ending it with his own hands. What effect would this difference make in the lives of others?

This is what the Apostle Paul says in 2 Timothy 4:6-8:

"For I am already being poured out like a drink offering, and the time for my departure is near. I have fought the good fight, I have finished the race, I have kept the faith. Now there is in store for me the crown of righteousness, which the Lord, the righteous Judge, will award to me on that day – and not only to me, but also to all who have longed for his appearing" (NIV).

How different this text would read if Paul had decided after being beaten, stoned, shipwrecked, falsely imprisoned, and more, that he had had enough suffering and wanted to escape by taking his own life. I imagine it would read something like this:

"The time has come for me to leave this world because I have had enough of the problems associated with ministry. I've been beaten with thirty-nine lashes, stoned and left for dead, deserted by my fellow workers, and shipwrecked. I was even put in prison for preaching the Gospel! My life is so miserable that I cannot take it any longer! I know I have not completed the assignment that God gave me to do – to preach the Gospel to the Gentiles and to write much of the New Testament. I just want to die and go to Heaven to be with God. That's a far better place, and I want to go there so that I don't have to deal with the problems of life anymore! I am burned out! Somebody else can take up the task of writing all the books of the New Testament that God wants me to write because I just can't do it!"

Notice what Paul actually says in Philippians 1:20-26, written from his prison cell:

"I eagerly expect and hope that I will in no way be ashamed, but will have sufficient courage so that now as always Christ will be exalted in my body, whether by life or by death. For to me, to live is Christ and to die is gain. If I am to go on living in the body, this will mean fruitful labor for me. Yet what shall I choose? I do not know! I am torn between the two: I desire to depart and be with Christ, which is better by far; but it is more necessary for you that I remain in the body. Convinced of this, I know that I will remain, and I will continue with all of you for your progress and joy in the faith, so that through my being with you again your boasting in Christ Jesus will abound on account of me" (NIV).

Let's sort out Paul's feelings about whether he should live or die.

1. He wants to exalt Christ in his body, whether he lives or dies. **The most important thing to him is not whether he lives or dies but that he exalts Christ.**

2. Living means fruitful labor for himself. I think this refers to a spiritual harvest that he knows he will take to Heaven with him. He is thinking about his eternal rewards for his ministry on Earth – specifically his work with the believers at Philippi.

3. He is torn between living and dying.

4. He wants to go to be with Christ in Heaven, which is better than living here on Earth.

5. He knows that it is necessary for the believers in Philippi that he continues to live so that he can help them.

6. He is so convinced that his influence is necessary for the welfare of those believers that he is determined to keep living for their benefit.

7. He is thinking about **their** progress and **their** joy in the faith.

8. He wants to stay alive so that he can be a benefit to those believers. He sees this as a very worthwhile reason to keep living, even though he would prefer to die and be with the Lord.

We see the selfless attitude of Paul in this passage. He would like to die and go to Heaven so that he can be with Christ, but he is thinking about what pleases God and what is a benefit to others. This should always be our attitude as well. Anything that I want more than glorifying God is an **idol** in my life.

This is actually the secret to happiness and fulfillment. God did not create us to live merely for ourselves. A life lived primarily for oneself brings heartache and emptiness; it is a life wasted on something merely temporal rather than something of eternal value.

8. I am wiser than God; I know better than He does what is best for me.

Not so! "For the foolishness of God is wiser than human wisdom, and the weakness of God is stronger than human strength" (1 Corinthians 1:25 NIV). Remember Proverbs 3:5 & 6: "Trust in the LORD with all thine heart and lean not unto thine own understanding. In all thy ways acknowledge him, and he shall direct thy paths" (KJV). Why are we told to not lean on our own understanding? It is because our understanding is limited and tainted by sin. His understanding is perfect. He knows what is best!

If the verses quoted so far do not bring you any conviction, I would have to say that you are probably not a born-again believer. It is God who is speaking through these verses. If your heart is not stirred at all towards obedience when reading the Word of God, then you probably are not His child. John 10:27 says, "**My sheep listen to my voice; I know them, and they follow me**" [emphasis added] (NIV).

Chapter Four

A Foiled Plan

Gina's* plan for that snowy evening just before Christmas was to take her own life.

She had been living with chronic pain and was diagnosed with CRPS (Complex regional pain syndrome). Her doctors told her that her condition would never improve; she would have to learn to live with the pain every day. She had already dealt with the condition for fourteen years. She believed that, due to her condition, she was a burden to her husband. It was not fair to him, she reasoned, to have to deal with the financial strain and with her depression, both brought on by her condition.

So that night she got into her car and started driving north. She figured that after running out of gas, she would simply freeze to death on the side of the road. It was a brutal winter, and the night's forecast was -20 degrees Fahrenheit. She had left her house without a coat or any provisions.

As she drove with the determination to end her life that night, she was distracted by the snowflake Christmas decorations hanging on the overhead street lights. They began to look like halos. This sight startled and perplexed her. She blinked to clear her vision but continued to see halos rather than snowflakes. Halos reminded her of angels. Angels reminded her of Heaven. Heaven reminded her of God. Then she began to feel conviction about what she was planning to do.

She decided to pull into a gas station to compose herself. As she sat in the car, the attendant looked over at her, and their eyes met. Something about the attendant's gaze gave Gina pause. She sensed that the attendant was being used by God to get her attention and cause her to rethink her plans. Three times, the oblivious attendant looked directly at Gina.

"The Lord caused this to bring attention to what I was doing – to think things over some more. I am convinced that the Spirit was pulling me," she relates years later.

Moments after arriving at the gas station, she left and continued driving. Yet, the sight of those halos haunted her. She was so overwhelmed by the power of God's conviction that she decided she needed to be with other people. "If not, I would have probably moved forward. It was an immediate conviction to be around people."

Gina's thought was to go to the TJ Maxx store so that she would be distracted by the bounty of Christmas merchandise and be around other people. She drove to the retail store which was open for extended hours due to Christmas shopping. She got out of the car and went inside the store. While in the store, she was crying. The Lord was convicting her to just get the thought of suicide out of her head.

A horrible realization suddenly came to her mind: "I'm going to do this right before Christmas and ruin the celebration of Jesus' birth. I will taint Christmas for my family for the rest of their lives!"

Then the merchandise in the store began to catch her attention. "Wouldn't that be a nice gift for so and so," she thought, still wrestling with the idea of ending her life. God used things in the store to convict her further. "Oh my! My brother would love that hat!" Then, seeing other items, she thought, "I could buy that for Matt! Tyler would love that hoodie!" God used those things to show her that her family needs her.

"But I need you, too," came the thought. "I still have a purpose for you; I'm not finished with you yet." She was convinced that it was the Holy Spirit telling her spirit that God wanted her to stay alive to continue to serve Him.

The resolution came pouring over her. "When I leave here, I need to get gas and go home." She kept telling herself that. "When you leave the store, you are going to get gas, and you're going home!"

The next day was Monday, and Gina called her doctor's office for an appointment. The office had added a new resource – a woman counselor. She was available that day, so Gina was able to see her.

The day after meeting with the counselor, Gina broke down and confessed to her husband that she had almost taken her own life a couple of days before. He was shocked. He knew that she had been depressed, but he never imagined that her depression was that severe.

I asked Gina to look back and recall what she would have missed most if she had been successful in ending her life that night many years earlier. She immediately told me that she would have missed seeing her son graduate from high school. She also would have missed facilitating the finding of the answer to his baffling physical ailment.

He had been sick from birth. Whenever he got sick, he ended up with pneumonia – sometimes double pneumonia. His ears would get infected. Consequently, he missed a lot of school. According to Gina, the doctors dismissed his symptoms because they could not find answers on the tests. They said his symptoms must be due to depression.

"I would have missed advocating for him. We went to several different doctors. They suspected that something wasn't right. They did a ton of tests and blood work. Eventually, the doctor suspected that something was wrong with his lungs."

They discovered that part of one of his lungs had not developed. "Whenever he would get sick and it would get into his lungs, stuff would basically get trapped and that is why he was constantly sick; the infection was deep within the lung." They had been blaming his illness sometimes on his asthma. "If I had moved onward [with her plan to kill herself], my child would not have gotten the information we needed for him to have a healthier life. A huge boulder was lifted from my shoulder." He now takes medicine every day, on a regular schedule.

Gina recalls a comment her husband had made one night many years ago after watching a movie together as a family. He said that suicide is a very selfish thing to do. She was taken aback. He was not aware that she had been thinking about taking her own life. Her desire to end her life was the result of viewing it as a burden to him. Her suicide, she reasoned, would be a noble thing because she was thinking of his welfare – that he would be better off without her.

She was not realizing, however, the negative impact that her absence would have on her husband or other family members. But that snowy night just before Christmas many years later, she came to understand that, though her death might alleviate her husband of the financial and the emotional burden of her depression due to her condition, her absence would also hurt him. He needed her!

It is apparent that one of the tactics Satan uses to cause some people to kill themselves is to convince them that their families and friends would be better off without them. I have heard this sentiment expressed by struggling people several times.

Today, in 2022, Gina and her husband are working on their marriage and have seen God work in amazing ways. Their son is in his second year of college and is doing well. She is thankful that God prevented her from taking her own life many years earlier. She looks forward to fulfilling God's plans for her life, and she is depending upon Him for the wherewithal to do what He has called her to do.

*Pseudonyms have been used to protect this family's privacy.

Chapter Five

A Mother's Rescue

Savannah* was not depressed, just overwhelmed. In addition to the usual tasks of being a wife and mother, this young homeschooling woman was also dealing with health issues in her family and teaching challenges. She was handling most of this by herself since her husband's job kept him away from home several days a week.

Savannah felt inundated with all these heavy responsibilities. "I was slowly becoming overwhelmed with everything that I felt 'I' needed to accomplish." The stress was taking a toll on Savannah. "I was struggling to just make it through the day and felt like a complete failure in every area of life. I felt like I wasn't measuring up in being a wife, mom, or teacher. Never mind the responsibilities at church."

"I would say the feelings of inadequacy came slowly over time. Then probably over a period of a week or two, I just strongly felt I wasn't enough. My family would be better off with someone else who could manage everything better than what I could. These feelings progressively got stronger until it culminated in my feelings of just ending it all. I truly felt that if I just ended it all, everyone would be so much better off. I was in my laundry room doing laundry one day, feeling all the weight and contemplating how I could end it. I remember my biggest fear was

I didn't want the kids to find me. The feelings were so strong and I knew they were not of Christ, but it felt like the perfect answer for my family."

Savannah eventually called out to God for help when she felt that she "just couldn't do life anymore." The answer came one night while she was in bed trying to fall asleep as her struggles occupied her mind. She sensed God was leading her to get up and start writing Scripture. Though she did not feel like doing that, she got up anyway, not knowing where to start. Again, she felt God's leading; He was impressing upon her to start writing out the book of James.

"And so I started writing James out. Just poring over it as I was writing. Absorbing it. God knew that was what I needed. James was exactly what I needed at that moment. I could endure Satan's temptation [to end her own life] but only through Christ!"

So began Savannah's habit of writing out Scripture every night before going to bed. As she did, she soon realized that the stresses of life had hindered her devotional life. "As I started studying God's Word again, those feelings of inadequacy, failure, and helplessness started diminishing, and I could see clearly again. I was able to share with my family my struggles, and they helped me in many areas I felt overwhelmed in."

Years later, Savannah still writes out Scripture when she feels like the pressures of life are getting heavy. "It helps me realign and focus on the One who knows my every need. Had I taken all my pressures to Him at the beginning and given my heavy heart's burdens to Him and not tried to carry them myself, I probably wouldn't have had the feelings of ending it that I did. But I can look back and say that I'm thankful for the things I learned through this time."

It appears that Savannah learned these lessons through this experience:

1. Resist the pressure to be perfect. Do the best you can at the time.

2. Resist the urge to carry your heavy burdens by yourself. First, call upon God to help you, and listen to what He is telling you to do. (He will not tell you to do anything that is contrary to His Word! If a thought comes to you that is not biblical, it is **not** from Him!) Second, ask for help from trusted loved ones when you are feeling overwhelmed.

3. Refuse to take on additional responsibilities at the time you are already overwhelmed.

4. Don't neglect your personal devotions (time reading and meditating upon the Bible and time praying).

I would add some things that Savannah did not mention. First, her family would **not** have been better off without her! Who could have replaced her? Who would love her family as much as she does? Who could have handled the pressures any better? No woman is a superhero who can handle the pressures of life day after day without eventually feeling overwhelmed at times.

In addition, in this story God's Word was victorious over human feelings! This is glorious! Savannah **knew** that her thoughts about ending her own life were not from Christ, yet she **felt** that it was the "perfect answer" for her family. Thank God that Savannah did not allow her feelings to dictate her actions! **The Word of God should never be subordinate to our feelings, which are sometimes flawed and fickle. Rather, our decisions and behavior should always be guided by God's infallible Word!** It was after Savannah began to immerse herself in Scripture that the feeling that it would be best for her family if she ended her life lost its grip.

It is interesting to know, as I watch her life today, that Savannah faced such struggles in the past. I know that she and her family are a blessing to their church where they are active in ministry. I praise God that in her time of desperation, He **saw** Savannah in her distress, and He **answered** her call for help! I am glad that she is alive today. I hope her story inspires some struggling souls to hang in there, and to call upon God for help rather than taking matters into their own hands!

*A pseudonym has been used to protect this family's privacy.

Chapter Six

A Wife and Child's Aftermath (Written in 2012)

Sarah is my brother's wife (widow) and Emily is their daughter. When my brother took his own life, he left them to deal with the problems he left behind. And new ones were created in that one act.

Emily was only two years old when she lost her father, so she has no recollection of him. This girl has a whole set of problems to deal with now that her daddy is gone. Fortunately, she has a dedicated mother and other family to help her deal with her loss.

Sarah recently told me that Emily used to want "my daddy" back and would ask questions about his death. She does not yet realize that she lost her father because he chose to not go on living. After the passing of time, she has come to just want "a daddy." Most of her friends and classmates have a father, but she does not. She has had to deal with feelings of being different and being left out.

Shortly after Emily turned ten, she and Sarah came to Michigan to see the cemetery where Emily's dad and her grandmother are buried. We also drove to the house where my family lived for many years – the house where her dad grew up. These things are all a mystery to her. To a ten-year-old, the state of Michigan probably seems like a million miles away from her home in Minnesota. I am glad that she got to briefly visit the town where her dad was born, grew up, and is buried. I hope that it brings her some closure and some peace finding some pieces to the puzzle of this mystery man – her father!

I am sure that Emily would rather have lived with the problems of my brother's life than living with **never** having a memory of her dad's embrace and loving words. I know that he would have given her that, even if he was jobless and in financial crisis. I know he loved her! He displayed that love at a family reunion in Florida a year or so before he died. He called her his little bunny. I am sure that she would love to hear those sweet words from him today!

I know that with God's grace, Emily can heal. She seems like a well-adjusted, normal kid who is concerned about typical ten-year-old stuff. With God's grace, she can move past the stigma of having no father. She can, with His help, accept her circumstances and become a responsible adult. But she will forever have to live with the fact that she does not really know her biological father. He won't walk her down the aisle someday. I am sure that some male in Emily's life will stand in David's stead. But nobody can **really** take his unique place! She will adjust, I am hopeful, but I am sorry that she has to adjust to what she would gladly change. The most precious gift a parent can give his child is himself. It is harmful to a child to forever take that away from him. No one will ever take the place of the only man in the entire universe who fathered her and whose genes she shares!

I hope that Emily never doubts her father's love for her or ever senses that it is in any way her fault that he is not here for her. God can be a husband to the widow and a father to the fatherless (Psalm 68:5 & 6). Her unique circumstance does not have to define her or keep her from becoming a healthy, happy woman. But she will have to deal with her loss the rest of her life, and I know that it would have been better for her if her father were still here.

Emily is not David's only child. Brittany*, Emily's half-sister, was eighteen when her dad died. At her father's funeral, Brittany cried out, "Daddy! Oh, Daddy, why did you do that?" I don't have contact with Brittany, so I am not sure how she is adjusting.

Sarah, too, has been affected by my brother's decision to end his own life. Parenting is difficult enough with a committed mother and father. When one parent is missing, it puts added responsibility and pressure upon the parent who is still present in the life of the child.

Update: We were able to see Sarah and Emily briefly in 2023. Both seem to be doing well. They smile and laugh easily, and have carried on, living responsible lives. Sarah has a good-paying job, and Emily has completed a couple of years of college. They appear to have a close, loving relationship. Emily now knows how her father died, and she does not seem to be uncomfortable hearing our family reminisce about life with David.

I am glad that they have been able to put the past behind them and move on with their lives. I just wish that David was here to share their lives with them. It shouldn't have ended this way!

*A pseudonym has been used to protect the family's privacy.

Chapter Seven

A Father's Cry
(Written in 2012)

My dad has had to deal with the heartbreak of losing his only son. I know it was not easy dealing with David's problems throughout life. (Is it ever easy being a parent?) Dad had to juggle trying to help David deal with his problems, complicated by David's intoxication, and take care of my dying mother. And David thought everybody would be better off without him. He knew he was a burden and thought that his absence would help people get on with their own lives. He told me that. When I pointed out to David shortly before his death that it would deeply hurt Dad and Mom if he took his own life, he said that though it initially would be painful for them, they would adjust and be better off without him and his problems.

Not long ago, Dad was here for a quick weekend visit. My daughter and her four children came over to see him. We were sitting around my living room talking when the conversation turned to my daughter's birthday, which we had recently celebrated. My dad asked her how old she had turned on this year's birthday. "Thirty-nine" was the answer. Those two words struck Dad like a dagger. David was thirty-nine when he died. Such a simple, innocent, and otherwise happy event was a painful reminder that he had lost his son at such a relatively young age. And he lost him in a most horrifying way!

There is no getting around the frequent reminders of the pain of losing a loved one prematurely through this gruesome act!

Dad had to deal with David's business once he was gone. He had to contact the coroner and David's landlord. Though he was living in Florida, he had to get David's stuff out of his apartment in Minnesota. He had to figure out what to do with the quilt my mother made for David. He paid off David's debts and purchased a burial plot and coffin. And worst of all, he had to view his son lying in a casket, with only his face visible, the rest of his body hidden to protect us from seeing the grotesque effects on his body from hanging. Further, he had to stand before family, friends, and strangers at David's funeral, explaining that his son was dead because he had committed suicide! All of this took place while my mother was so close to her own departure from this world, and Dad took care of her around the clock, with the exception of some hospice care at the very end.

Dad told me that he laments that he did not get to see David live up to his full potential. David was smart and had many abilities. In cutting short his own life, he denied his father of seeing his son accomplish the great things of which he was capable. What a disappointment! What a way to end life – in defeat and despair!

Dad has a mature, healthy acceptance of what happened that stormy day in January of 2005. His attitude is one of gratefulness for having had David for those thirty-nine crazy, tumultuous, fun, yet sometimes troubled years. Though not stoic, he has accepted the situation and moved on with life. I know he wishes that things would have been different – that David would have continued to live and work out his problems. I am sure he would love to sit down with his smart, witty son today and talk. Yes, though deeply troubled, David was a funny guy. Despite the problems, Dad enjoyed being with his son and misses him to this day. Nothing can bring David back, of course, so Dad moves on. What is done is done, so there is no use sitting around wishing things were different. It is a sad story, but things could have been worse, he reasons.

Thank God that He has protected Dad from bitterness or despair! Suicide, I know, can have a domino effect. "I have lost my loved one, so I cannot go on either. The only escape from this pain is ending my own life, too!" But Dad chose a different way of dealing with his problems. He is still here today, seven years after losing his only son and his wife of more than fifty years. He is a well-adjusted, responsible adult who has continued to live the best life he can.

Life is strikingly different for Dad today than it was when David and Mom were alive. He lives alone. (Years later, one of my sisters moved in with Dad to take care of him.) I am sure he must sometimes get lonely. But he has chosen to live and face his problems rather than escaping from them. His children's pain of losing their brother and their mother six months later would have been compounded had he chosen to end his life, too.

Update: Right to the end of his life at age 94, Dad continued to live for Jesus! He led the congregational singing at his little church in Florida until the week before he died. My sister told me that his tithe check was in his Bible ready for the next day. (He died on a Saturday.)

Dad is a testament to my objections to suicide. God's grace is sufficient to carry us through even the most difficult circumstances. Escaping our problems through suicide cheats us out of the chance to prove that fact to others in the context of our own complicated, painful lives! And I value that a lot more than a pain-free life! I am sure that my dad did, too.

Chapter Eight

A Husband's Healing

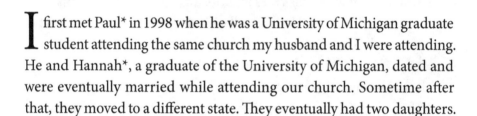

I first met Paul* in 1998 when he was a University of Michigan graduate student attending the same church my husband and I were attending. He and Hannah*, a graduate of the University of Michigan, dated and were eventually married while attending our church. Sometime after that, they moved to a different state. They eventually had two daughters.

While I was on Facebook one day in the fall of 2009, I read a message from Paul to all of his Facebook friends asking them to pray because a really terrible thing had happened to his family. Many of his Facebook friends responded that they would indeed pray. A couple of days later, we received another message from Paul, filling us in on the details of the event that so shook his family. Hannah, age thirty-two, had taken her own life!

Though I was reading Paul's subsequent messages on Facebook and not talking to him personally, I could detect the pain and despair in his "voice." He had just lost his one true love, his partner in life, and the mother of his children! He now had to care for these children by himself. He had to be the father and the mother to these two little girls – one age three years and the other age four months.

As his Facebook friends read his messages, we eventually witnessed God supplying all of Paul's needs, as well as those of his two little girls. It has been a wonderful journey to witness from afar! He has gone from despair to hope and from hope to joy!

Years after Hannah's suicide, Paul recounted to me the struggles he faced after his wife's death. The first three months, he experienced numbness.

The next three months, he felt the full depth of the loss. "It was very dramatic and painful." During those months, he felt very isolated because "nobody knew what to say. Nobody wanted to talk about it because they did not want to say the wrong thing, so people didn't say anything." That left him feeling alone.

When he really started feeling his emotions, he longed for the numbness again. "It feels like you bury your spouse one thousand times." He dealt with his emotions and his children as he grieved his spouse one little bit at a time. It felt like "walking through a wall of fire, but that is the only way to get through it. You bury them, in your mind, and then grieve, and the whole process starts over again. Bury – grieve – heal – bury – grieve – heal over and over again. Repeat nine hundred and ninety-nine times."

"What a long and arduous journey grieving was. Food lost its flavor." He learned one step at a time, one minute at a time. He learned to hold onto the Lord's grace minute by minute. Healing came, and so did hope. Eventually his desire to fully live again returned. He slowly gained the desire to completely work through the grief and to rebuild his life. "It was still a long way away, but hope returns slowly." Along the way, he shed many tears.

Paul described the following 12-36 months: "This was a whole new season of grieving for me. It was grieving the loss of who I was before with Hannah and learning to embrace the blank canvas that was in front of me. I also had to deal a little with the hurt of the suicide." Even though he would not have chosen for Hannah to die, he had to deal with that reality. In addition, he had to deal with the rejection he felt inside and the insecurity it made him feel. When considering dating again, he wondered who could ever love someone whose wife killed herself. "Yikes! Yeah, I had to face that."

Paul did not expect the second year to be so hard, but he says that it was still a good year. "This was the year I found myself blossoming and learning to fully live again. I did begin to date again at this time. This happened slowly." During this time, he learned more about the person he was now becoming.

Paul reflects on the act of suicide: "My opinion is that suicide is often a result of the brain not functioning properly." He acknowledges that suicide is a sin but that God can forgive any and all sins. "I always imagine Hannah entering Heaven and fully seeing everything and crying so many tears only to have the Lord wipe them away. He paid for that sin like all of the others."

Paul says that to those left behind, suicide is "an atomic bomb of devastation. It is brutal and devastating on so many levels. It leaves you confused and hurt and feeling broken, and that it is your fault. All this on top of losing them [a loved one]. Suicide loss is, in my opinion, one of the harder ones, especially a spouse. Every loss is hard, but that is a special type of pain and rejection you must work through that adds a whole unique challenge to it. It feels so shameful, and that makes it hard to talk about as well. Oh, man, just remembering the feelings still makes me misty-eyed."

Paul recounts that the Lord helped him in so many ways as he worked through those early days of the loss of Hannah.

"The day and night before we lost her, Hannah and I talked about so much. What a fantastic day and evening. She was all there. I remember talking about casting our cares on the Lord and the story of the disciples in the boat when the storm came up and Jesus was asleep. They must have tried everything as fishermen who grew up there, but [they] **never asked for help**. They just basically cursed Jesus for not caring that they were about to die. Only Matthew, the tax collector, is recorded as saying, 'Lord, help us!' But I was like, we do that, too, in trials. We try everything ourselves and get angry at God when our plans don't work. We have to look to Him and cast our cares and trust Him to be in control. This means letting go of our burdens."

"Well, twenty-four hours later, it was me in the storm, and I remember falling to my knees and saying, 'Oh, Lord help! I'm drowning. Save us, oh Lord! We are perishing!'"

"A few months later, the kids were sick, and it's so hard to ask for help as a single dad, the only parent. Your needs are messy and not as easy to help. It was late. I had a list of ten folks on call anytime for help. I finally humbled myself to call. I was desperate. The first person I called said, 'I'm sorry. I can't right now.'" The second person said the same thing. Paul called through the list of ten people, and none of them was available to help. "I was devastated and hung up crying. 'Lord, what the heck? I asked, right?'"

"'Did you ask me for help, Paul?' Crickets. 'Uh no, Lord. Lord, please help me! I'm desperate and in need of help!' The kids' fevers broke minutes later and all was well."

"A month after that, I hardly ever got out. It was so hard and I was so busy. To get out was glorious. I got invited to a luncheon, but I have a long truck and am running late. I'm five minutes away and am like

'Oh no, Lord! I'll never find parking for this thing!' I almost broke down, crying that I might not be able to go. And again, I hear, 'Ask me for help.'"

"'Okay, Lord, please help me.' I pulled in and right away someone in one of the only five spots that I could park pulled out. 'Oh Lord, thank you!'"

"He really showed me that He loved me and that He cared and to look to Him, not to myself or others in my need. Wow. I will never forget those lessons that he specifically taught me."

Update: In 2022, Paul celebrated ten years of marriage with his second wife, Sheila*! Paul and Sheila often post pictures on Facebook of themselves and the two girls, now teenagers. It sure looks like Sheila has become the mother to these two girls. There seems to be joy in the household as they face the blessings and the trials of life. This is another story where God redeemed a broken, devastating situation and brought new life!

Praise be to the true and living God!

*Pseudonyms have been used to protect this family's privacy.

Chapter Nine

Practical Help for the Desperate

Focus on the Family free counseling:
1-855-771 (HELP) 4357
Available weekdays 6:00 AM-8:00 PM Mountain Time

National Suicide Hotline: 988
Available 24 hours

Now that some biblical reasons why suicide is wrong have been presented, you may feel stuck. You realize that you cannot take your own life, but you are not at all happy about the prospect of living. It is very distasteful to you. The thought that you may have to live another twenty, thirty, forty years or more of torture is the reason that you want to end your life now. I do understand the anguish of living with circumstances that you find unbearable – yes, even impossible. You feel stuck because you know that you cannot die, but neither do you feel that you can live! That **is** a miserable existence!

So, what do you do if you find yourself in this position of realizing that you cannot die and yet thinking that you are not able to live?

First, if you are a believer in Jesus Christ – if you claim Him as your Savior and Lord – you run to Him and pour out your heart to Him and ask for His help. You must confess and turn away from any sin in your life, whether it is sin of behavior or attitude. Maybe you have already done that, but you still feel very burdened and are tempted to end it all. You cannot seem to get relief from the pain. Perhaps you wonder if God **wants** you to live in misery for the rest of your life. You conclude that He must **want** you to be unhappy because nothing seems to change. You can only foresee misery the rest of the days of your life.

Well, after you have pleaded for God's help and turned from your sin, you have to believe that He has heard your prayer, that He wants to help you, and that He is able to do so! When we really understand who God is, then we can trust Him to help us. His hands are not tied. He is not helpless to give you aid. He is not unaware of what is happening in your life or unaware of your strong feelings of death. He has every resource available to help you. He does not lack wisdom or knowledge or power or any other resource. And He has compassion for you in your distress! Relinquish your desire to take matters into your own hands, and resolve that you are going to be obedient to God in all things – even the matter of when you leave this world.

Listen to the words of Psalm 103, my favorite psalm and one of the passages that helped me most years ago when I was in a depressed state.

> "Praise the LORD, my soul; all my inmost being, praise his holy name. Praise the LORD, my soul, and forget not all his benefits – who forgives all your sins and heals all your diseases, who redeems your life from the pit and crowns you with love and compassion, who satisfies your desires with good things so that your youth is renewed like the eagle's. The LORD works righteousness and justice for all the oppressed. He made known his ways to Moses, his deeds to the people of Israel: The LORD is compassionate and gracious, slow to anger, abounding in love. He will not always accuse, nor will he harbor his anger forever;

he does not treat us as our sins deserve or repay us according to our iniquities. For as high as the heavens are above the earth, so great is his love for those who fear him; as far as the east is from the west, so far has he removed our transgressions from us. As a father has compassion on his children, so the LORD has compassion on those who fear him; for he knows how we are formed, he remembers that we are dust. The life of mortals is like grass, they flourish like a flower of the field; the wind blows over it and it is gone, and its place remembers it no more. But from everlasting to everlasting the LORD's love is with those who fear him, and his righteousness with their children's children – with those who keep his covenant and remember to obey his precepts. The LORD has established his throne in heaven, and his kingdom rules over all. Praise the LORD, you his angels, you mighty ones who do his bidding, who obey his word. Praise the LORD, all his heavenly hosts, you his servants who do his will. Praise the LORD, all his works everywhere in his dominion. Praise the LORD, my soul" (NIV).

This morning I was reading a portion of 1 Samuel in my devotions, and I want to include this passage as an additional encouragement. Hannah was one of Elkanah's two wives. His other wife had children, but Hannah did not. She was constantly derided by Elkanah's other wife for her barrenness. What did Hannah do? Did she sit around feeling sorry for herself? Did she take revenge on her abuser? Did she end her own life? No, she did none of these things. Though she did grieve, she did something positive with her grief. She did not seek revenge on her rival or take her own life. **She went directly to God and asked Him to give her a son**. And He did! In fact, He gave her three sons and two daughters! Here is part of Hannah's prayer after God opened her womb:

> "The bows of the mighty men are broken, and they that stumbled are girded with strength. They that were full have hired out

themselves for bread; and they that were hungry ceased: so that the barren hath born seven; and she that hath many children is waxed feeble. The LORD killeth, and maketh alive: he bringeth down to the grave, and bringeth up. The LORD maketh poor, and maketh rich: he bringeth low, and lifteth up. He raiseth up the poor out of the dust, and lifteth up the beggar from the dunghill, to set them among princes, and to make them inherit the throne of glory: for the pillars of the earth are the LORD's, and he hath set the world upon them. He will keep the feet of his saints, and the wicked shall be silent in darkness; for by strength shall no man prevail" (1 Samuel 2:4-9 KJV).

Do you see what Hannah is saying? She is acknowledging that it is God who determines our welfare. He changes the circumstances of the impoverished and the barren. He also changes the circumstances of the mighty and the wealthy. He raises up, and He casts down. He is the One who gives life and the One who takes life. Hannah knows that it is God who can open her womb and give her children, so she goes to Him in prayer, asking for His favor. I encourage you to do the same on your own behalf. Ask God to give you what you need.

It is very helpful to immerse yourself in other Scriptures about God's goodness and greatness. Renew your mind so that you can be transformed (Romans 12:2). Your mind (or maybe Satan or one of his demons) is telling you that there is no hope or that life is not worth living or that life is too painful. Reading and meditating on Scripture, especially meditating on the greatness and character of God, will fill your heart with hope and bring some relief. Focus on Christ and the blessings of being His child. Refer to chapter thirty-two in this book which lists attributes of the true and living God.

Another extremely helpful solution is sharing your burdens with a trusted brother or sister in Christ – one who knows the Word of God very well and is adept at handling the Word. Such a person can help apply Scripture to you and your situation, which should greatly encourage your heart. Our enemy, Satan, loves to tell us lies so that we become disheartened and lose hope. If you keep these struggles to yourself, you will probably be defeated. But with the help of a mature believer who knows Scripture and how to apply it, you can ward off Satan and his lies, at least temporarily. If you bring your struggles to light, it will expose the lies of Satan, and much of your hopelessness should dissipate.

In addition, inform the leadership of your church about your struggles. They will very likely be able to help you by praying with and for you and offering financial and other practical help, when needed. They can also hold you accountable and look after you so that you do not do something alone out of desperation. It is wise to not struggle by yourself. You will be more successful solving the difficulties which are weighing you down if others come alongside you and help you. Ecclesiastes 4:9-12 says, "Two are better than one; because they have a good reward for their labour. For if they fall, the one will lift up his fellow: but woe to him that is alone when he falleth; for he hath not another to help him up. Again, if two lie together, then they have heat: but how can one be warm alone? And if one prevail against him, two shall withstand him; and a threefold cord is not quickly broken" (KJV).

You should also solicit the prayers of some faithful prayer warriors. This is another way that someone else coming alongside you can strengthen you as you struggle. Others calling on God's help on your behalf can be a great blessing!

Of course, it is possible that you are experiencing anguish because of unconfessed and unrepented sin. Guilt feelings, intended by God to lead you to confession and repentance, might be causing your mental anguish. The treatment is to confess your sin to God and to receive His cleansing (1 John 1:9). Repenting of sin means agreeing with God about your sin and turning away totally from that sin, whether it be sin of behavior, of speech, or of thought. God will not give you hope and a clear reason for living if you refuse to repent of your sin. Stubbornly holding on to your sin is a sure way to sink deeper into the abyss of hopelessness and meaninglessness. I can say with assurance that this is not what God wants for you. Repent of your sin, make every effort to live for the glory of God, and watch your hopelessness and meaninglessness fizzle like a defective firecracker! You cannot experience intimate, peaceful fellowship with the true and living God if you fail to acknowledge your sin before Him. He wants to expose your sin to you, not to make you feel worthless and guilt-ridden but to cause you to repent and be healed. He is eager to forgive and heal you when you come to Him with a contrite heart (Psalm 51:17; Isaiah 66:2).

It is tempting when I am being squeezed by a painful trial to do one or more of the following. All are devices of the flesh rather than the Spirit and, therefore, do not glorify God and are ineffective long-term solutions:

- withdraw from others and from productive activity
- fret and worry about my problems
- engage in self-pity
- brood over perceived mistreatment by others
- become angry, resentful, bitter
- wallow in hopelessness
- become obsessed with myself, my problems, my feelings
- become jealous, combative, revengeful
- pursue the attention of others so as to soothe my own ego
- concentrate on getting what I want rather than concentrating on ministering to others
- build up walls of protection
- sit around waiting for my circumstance to change so that I feel well enough to get up and be productive

Do you see how pathetically ineffective these attitudes and behaviors are?

It is when I persist in doing the **right** things and thinking the **right** thoughts that the flesh loosens its grip on me. The only way to combat the power of the flesh is to make use of the power of the Holy Spirit, for the Spirit is even more powerful than my stubborn flesh!

One of the things that I realized about myself a long time ago was that when I was struggling with my emotions, I tended to become less productive. I did not **feel** like doing whatever tasks needed to be done. My thinking was that when I felt better, I would get up and do those necessary tasks, or do something to make either my life or someone else's life better. But as I sat around thinking about my problems and my feelings, instead of eventually feeling better, I actually felt worse. I have found that to feel better, I have to fight against my negative feelings and get up and start working on something worthwhile. When I do, I begin to feel better. **The sense of accomplishment that I feel is a great encouragement.**

For example, years ago we experienced some financial setbacks. We had major work done on our car, costing $1,500, the washing machine failed to spin the clothes properly so that they were dripping wet when the spin cycle was over, the refrigerator was leaking water so that the top shelves had a puddle of water on them, medical bills had piled up, and lightning hit the big tree in the front yard causing a huge branch to fall down across the yard. These things all happened within a short period of time. You know what I am talking about! The temptation was to become overwhelmed with discouragement and to sit around doing nothing. But it is amazing how much better I felt when I got up and began working on some of those tasks. Obviously, I could not work on all of these problems at one time, but as I took little steps to do the work that needed to be done, it actually began to relieve the oppressive feelings that had squeezed me and left me feeling helpless and hopeless.

When we were contending with the problems of the washing machine, the refrigerator, and the fallen tree limb, and we were working on paying off the medical bills, we still had much for which to be grateful. We were thankful that we now had a working car, we had a refrigerator that kept our food cold, a yard with a tree, and I had a husband with less shoulder pain (hence the medical bills). We were also grateful that the heavy tree limb had not fallen on our house or car – or our neighbor's car! Yikes!

Another result of working despite my negative feelings is that I see how good it feels to get a job done, and I become grateful for the things that do work properly and for the things in my life that I do enjoy. For example, during this time of upheaval with the car, the appliances, medical problems, and the debris all over the front yard from the fallen tree, I was able to get other jobs done around the house that I had been wanting to do. The rolls of fabric and the packaged curtain rods which had been lying on our bedroom floor for years were now beautiful window treatments framing the new windows we recently had installed. The picture that I bought for $1 at a yard sale was now hanging in the perfect frame I purchased with a coupon from a craft store. It looks beautiful on the wall painted the same color as the sky in the picture.

As I sit here typing on my computer, I am enjoying the desk I purchased at my favorite antique store with money that my church gave me to show their appreciation for my work as choir director. (A picture of my desk is on the front cover of this book.) If I had let my feelings rule, I would not have done the work in that ministry, which in itself is success. But also, I would not have my desk that is a perfect reflection of my taste. My desk is a reminder of this principle of working despite my feelings.

After leading the church choir for a few years, I had to cancel the choir for about a year because we did not have enough men to sing the tenor and bass parts. So as summer came in 2011, I had to make a decision. Should I proceed with choir this coming year? I decided to go ahead and make plans to start up choir again, not really knowing if we would have enough people. I chose a Christmas musical. It would be a challenging one for our choir, partly because it contained quite a bit of drama. But it was the best musical, I felt, of the ten from which I had to choose. I began to set into motion the plans, working through many issues. It took me a while to fill all the characters in the drama, but I kept at the task.

Then in early October, someone outside of my church said something to me that so devastated, angered, and consumed me that I wanted to resort to some of the fleshly behavior which I referred to earlier. I wanted to sit around feeling sorry for myself. I did not feel like working on this musical. I had to get up in front of the choir every week with my raw feelings eating away at me, and I just wanted to run away!

Recognizing that Satan was trying to derail me, I called several sisters in Christ and asked them to pray for me. Then I cautiously but immediately pushed myself to do the necessary tasks of getting ready for the Christmas musical. There were so many problems to work out, but I kept pushing through them one at a time, seeking God's help. I felt like the story of this musical was so good that it would certainly bring glory to God, even if it was not a perfect production. As I moved through the days and the weeks of practice and the implementation of my plans, I began to **feel** more like working on this project. The hurtful comment that was said to me weeks earlier began to lose its grip.

The end of the story is that the choir and actors put on an amazing presentation of the Christmas musical, and it was a great blessing to our church. And as I sit at my desk, I am reminded of what a blessing it was to watch God help us through all the difficulties and present a program that was a blessing to so many people. My desk is a reminding testament to how God helped me, as I began to take the steps necessary to go all the way from the idea of our choir presenting this musical to the full, successful, presentation of it before a live audience of 477 people. I was in awe as I watched what God did with my simple steps of obedience when I did not **feel** like doing anything! What a wonderful blessing I would have missed had I given up! **Instead, I worked through my feelings because I knew that was the right thing to do.** I had to work hard against many obstacles for a couple of months before I could receive the final blessing, but it was so worth it! This is victory! The memory of that triumph gives me encouragement as I work through the issues that face me today. There are new challenges, new struggles, but I choose to work through them rather than giving way to my feelings. Allowing my feelings to rule my life is idolatry.

Do not believe the lie that it is God who is encouraging you to end your own life. That is not the Spirit of God prompting you but rather the spirit of the antichrist – Satan! When God wants your life to end, He will take you home; He does not need your help. You are still alive because God wants you to be alive, and He wants you to live for Him. It is Satan who wants to take your life. He seeks to kill, steal, and destroy. It is he who is whispering to you to escape your pain and your problems by taking your own life. God wants you to live, to experience His help and His power to triumphantly get through whatever it is you are facing. Your problems may be far more daunting and oppressive than mine, but God still has the power to help you through them! And He receives a lot of glory when we live victoriously, despite our circumstances and our feelings.

And that, dear friend, makes life worth living. Bringing glory to God is the most important, fulfilling, fruitful thing anyone can do in this life. And you can bring glory to God by living through those tough days when all seems dark and hopeless. Hopelessness is another lie from Satan! God is still on His throne and will remain on His throne, sovereign over every aspect of your life, and so there is **abundant** hope! But you cannot sit around waiting for circumstances to change so that you can become hopeful. You need to get up and get going, doing whatever He has called you to do today, leaning on His everlasting arms for support! You can live a fruitful, victorious life for His glory, through the same power from God that raised Jesus from the dead (Ephesians 1:18-20).

Please do not throw away your life as you would a half-finished research paper or painting or building project with which you have become frustrated! Your life has value, even though it is flawed!

Chapter Ten

An Outcome Worse Than a Difficult Life

This book has been written primarily for Christians – for believers in and followers of Jesus Christ. Maybe you are a true believer, but perhaps you are not. Some people think they are Christians because they believe that Christ existed and that He was the Son of God. But there is more to being a Christian than that.

Perhaps you do not even claim to be a Christian, but you have read this book anyway. If that is the case, probably much of this makes little sense to you. And that is understandable; only true believers can really understand the Bible.

But let me warn you, on the authority of the true and living God, that **taking your own life is no true escape if you are not a Christian.** Yes, suicide allows you to escape from this earthy world of pain and problems. That is true. But if you are not a believer in Christ, when you die you will be placing yourself in a vastly more painful situation, one from which you can never, ever escape! It is the proverbial "jumping from the frying pan into the fire," so to speak. Why do I say this?

It is because the Bible clearly says that only Christians, true believers in Christ, will enter Heaven when they die. All others will be condemned to Hell, which is described in the Bible as an awful place!

This description of Hell is given throughout the New Testament: "eternal punishment" (Matthew 25:46); "weeping and gnashing of teeth" (Matthew 25:30); "eternal fire" (Matthew 25:41); "unquenchable fire" (Mark 9:43 & 48); "their worm does not die" (Mark 9:48); "torment" (Luke 16:28); "outpouring of God's wrath" (Revelation 14:9-11); "torment with fire and sulfur" (Revelation 14:9-11); "no rest day or night" (Revelation 14:9-11).

It is a horrible thought, but Hell is a real place where those without Christ will spend eternity! And Hell is a vastly more terrible place than most people realize. The Bible's description of Hell should wipe away any thought that suffering souls can find camaraderie in revelry and debauchery in that cursed place! You will derive no comfort from the other languishing souls who are consumed by their own misery! Satan and his demons will be there, pouring out hate and cruelty. Those who worshiped Satan in this life will experience no enjoyment from him in this place of punishment. Unlike life on Earth, he will not be able to offer you anything in exchange for your soul, for it will already be his. His mask will come off, and the terror of his nature will be fully exposed. God has already told us that he is a liar and a deceiver, masquerading as an angel of light (John 8:44; 2 Corinthians 11:14).

Lest you think that Hell will not be all that terrible, reflect upon this. In Matthew 18:5 & 6, Jesus says this: "And whoso shall receive one such little child in my name receiveth me. But whoso shall offend one of these little ones which believe in me, it were better for him that a millstone [a heavy stone weighing a couple thousand pounds] were hanged about his neck, and that he were drowned in the depth of the sea" (KJV). Though you may not be guilty of the particular sin that is mentioned here, you are guilty of other sins, and God's wrath abides on you unless you have placed your faith in Jesus Christ and have therefore been forgiven of all your sins.

My purpose for using this passage is to get you to think about the horror of experiencing the wrath of God. God's anger is worse than being thrown into the deep part of the sea with a millstone around your neck. Think of the terror of drowning due to that heavy weight tied around your neck as you futilely flail and gasp for breath. How indescribably terrible! Even if you were an excellent swimmer, you would be absolutely powerless to save yourself! That heavy millstone would drag you down to the bottom of the sea, and there you would stay as your lungs filled with water and you drowned. How frightening! As horrific as that experience would be, it pales in comparison to encountering the fury of God's wrath, according to Matthew 18:6.

Christians, however, will not face the wrath of God. His wrath has been appeased by the sacrificial death of Jesus Christ in payment for sin. The question is, then, "How does one become a true Christian?" The Bible gives the answer to this question!

God tells us in the Bible that every person in the world and throughout time is born a sinner because we have all inherited a sin nature from our first parents, Adam and Eve. Further, we are all guilty of willfully sinning in thought, word, and deed our whole lives. "For all have sinned, and come short of the glory of God" (Romans 3:23 KJV). Sin is the breaking of God's laws. God has established laws for the creatures He created – all human beings. We have all broken His laws and are guilty before Him. 1 John 1:8 says that we deceive ourselves if we claim that we have not sinned. God is holy and cannot stand sin, which is an offense against His character. God says that the wages, or the payment of sin is death (Romans 6:23). Ezekiel 18:4 says that the soul who sins will die. We all deserve death in Hell because we have all broken His laws in many ways throughout our lives.

Humans tend to think that, though we have sinned, if our goodness outweighs our sin, God will surely let us into Heaven. Those with that perspective fail to realize that the standard for getting into Heaven is perfection – perfect conformity to all of God's laws in thought, word, and deed, without fail – even once! That disqualifies us all from Heaven!

God's moral law, the ten commandments, condemns us all! There is no getting around it. We are all guilty of breaking His commandments. Jesus said that even having hatred in one's heart is murder. Looking upon a man or a woman with lust makes us guilty of sexual sin. Using God's name or His role of God lightly or disrespectfully makes us guilty of blasphemy. Don't fool yourself; God will by no means clear the guilty (Exodus 34:7). "The Lord is slow to anger and great in power, and the Lord will by no means clear the guilty. His way is in whirlwind and storm, and the clouds are the dust of his feet" (Nahum 1:3 ESV).

Even though we deserve death and can do nothing that will cause God to overlook our sin and look favorably upon us, He loves us and offers us a way to escape the otherwise sure condemnation to Hell. He provided a way to maintain His justice (His justice demands that He punish sin) and to forgive us of our sin and escape the penalty of Hell.

He provided a substitute for us — Jesus Christ — whose death on the cross was the payment for our sin. Jesus Christ was fully God and fully man. Jesus Christ, who knew no sin, became sin by taking upon Himself our sin and paying the just penalty for our sin by His sacrificial death on the cross (2 Corinthians 5:21). He did not die for His own sins, because He had none. He was the only One qualified to die on our behalf because He had no sin of His own.

God is completely satisfied with Jesus' sacrifice on the cross as payment for the penalty of our sin. Just before Jesus died, He uttered the Greek word "tetelestai", which means, "It is finished/complete" or "paid in full." After Jesus ascended into Heaven once He rose from the grave, He now sits at the right hand of God the Father, indicating that God has accepted Jesus' sacrifice as payment for our sin.

But Jesus' payment for sin can be applied to you personally only if you repent, which means to turn from your sin, and place your faith in Jesus' sacrifice for you instead of trying to be good enough yourself to get into Heaven. You will never make it if you trust in your own goodness. Remember that the standard is perfection. Even one sin will keep you out of Heaven. Admit to God that you have broken His laws and deserve His punishment. Call upon Jesus to save you. He is your only hope to avert the wrath of God. If you do not take refuge in the cross of Christ, your sin will be on your own head, and God will unquestionably condemn you to Hell. John 3:18 says, "He that believeth on him [Jesus] is not condemned: but he that believeth not is condemned already, because he hath not believed in the name of the only begotten Son of God" (KJV).

If you have not already done so, I plead with you to get right with God by calling upon Jesus to save you from the penalty of sin. "For whosoever shall call upon the name of the Lord shall be saved" (Romans 10:13 KJV). Those who are in Christ Jesus are no longer under condemnation, God promises (Romans 8:1)!

After you call upon Jesus to save you, seek out a church where Jesus Christ and His Word, the Bible, are honored, taught and preached. Let the pastor of that church know that you are a new believer in Christ and ask for help to grow in Christ and live for Him.

Chapter Eleven

Conclusion

Suicide is often a selfish act that interferes with God working in one's life for his good and God's glory. It is the end of the self-murder's story which can never be redeemed and changed for the better. It is a sinful act because it is unbiblical in many ways. It shortchanges oneself, his family, friends, and associates, and God Himself. It gives the world a weak view of Almighty God if the self-murderer is a professing believer. Rather than glorifying God, suicide glorifies Satan who reigns over the kingdom of death.

The believer who takes his own life deprives himself of possible additional eternal rewards. The true believer will enter Heaven when he dies. As long as he trusted in Christ alone to absolve his sins and he is not trusting in any of his own goodness to get into Heaven, he can be assured of seeing Jesus Christ on the other side of this life. Jesus will usher him into Heaven with welcoming arms only because his sins have been covered by the sacrificial death of Jesus Christ. However, whatever additional rewards he could have stored up for himself will be lost to him. That is a very sad thing that can never be changed (Matthew 6:19-21).

There is something that is far, far worse than that ending, however. The person who dies without Jesus Christ will immediately go to

Hell where there is extreme torment for all eternity. That person will experience God's justified, full wrath forever. Hell is a place of misery and gloom. There is no light, no joy, no quenching of one's mind-numbing thirst.

In His mercy, God has provided a way to escape this gloomy fate that all of us deserve. God hates sin and will not overlook it. He is completely just; He says that the wages of sin is death, and He guarantees that all sinners will go to Hell for eternity unless they accept His free offer of escape. Jesus Christ, who is God, lived an absolutely sinless life which completely met the requirements for getting into Heaven – sinless perfection in thought, word, and deed. He died on the cross as payment for the penalty of my sins and the sins of all who will call upon Him and place their trust solely in His sacrificial death as payment for our sins. He who knew no sin took our sin upon Himself and offers us His righteousness (goodness, rightness). That is the only way to get into Heaven. Heaven is for those who have perfect righteousness, and in myself and in yourself, we do not have that at all. The only way to get into Heaven is having the sinless perfection of Jesus Christ. He offers that as a free gift to all who recognize their need for a savior – those who recognize that they have the guilt of sin which can be washed away only through the blood of Jesus Christ.

If you die without Christ, you will be facing something far worse than anything you experienced on Earth. If you think you have problems now, just wait until you get to Hell where there is no possible relief from your problems and your aching heart. You will be absolutely helpless to ever improve your situation. I plead with you to not make this irreversible mistake! Call upon Jesus Christ to save you from the penalty of your sins. That is just the beginning of the blessings of being "in Christ."

Part 2

How to Biblically Handle Disappointment, Discouragement, Defeat, Depression, and Despair

"Trust in the LORD with all your heart,
and do not lean on your own understanding.
In all your ways acknowledge him,
and he will make straight your paths."
(Proverbs 3:5 & 6 ESV)

Chapter Twelve

How to Biblically Handle Disappointment, Discouragement, Defeat, Depression and Despair

Introduction

Do you struggle with any of these joy killers? Though God understands our human frailties and our struggles, He does not want our lives to be overtaken by any of these human emotions; rather, He wants us to live victoriously in spite of them. So how should we respond to our negative emotions so that we can live victoriously and bring glory to God? Learn what Scripture says about this.

All of the real-life characters in the Bible struggled with one or more negative human emotions such as disappointment, discouragement, defeat, depression and despair. Even Jesus Christ, who was fully God, experienced human emotions such as agony and sorrow, because He was also fully human.

In Part 2 of this book, we will examine the struggles of several of these Bible characters to see how they handled their problems and conclude what we can learn from them, whether they were good examples or bad. Several of these characters, many of whom were godly people, expressed their desire to die because of their difficult circumstances that seemed at times to overwhelm them. Did they resort to taking their own lives? We shall see.

Dictionary definitions:

disappoint[1] – 1. to fail to satisfy the hope, desire, or expectation of 2. to frustrate or thwart

discouragement[2] – 1. to deprive of confidence, hope, or spirit 2. to dissuade or deter (someone) from doing something

defeat[3] – 1. to prevent the success of; thwart 2. to dishearten or dispirit

depress[4] – to lower the spirits; deject

despair[5] – 1. to lose all hope 2. to be overcome by a sense of futility or defeat

There are many ways in which people attempt to deal with disappointment, discouragement, defeat, depression, and despair. The following is a list of some of them. Many of these ways are ineffective, sinful, destructive, and/or financially expensive.

---

[1] The American Heritage Dictionary of the English Language (Boston: Houghton Mifflin Harcourt Publishing Company, 2016), p. 513.
[2] Ibid., p. 515.
[3] Ibid., p. 475.
[4] Ibid., p. 488.
[5] Ibid., p. 492.

recreational or other drugs	anger
	complaining
excessive behavior (shopping, eating, drinking alcohol, engaging in social media and playing computer games)	self-absorption
illicit sex (fornication or adultery)	self-pity
risky behavior	worry and anxiety
gambling	bitterness
unbiblical, secular counsel	debilitating fear
withdrawal from people and/or life	fascination or involvement with the demonic spirit world
blame shifting	thoughts of suicide

1. Most people face one or more of these emotions or states of being at some time in their lives. It is a natural occurrence in the life of most human beings – even godly people who are in close fellowship with the Lord.

The following are some examples of characters from the Bible who were in distress. See if you can guess what Bible character made the following statements or is being described. (All of the verses are from the NIV version.)

A. "…was seized with remorse…went away and hanged himself."
_____

B. "The matter distressed _____ greatly because it concerned his son."

C. "Whenever the spirit from God came on _____-, _____ would take up his lyre and play. Then relief would come to _____; he would feel better, and the evil spirit would leave him."

D. "And he went outside and wept bitterly."
   _____

E. "Why did I not perish at birth, and die as I came from the womb? Why were there knees to receive me and breasts that I might be nursed? For now I would be lying down in peace; I would be asleep and at rest with kings and rulers of the earth..."
   _____

F. "I am a woman who is deeply troubled. I have not been drinking wine or beer; I was pouring out my soul to the LORD. Do not take your servant for a wicked woman; I have been praying here out of my great anguish and grief."
   _____

G. "I am in great distress," _____ said. 'The Philistines are fighting against me, and God has departed from me. He no longer answers me, either by prophets or by dreams. So I have called on you to tell me what to do."

H. "We are hard pressed on every side, but not crushed; perplexed, but not in despair; persecuted, but not abandoned; struck down, but not destroyed."
   _____

I. "I am worn out from my groaning. All night long I flood my bed with weeping and drench my couch with tears. My eyes grow weak with sorrow; they fail because of all my foes."

_____

J. "Don't call me _____," she told them. "Call me Mara, because the Almighty has made my life very bitter. I went away full, but the LORD has brought me back empty. Why call me _____? The LORD has afflicted me; the Almighty has brought misfortune upon me."

K. "When the sun rose, God provided a scorching east wind, and the sun blazed on _____'s head so that he grew faint. He wanted to die, and said, 'It would be better for me to die than to live.'"

L. "He came to a broom bush, sat down under it and prayed that he might die. 'I have had enough, LORD,' he said. 'Take my life; I am no better than my ancestors.' Then he lay down under the bush and fell asleep."

_____

M. "When the water in the skin was gone, she put the boy under one of the bushes. Then she went off and sat down about a bowshot away, for she thought, 'I cannot watch the boy die.' And as she sat there, she began to sob."

_____

N. "He has besieged me and surrounded me with bitterness and hardship. He has made me dwell in darkness like those long dead. He has walled me in so I cannot escape; he has weighed me down with chains. Even when I call out or cry for help, he shuts out my prayer. He has barred my way with blocks of stone; he has made my paths crooked."

_____

O. "Then _____ said to _____, 'I'm disgusted with living because of these Hittite women. If _____ takes a wife from among the women of this land, from Hittite women like these, my life will not be worth living.'"

P. "When _____ saw that she was not bearing_____ any children, she became jealous of her sister. So she said to _____, "Give me children, or I'll die!'"

Q. "Then _____ tore his clothes, put on sackcloth and mourned for his son many days. All his sons and daughters came to comfort him, but he refused to be comforted. 'No,' he said, 'I will continue to mourn until I join my son in the grave.' So his father wept for him."

R. "'Cursed be the day I was born! May the day my mother bore me not be blessed! Cursed be the man who brought my father the news, who made him very glad, saying, 'A child is born to you – a son!' May that man be like the towns the LORD overthrew without pity. May he hear wailing in the morning, a battle cry at noon. For he did not kill me in the womb, with my mother as my grave, her womb enlarged forever. Why did I ever come out of the womb to see trouble and sorrow and to end my days in shame?'"

S. "The waves of death swirled about me; the torrents of destruction overwhelmed me. The cords of the grave coiled around me; the snares of death confronted me. In my distress I called to the LORD; I called out to my God. From his temple he heard my voice; my cry came to his ears."

(Answers):
A. Judas Iscariot (Matthew 27:3-5)
B. Abraham (Genesis 21:11)
C. Saul, David, Saul (1 Samuel 16:23)
D. Peter (Matthew 26:75)
E. Job (Job 3:11-14)
F. Hannah (1 Samuel 1:15 & 16)
G. Saul (1 Samuel 28:15)
H. Paul (2 Corinthians 4: 8 & 9)
I. David (Psalms 6:6 & 7)
J. Naomi, Naomi (Ruth 1:20 & 21)
K. Jonah (Jonah 4:8)
L. Elijah (1 Kings 19:4 & 5)
M. Hagar (Genesis 21:15 & 16)
N. The writer of Lamentations – possibly Jeremiah (Lamentations 3:5-9)
O. Rebekah, Isaac, Jacob (Genesis 27:46)
P. Rachel, Jacob, Jacob (Genesis 30:1)
Q. Jacob (Genesis 37:34 & 35)
R. Jeremiah (Jeremiah 20:14-18)
S. David (2 Samuel 22:5-7)

2. The emotions of disappointment, discouragement, defeat, depression, and despair are very real in the minds of the people who are experiencing them. We should attempt to never belittle or minimize the feelings of others.

3. Depression has many causes, some of which are physical. I will focus on spiritual depression. **Regardless of the cause of a believer's depression, he is responsible to handle the problem biblically. No amount of adversity, confusion, fear, frustration, anxiety, or depression justifies acting or reacting sinfully.**

4. With spiritual depression, often the thinking of the depressed person needs to change. He may very well not be thinking biblically, and real help can be found when he learns to think biblically. Our thinking influences our behavior.

5. Be honest about your struggles. There is no shame in struggling with these emotions. And there is nothing to be gained if you are not honest about your struggles. It is only when we admit that we have a problem with these negative emotions that we can find help. It is not the struggle with these emotions that is the problem. It is when we cannot seem to find victory over them and they begin to control us that we know we have a real problem.

6. Words and body language can hurt or heal, discourage or encourage. When I struggled with depression many years ago, I longed for encouraging words. When I heard them, they were like medicine to my soul! Sometimes in an attempt to be helpful, people said things to me that actually caused me more grief! **We should never tell a hurting person things that are not true just so that he will feel better; nor should we refrain from gently and lovingly telling him the truths that he needs to hear to begin thinking more biblically. It is not helpful to tell a hurting person to just stop feeling this way or to pretend that he is not hurting. A listening ear and gentle, helpful words can bring temporary relief. Sometimes a hurting person wants to talk about his painful feelings rather than talking about something more lighthearted. Listen patiently to his feelings without giving advice at first or changing the subject. Display your compassion with your body language. Eventually, the hurting believer needs to hear the counsel of Scripture from another believer who knows how to apply that Scripture to the circumstances at hand. And often that means gently, yet firmly, confronting the hurting person about his thinking and/or behavior that is unbiblical.**

Suicide – The Biblical View

7. You may not find some of these lessons to be immediately helpful. But stick with them. Over time, they will build up a framework of thinking that should help any believer in Christ who is struggling with disappointment, discouragement, defeat, depression and despair.

8. There is always hope! Cling to that! There is always hope because there is GOD!

Romans 15:4:

> "For whatever was written in former days was written for our instruction, that through endurance and through the encouragement of the Scriptures we might have hope" (ESV).

The Scriptures offer hope!

Chapter Thirteen

The Study of Hagar

"So she called the name of the LORD who spoke to her, 'You are a God of seeing,' for she said, 'Truly here I have seen him who looks after me.'"
Genesis 16:13 ESV

This lesson is a story from the Old Testament about a woman named Hagar. I chose this story to study because it shows the true and living God intervening with compassion in the life of this destitute Egyptian slave who knew that her son was about to die in the wilderness without food and water.

The lessons in this book have been designed to correct our thinking about God or to remind us of what we already correctly believe about Him. The more we understand about the true and living God, the better we will understand how to biblically deal with disappointment, discouragement, defeat, depression, and despair.

It is of utmost importance to deal biblically with these emotions if we desire to follow Christ. True believers in Jesus Christ should have the desire to follow Him in obedience to His written Word. God's Word offers solutions to our troubles, solutions which are far superior to our own fallen human thinking.

With all this in mind, read the true-life story about Hagar and what she did when she was in desperation.

Genesis 16:

1 Now Sarai, Abram's wife, had borne him no children. She had a female Egyptian servant whose name was Hagar. **2** And Sarai said to Abram, "Behold now, the Lord has prevented me from bearing children. Go in to my servant; it may be that I shall obtain children by her." And Abram listened to the voice of Sarai. **3** So, after Abram had lived ten years in the land of Canaan, Sarai, Abram's wife, took Hagar the Egyptian, her servant, and gave her to Abram her husband as a wife. **4** And he went in to Hagar, and she conceived. And when she saw that she had conceived, she looked with contempt on her mistress. **5** And Sarai said to Abram, "May the wrong done to me be on you! I gave my servant to your embrace, and when she saw that she had conceived, she looked on me with contempt. May the Lord judge between you and me!" **6** But Abram said to Sarai, "Behold, your servant is in your power; do to her as you please." Then Sarai dealt harshly with her, and she fled from her.

7 The angel of the Lord found her by a spring of water in the wilderness, the spring on the way to Shur. **8** And he said, "Hagar, servant of Sarai, where have you come from and where are you going?" She said, "I am fleeing from my mistress Sarai." **9** The angel of the Lord said to her, "Return to your mistress and submit to her." **10** The angel of the Lord also said to her, "I will surely multiply your offspring so that they cannot be numbered for multitude." **11** And the angel of the Lord said to her,

"Behold, you are pregnant
and shall bear a son.
You shall call his name Ishmael,
because the Lord has listened to your affliction.

12 He shall be a wild donkey of a man,
his hand against everyone
and everyone's hand against him,
and he shall dwell over against all his kinsmen."

13 So she called the name of the Lord who spoke to her, "You are a God of seeing," for she said, "Truly here I have seen him who looks after me." **14** Therefore the well was called Beer-lahai-roi; it lies between Kadesh and Bered.

15 And Hagar bore Abram a son, and Abram called the name of his son, whom Hagar bore, Ishmael. **16** Abram was eighty-six years old when Hagar bore Ishmael to Abram.

Genesis 21:

1 The Lord visited Sarah as he had said, and the Lord did to Sarah as he had promised. **2** And Sarah conceived and bore Abraham a son in his old age at the time of which God had spoken to him. **3** Abraham called the name of his son who was born to him, whom Sarah bore him, Isaac. **4** And Abraham circumcised his son Isaac when he was eight days old, as God had commanded him. **5** Abraham was a hundred years old when his son Isaac was born to him. **6** And Sarah said, "God has made laughter for me; everyone who hears will laugh over me." **7** And she said, "Who would have said to Abraham that Sarah would nurse children? Yet I have borne him a son in his old age."

8 And the child grew and was weaned. And Abraham made a great feast on the day that Isaac was weaned. **9** But Sarah saw the son of Hagar the Egyptian, whom she had borne to Abraham, laughing. **10** So she said to Abraham, "Cast out this slave woman with her son, for the son of this slave woman shall not be heir with my son Isaac." **11** And the thing was very displeasing to Abraham on account of his son. **12** But God said to

Abraham, "Be not displeased because of the boy and because of your slave woman. Whatever Sarah says to you, do as she tells you, for through Isaac shall your offspring be named. **13** And I will make a nation of the son of the slave woman also, because he is your offspring." **14** So Abraham rose early in the morning and took bread and a skin of water and gave it to Hagar, putting it on her shoulder, along with the child, and sent her away. And she departed and wandered in the wilderness of Beersheba.

15 When the water in the skin was gone, she put the child under one of the bushes. **16** Then she went and sat down opposite him a good way off, about the distance of a bowshot, for she said, "Let me not look on the death of the child." And as she sat opposite him, she lifted up her voice and wept. **17** And God heard the voice of the boy, and the angel of God called to Hagar from Heaven and said to her, "What troubles you, Hagar? Fear not, for God has heard the voice of the boy where he is. **18** Up! Lift up the boy, and hold him fast with your hand, for I will make him into a great nation." **19** Then God opened her eyes, and she saw a well of water. And she went and filled the skin with water and gave the boy a drink. **20** And God was with the boy, and he grew up. He lived in the wilderness and became an expert with the bow. **21** He lived in the wilderness of Paran, and his mother took a wife for him from the land of Egypt.

22 At that time Abimelech and Phicol the commander of his army said to Abraham, "God is with you in all that you do. **23** Now therefore swear to me here by God that you will not deal falsely with me or with my descendants or with my posterity, but as I have dealt kindly with you, so you will deal with me and with the land where you have sojourned." **24** And Abraham said, "I will swear."

25 When Abraham reproved Abimelech about a well of water that Abimelech's servants had seized, **26** Abimelech said, "I do not know who has done this thing; you did not tell me, and I have not heard of it until today." **27** So Abraham took sheep and oxen and gave them to

Abimelech, and the two men made a covenant. **28** Abraham set seven ewe lambs of the flock apart. **29** And Abimelech said to Abraham, "What is the meaning of these seven ewe lambs that you have set apart?" **30** He said, "These seven ewe lambs you will take from my hand, that this may be a witness for me that I dug this well." **31** Therefore that place was called Beersheba, because there both of them swore an oath. **32** So they made a covenant at Beersheba. Then Abimelech and Phicol the commander of his army rose up and returned to the land of the Philistines. **33** Abraham planted a tamarisk tree in Beersheba and called there on the name of the Lord, the Everlasting God. **34** And Abraham sojourned many days in the land of the Philistines (NIV).

Observations about the story of Hagar:

1. God sees what is going on between Abram, Sarai, and Hagar. God is omniscient; that means He knows what is happening everywhere at all times. Consider these passages of Scripture that reveal this aspect of God to us:

Hebrews 4:13:

> "And no creature is hidden from his sight, but all are naked and exposed to the eyes of him to whom we must give account" (ESV).

Psalm 139:2-4:

> "You know when I sit down and when I rise up;
> you discern my thoughts from afar.
> You search out my path and my lying down
> and are acquainted with all my ways.
> Even before a word is on my tongue,
> behold, O LORD, you know it altogether" (ESV).

So, God certainly saw what was happening in this human drama between Abram, Sarai, and Hagar. I imagine that as an Egyptian who probably worshiped numerous gods – worthless gods who could not see – Hagar was surprised to realize that the true and living God could actually see her alone in the wilderness. He also saw her and her son Ishmael later in the wilderness. She named Him "a God of seeing" or "the God who sees me."

2. God seeks out Hagar. He obviously already knows where she is, but He comes to her and initiates the conversation.

3. God intervenes in the affairs of these people.

4. The Lord hears Hagar in her misery. He is aware of her troubled heart.

5. The Lord hears Ishmael crying. He is aware of Ishmael's troubled heart.

6. The angel of God comforts Hagar from Heaven.

7. God opens Hagar's eyes, and she sees a well of water. God saves her life and her son's life!

Conclusion:

God **sees** Hagar and Ishmael and is very mindful of their distress. He cares for them. Likewise, God **sees** you! God is very mindful of you and cares for you. Regardless of your situation, God can help you! If He helped Hagar and Ishmael in their distress, He will certainly help you.

Years later, God also saw the hardships of the Israelites who were in bondage in Egypt.

Exodus 3:7-10:

> "Then the LORD said, 'I have surely seen the affliction of my people who are in Egypt and have heard their cry because of their taskmasters. I know their sufferings, and I have come down to deliver them out of the hand of the Egyptians and to bring them up out of that land to a good and broad land, a land flowing with milk and honey, to the place of the Canaanites, the Hittites, the Amorites, the Perizzites, the Hivites, and the Jebusites. And now, behold, the cry of the people of Israel has come to me, and I have also seen the oppression with which the Egyptians oppress them. Come, I will send you to Pharaoh that you may bring my people, the children of Israel, out of Egypt'" (ESV).

Observations about the story of the Israelites:

1. God sees the misery of the Israelites and hears their cries.
2. God is concerned about their suffering.
3. God rescues them.
4. God brings them into a good land.

Conclusion:

I realize that the fact that God sees us and knows our suffering and is able to help us is a simple truth that most of us probably already know. However, sometimes we need to be reminded of simple truths.

God is not unaware of or indifferent about your suffering. He sees and knows about your suffering, and He is concerned about it. God can rescue you from your suffering and bring good to you. Be patient and wait for His deliverance!

Chapter Fourteen

The Study of Job

> "'Naked I came from my mother's womb, and naked I will depart.
> The LORD gave and the LORD has taken away;
> may the name of the LORD be praised.'"
> Job 1:21 NIV

There are some lessons from the book of Job that can help us learn how to biblically handle disappointment, discouragement, defeat, depression, and despair. Since the book of Job is too long to cover here, I am including only four chapters, thereby omitting Job's friends' foolish arguments with him and most of Job's reaction to his friends' advice.

The book of Job is considered to be one of the oldest books, if not the oldest book, in the Bible. Job and his family lived around the time of the patriarchs (Abraham, Isaac, and Jacob).

Job 1:

1 In the land of Uz there lived a man whose name was Job. This man was blameless and upright; he feared God and shunned evil. **2** He had seven sons and three daughters, **3** and he owned seven thousand sheep, three thousand camels, five hundred yoke of oxen and five hundred donkeys, and had a large number of servants. He was the greatest man among all the people of the East.

4 His sons used to hold feasts in their homes on their birthdays, and they would invite their three sisters to eat and drink with them. **5** When a period of feasting had run its course, Job would make arrangements for them to be purified. Early in the morning he would sacrifice a burnt offering for each of them, thinking, "Perhaps my children have sinned and cursed God in their hearts." This was Job's regular custom.

6 One day the angels came to present themselves before the Lord, and Satan also came with them. **7** The Lord said to Satan, "Where have you come from?"

Satan answered the Lord, "From roaming throughout the earth, going back and forth on it."

8 Then the Lord said to Satan, "Have you considered my servant Job? There is no one on earth like him; he is blameless and upright, a man who fears God and shuns evil."

9 "Does Job fear God for nothing?" Satan replied. **10** "Have you not put a hedge around him and his household and everything he has? You have blessed the work of his hands, so that his flocks and herds are spread throughout the land. **11** But now stretch out your hand and strike everything he has, and he will surely curse you to your face."

12 The Lord said to Satan, "Very well, then, everything he has is in your power, but on the man himself do not lay a finger."

Then Satan went out from the presence of the Lord.

13 One day when Job's sons and daughters were feasting and drinking wine at the oldest brother's house, **14** a messenger came to Job and said, "The oxen were plowing and the donkeys were grazing nearby, **15** and the Sabeans attacked and made off with them. They put the servants to the sword, and I am the only one who has escaped to tell you!"

16 While he was still speaking, another messenger came and said, "The fire of God fell from the heavens and burned up the sheep and the servants, and I am the only one who has escaped to tell you!"

17 While he was still speaking, another messenger came and said, "The Chaldeans formed three raiding parties and swept down on your camels and made off with them. They put the servants to the sword, and I am the only one who has escaped to tell you!"

18 While he was still speaking, yet another messenger came and said, "Your sons and daughters were feasting and drinking wine at the oldest brother's house, **19** when suddenly a mighty wind swept in from the desert and struck the four corners of the house. It collapsed on them and they are dead, and I am the only one who has escaped to tell you!"

20 At this, Job got up and tore his robe and shaved his head. Then he fell to the ground in worship **21** and said:

"Naked I came from my mother's womb,
 and naked I will depart.
The Lord gave and the Lord has taken away;
 may the name of the Lord be praised."
22 In all this, Job did not sin by charging God with wrongdoing.

Job 2:

1 On another day the angels came to present themselves before the Lord, and Satan also came with them to present himself before him. **2** And the Lord said to Satan, "Where have you come from?"

Satan answered the Lord, "From roaming throughout the earth, going back and forth on it."

3 Then the Lord said to Satan, "Have you considered my servant Job? There is no one on earth like him; he is blameless and upright, a man who fears God and shuns evil. And he still maintains his integrity, though you incited me against him to ruin him without any reason."

4 "Skin for skin!" Satan replied. "A man will give all he has for his own life. **5** But now stretch out your hand and strike his flesh and bones, and he will surely curse you to your face."

6 The Lord said to Satan, "Very well, then, he is in your hands; but you must spare his life."

7 So Satan went out from the presence of the Lord and afflicted Job with painful sores from the soles of his feet to the crown of his head. **8** Then Job took a piece of broken pottery and scraped himself with it as he sat among the ashes.

9 His wife said to him, "Are you still maintaining your integrity? Curse God and die!"

10 He replied, "You are talking like a foolish woman. Shall we accept good from God, and not trouble?"

In all this, Job did not sin in what he said.

11 When Job's three friends, Eliphaz the Temanite, Bildad the Shuhite and Zophar the Naamathite, heard about all the troubles that had come upon him, they set out from their homes and met together by agreement to go and sympathize with him and comfort him. **12** When they saw him from a distance, they could hardly recognize him; they began to weep aloud, and they tore their robes and sprinkled dust on their heads. **13** Then they sat on the ground with him for seven days and seven nights. No one said a word to him, because they saw how great his suffering was.

Job 3:

1 After this, Job opened his mouth and cursed the day of his birth. **2** He said:

3 "May the day of my birth perish, and the night that said, 'A boy is conceived!'

4 That day—may it turn to darkness; may God above not care about it; may no light shine on it.

5 May gloom and utter darkness claim it once more; may a cloud settle over it; may blackness overwhelm it.

6 That night—may thick darkness seize it; may it not be included among the days of the year nor be entered in any of the months.

7 May that night be barren; may no shout of joy be heard in it.

8 May those who curse days curse that day, those who are ready to rouse Leviathan.

9 May its morning stars become dark; may it wait for daylight in vain and not see the first rays of dawn,

10 for it did not shut the doors of the womb on me to hide trouble from my eyes.

11 "Why did I not perish at birth, and die as I came from the womb?

12 Why were there knees to receive me and breasts that I might be nursed?

13 For now I would be lying down in peace; I would be asleep and at rest

14 with kings and rulers of the earth, who built for themselves places now lying in ruins,

15 with princes who had gold, who filled their houses with silver.

16 Or why was I not hidden away in the ground like a stillborn child, like an infant who never saw the light of day?

17 There the wicked cease from turmoil, and there the weary are at rest.

18 Captives also enjoy their ease; they no longer hear the slave driver's shout.

19 The small and the great are there, and the slaves are freed from their owners.

20 "Why is light given to those in misery, and life to the bitter of soul,

21 to those who long for death that does not come, who search for it more than for hidden treasure,

22 who are filled with gladness and rejoice when they reach the grave?

23 Why is life given to a man whose way is hidden, whom God has hedged in?

24 For sighing has become my daily food; my groans pour out like water.

25 What I feared has come upon me; what I dreaded has happened to me.

26 I have no peace, no quietness; I have no rest, but only turmoil.

Job 42:

1 Then Job replied to the Lord:

2 "I know that you can do all things; no purpose of yours can be thwarted.

3 You asked, 'Who is this that obscures my plans without knowledge?' Surely I spoke of things I did not understand, things too wonderful for me to know.

4 "You said, 'Listen now, and I will speak; I will question you, and you shall answer me.'

5 My ears had heard of you but now my eyes have seen you.

6 Therefore I despise myself and repent in dust and ashes."

7 After the Lord had said these things to Job, he said to Eliphaz the Temanite, "I am angry with you and your two friends, because you have not spoken the truth about me, as my servant Job has. **8** So now take seven bulls and seven rams and go to my servant Job and sacrifice a burnt offering for yourselves. My servant Job will pray for you, and I will accept his prayer and not deal with you according to your folly. You have not spoken the truth about me, as my servant Job has." **9** So Eliphaz the Temanite, Bildad the Shuhite and Zophar the Naamathite did what the Lord told them; and the Lord accepted Job's prayer.

10 After Job had prayed for his friends, the Lord restored his fortunes and gave him twice as much as he had before. **11** All his brothers and sisters and everyone who had known him before came and ate with him in his house. They comforted and consoled him over all the trouble the Lord had brought on him, and each one gave him a piece of silver and a gold ring.

12 The Lord blessed the latter part of Job's life more than the former part. He had fourteen thousand sheep, six thousand camels, a thousand yoke of oxen and a thousand donkeys. **13** And he also had seven sons and three daughters. **14** The first daughter he named Jemimah, the second Keziah and the third Keren-Happuch. **15** Nowhere in all the land were there found women as beautiful as Job's daughters, and their father granted them an inheritance along with their brothers.

16 After this, Job lived a hundred and forty years; he saw his children and their children to the fourth generation. **17** And so Job died, an old man and full of years. (NIV)

Observations about the story of Job:

1. Job is godly; he fears God and rejects evil.

2. Job is wealthy and has many children.

3. Satan comes before the Lord along with the angels.

4. God initiates a conversation with Satan.

5. Satan has been roaming the earth. (We are told in 1 Peter 5:8 that the devil prowls around like a roaring lion, seeking someone to devour.)

6. God knows that Job is godly, and He points that fact out to Satan.

7. Satan claims that it is only because of what God does for Job, such as protecting and blessing him, that Job serves God. This appears to be an example of the accuser, Satan, our enemy, accusing a believer (Revelation 12:10).

8. Satan claims that Job would curse God if He took everything away from Job.

9. God gives Satan permission to take everything away from Job, except for his life.

10. Satan takes away all of Job's oxen, donkeys, sheep, camels, servants, and his sons and daughters.

11. Job worships and praises God. Job does not sin by charging God with wrongdoing. Job praises God **despite** his feelings! In fact, it appears that the first thing Job does upon learning of his losses is to fall down and worship the Lord (Job 1:20 & 21).

12. Satan again comes before the presence of the Lord with the angels.

13. God again initiates a conversation with Satan, pointing out that even though he was severely tested, Job still maintained his integrity.

14. Satan says that Job would certainly curse God if He inflicted Job's body.

15. God gives Satan permission to strike Job with illness but prohibits him from taking Job's life.

16. Satan afflicts Job's body with painful sores.

17. Job's wife tells him to curse God and die.

18. Job refuses her counsel. He accepts trouble from God as he accepts good from Him.

19. Job's three friends come to sympathize with him and comfort him.

20. Job expresses sorrow that he had ever been born.

21. Job admits that he spoke of things that he did not understand. He is deferring to God's wisdom as far superior to his own.

22. Job despises himself and repents in dust and ashes for presuming to know some things that he does not know.

23. God rebukes Job's three friends for their foolish counsel to Job and for misrepresenting God.

24. God blesses Job again – even more than He had before Job lost everything!

25. Job 42:11 says that the Lord brought all the trouble on Job. Read the verse: "All his brothers and sisters and everyone who had known him before came and ate with him in his house. They comforted and consoled him over all the trouble the LORD had brought on him, and each one gave him a piece of silver and a gold ring" (NIV).

What God says:

1. He is upset with those who have darkened His counsel with untruth. In other words, Job's three friends have misrepresented God (Job 38:2).

2. He asks if someone could correct the Almighty (Job 40:2).

3. He asks if Job would discredit God's justice (Job 40:8).

4. God intimates that Job cannot save himself (Job 40:14).

5. He asks who it is who could stand against God (Job 41:10).

6. He asks if He owes anything to anyone (Job 41:11).

7. He says that everything belongs to Himself (Job 41:11).

Conclusions:

1. Don't cling too tightly to anything except God. God gives good gifts for us to enjoy, but He sometimes takes them away. 1 Samuel 2:7 says, "The LORD sends poverty and wealth; he humbles and he exalts" (NIV). Anything I value more than God is an idol in my life. Idolatry is a sin (Exodus 20:2 & 3)! The only reason God sometimes takes things away from us is to accomplish a greater good, never because He is stingy, jealous, vindictive, capricious, or delights in our suffering. He

is not like human beings who sometimes do things out of childish or selfish motives.

God has at times taken things away from me – good things that I enjoyed. But it has been my experience that in time, He gave me something else in place of what He took away. This has been particularly true of some of the ministries in which I have been involved. He has taken away some very fruitful, fulfilling ministries, and at the time, I did not understand why. I am not sure that I understand why even to this day, but I know that after taking away a ministry, He always gave me another one in its place. I could not have participated in both ministries at the same time, so in losing one ministry, I was able to engage in the new ministry. This has blessed me with a wealth of experiences.

After several years of going to school to get a teaching certificate while raising two children, a teaching job at a Christian school fell into my lap. I taught high school English, speech, and home economics for three years. Then the school permanently closed.

It was a difficult time for many reasons. First, I no longer had a job. I did not know what I was going to do with my time and my education. I did not want to teach in a public school, and there were no other Christian schools nearby that were viable options. My children, who were students at the school where I taught, lost contact with the friends they had made while attending the school, and they had to adjust to a new school. In addition, my husband and I felt led to leave the church we had been attending for many years and search for a different church. I felt very uprooted and without direction. How was God going to provide for all these needs?

The answer came quickly! I thank God that He promptly gave us new direction. In April of the year that the Christian school closed, we came in contact with a pastor who was led by God to leave the church he had been pastoring to start a new church in a neighboring area. After talking with the pastor and his wife about their vision for this new church, we were confident that we were to be involved in helping to start this church. It became obvious to me very quickly that I would not have been able to continue teaching at the Christian school and also fulfill the roles that God was calling me to at this church-in-the-making. We became so busy with the start up of the church that I had no time or even a reason to mourn the loss of my job. Those days were so refreshing and exciting as we saw God raise up people to attend the new church and give us some prime property to build what quickly became a beautiful and very functional building! God had taken away my teaching position, but He gave me new roles in the new church. In the years that we were active members of that church, I was able to develop many skills which were useful in that church and in the one we now attend years later.

We never know how God will use our experiences in life as the foundation for other opportunities. Years ago, the mother of a friend of mine was in the hospital, and my friend requested that I go sing "Amazing Grace" to her. I had never met her mother, but I wanted to help my friend, so I went. There in the hospital, I sang "Amazing Grace" a cappella to the stranger who lay in bed with her eyes closed as her family stood around the room observing. I do not know if the patient even heard me. Once I finished the song, the family thanked me for coming and I left, not really thinking much more about it. I did not even dream of how God would later use that one small act of kindness to place me into one of my ministries.

Years later, I decided to stop at the local Christian school to inquire about substitute teaching. For several years, I had been watching four of my grandchildren during the day while my daughter worked at the local community college. Every day, I would drive past that Christian school on the way to my daughter and son-in-law's house. When the youngest of the four children started school, I figured that I might have time during the day when all the kids were in school to put in some hours teaching at that Christian school. It had been years since I had taught in a school, so I was not sure how I would be received. Setting aside those reservations, I proceeded with the application process. As it turned out, I was interviewed for the substitute teacher position by one of the people in that hospital room years earlier. The sister of my friend was responsible for hiring the substitute teachers at that school, and here I was, seeking that very position! She remembered me from our one-and-only encounter – that day years earlier in her mother's hospital room. Long story short, I was hired! She was also the one who placed the substitute teachers in their assignments, and I was privileged to teach fifth grade for a whole semester and the next year to teach elementary music for the whole year. I taught at the school for six years. I still marvel at how God arranged for me to have those gratifying, valuable opportunities, which also helped the school.

Job experienced God taking away some precious things from him as well, much more than He has taken away from me. God took away all his possessions and all his children, but in time, He gave Job even more possessions and the same number of children as he had before. Praise God for His goodness and His generosity! All good things come from God (James 1:17).

2. Satan can tempt me or bring harm to me only as our sovereign, loving God allows! Though Satan wants to bring things into my life to destroy me (John 10:10; 1 Peter 5:8), God will allow those things only to ultimately use them for my good! Satan is very powerful, but God is more powerful, and He is sovereign; He is in control, not Satan! God allows Satan to do only that which fulfills God's own purposes. And God's purposes are always good since God is always good! God can take what was intended by Satan for my destruction and use it for my good (Romans 8:28)!

3. Sometimes we might experience depression, not because we have sinned, but because of something else that is happening in the spiritual realm. Look at what is happening behind the scenes in the story of Job. Of course, Job knows nothing about these conversations between God and Satan. He therefore does not know the reason behind his trials. But he trusts God anyway. One of the themes of the book of Job is, "Why do the righteous suffer?" Job was used by God to silence Satan's accusations. Not only was Satan accusing Job, but he was also accusing God. In essence, he was saying that no one would serve God if there were nothing in it for himself – that having God alone is not sufficient. God disproved Satan's accusation through Job's faithfulness to God even when he lost everything and he did not realize why. This is an example of perseverance of the saints (Philippians 1:6; Jude 24).

A spiritual battle between good and evil is taking place every day all around us, and we often cannot perceive it. Ephesians 6:12 says, "For we do not wrestle against flesh and blood, but against the rulers, against the authorities, against the cosmic powers over this present darkness, against the spiritual forces of evil in the heavenly places" (ESV).

Years after attacking Job, Satan sought to destroy the faith of Jesus' disciples by shaking them physically. In the following passage, Jesus is speaking to Peter, but "you" is in the plural form, indicating that Satan's target was not only Peter but the other disciples as well. Peter must not have been aware of Satan's plan, or Jesus probably would not have told him about it. Luke 22:31 & 32 says, "Simon, Simon, [Peter] behold, Satan demanded to have you, that he might sift you like wheat, but I have prayed for you that your faith might not fail" (ESV). Jesus said this shortly before sweating drops of sweat that resembled blood as He contemplated dying on the cross. Not long after that, He was arrested. Hours later, Peter disowned Jesus.

Notice what Jesus did shortly before He was arrested, knowing all that would happen to Him. Despite the awfulness of what awaited Him, He was concerned about the faith of the disciples, and He prayed that they would not lose faith. He thought of the welfare of others, even in His most agonizing moments.

4. Sometimes depression comes from a satanic attack. Job 2:3 says that Satan incited God to ruin Job. Satan is my enemy, and he is always seeking ways to destroy me. One of his tactics is accusing me before God. Satanic oppression is real, and the key is resisting him and obeying God. James 4:7 & 8 says, "Submit yourselves therefore to God. Resist the devil, and he will flee from you. Draw nigh to God, and he will draw nigh to you" (KJV). 1 Peter 5:8 & 9 says, "Be sober-minded; be watchful. Your adversary the devil prowls around like a roaring lion, seeking someone to devour. Resist him, firm in your faith, knowing that the same kinds of suffering are being experienced by your brotherhood throughout the world" (ESV). Resist Satan by refusing to sin and by being obedient to Christ! Cling to the Lord through reading the Word and through prayer.

5. No one can accuse God of acting unjustly toward Job. Since God owns everything, He has the right to take away anything He has given to us. We are just temporary stewards, anyway. Further, since everyone is a sinner and deserves death, we do not deserve any good thing from God anyway. God gives good gifts to us, not because we deserve them, but because of His love and grace.

6. Do you withhold praise from God when things are not going your way? Or do you continue to praise Him for the great God that He is? Do you question His wisdom? Do you question His goodness? God commends Job for not charging Him with wrongdoing.

7. God had a good reason for the trials that tested Job. Job's trials, though meant by Satan to destroy Job and discredit God, brought about something of great worth! God is not capricious; He does not allow us to experience trials for no reason, nor does He take delight in watching His children suffer. Job's attitude towards the trials that God brought about in his life is reflected in Job 23:10: "But he knows the way that I take; when he has tested me, I will come forth as gold" (NIV). Job's trials also gave him a better understanding of God and a better understanding of himself. He says this in Job 42:5 & 6: "My ears had heard of you but now my eyes have seen you. Therefore I despise myself and repent in dust and ashes" (NIV).

In 1 Peter 1:7, the Apostle Peter says this about trials: "These [trials] have come so that the proven genuineness of your faith – of greater worth than gold, which perishes even though refined by fire – may result in praise, glory and honor when Jesus Christ is revealed" (NIV).

8. When we resist Satan, he flees for a time. God then brings times of refreshment. Persevere through the trial – remaining faithful to God and trusting Him and resisting Satan (James 4:7 & 8)!

9. Be sure you always correctly represent God! That means knowing who He is and what He is like which is revealed in the Bible. Give counsel to others only when you know God well enough through His Word to correctly represent Him.

10. God knows how to bring good from a bad situation. He can take any situation and turn it around. He can bring beauty from ashes (Isaiah 61:3) and restore the years that the locusts have eaten (Joel 2:25).

11. God is worthy to be praised when times are good for me and when times are bad – when I gain and when I lose. He gives and He takes away, and it is His right to do so. I should praise Him **despite** my feelings.

Often praise can change my feelings from discouragement or depression to encouragement and hope. Regardless of my feelings, I should praise Him! Don't praise God only when you feel like it; praise Him when you don't feel like it as well. Don't allow your feelings to control you. That would be idolatry!

These words of Habakkuk, an Old Testament prophet who prophesied the destruction of Judah by the Babylonians, remind me of some of Job's words.

Habakkuk 3:17 & 18:

> "Though the fig tree does not bud and there are no grapes on the vines, though the olive crop fails and the fields produce no food, though there are no sheep in the pen and no cattle in the stalls, yet I will rejoice in the LORD, I will be joyful in God my Savior" (NIV).

Both Job and Habakkuk seem to have realized that their praise and worship of God should not rely on their prosperity but on who God is. Both had the attitude that God should be worshiped and praised whether in prosperity or poverty. God is worth more than having many earthly possessions.

12. God is worth serving, even when He takes something away from me – even my life.

Job says, "Though he slay me, yet will I hope in him…" (Job 13:15 NIV). Job's resolve reminds me of the same attitude displayed by Shadrach, Meshach, and Abednego when they were commanded by King Nebuchadnezzar to bow down to the golden image he had made. If they refused to do so, they would be thrown into a fiery furnace. This was their response to the king: "King Nebuchadnezzar, we do not need to defend ourselves before you in this matter. If we are thrown into the blazing furnace, the God we serve is able to deliver us from it, and he will deliver us from Your Majesty's hand. But even if he does not, we want you to know, Your Majesty, that we will not serve your gods or worship the image of gold you have set up" (Daniel 3:16-18 NIV).

Shadrach, Meshach, and Abednego were confident that God could rescue them from the fiery furnace. However, even if God chose not to do so, they resolved that they would not bow down to the golden image. They would worship no god but the true God, even if that meant they would die. May we all be so resolved!

When you are in anguish due to a trial, will you, like Job, determine that no matter what happens, you will worship God and hope in Him? Job's anguish is clearly seen in chapter 3. However, his hope was founded on the true and living God who is sovereign over all and who can never be blamed with wrongdoing! You can trust Him, just like Job did.

Chapter Fifteen

The Study of Ruth

"The women said to Naomi: 'Praise be to the LORD, who this day has not left you without a guardian-redeemer. May he become famous throughout Israel! He will renew your life and sustain you in your old age. For your daughter-in-law, who loves you and who is better to you than seven sons, has given him birth.' Then Naomi took the child in her arms and cared for him."
Ruth 4:14-16 NIV

This lesson is centered around a love story from the Old Testament. It is much more than just a beautiful love story between a man and a woman, however. There are some lessons about the true and living God that we can learn from this story to help us know how to handle disappointment, discouragement, defeat, depression, and despair.

The love story is found in the Old Testament book of Ruth. This real-life drama took place well before 1000 B.C. in Judah, in the city of Bethlehem. The woman in this love story is Ruth. She was not an Israelite (a Jew) – not one of God's chosen people – and this is a very interesting and important fact that will shed light on the story and on God and His purposes throughout history. Ruth was from Moab, a region east of Israel, across the Dead Sea.

The Moabites originated from the incestuous relationship between a father, Lot, and his firstborn daughter (Genesis 19:30-38). This is a very wicked thing in the sight of the true and living God. The Moabites worshiped the false god Chemosh, and they practiced infant sacrifice to this god. This is another very offensive attitude and behavior in the sight of the true and living God. The Moabites were on-going enemies of the Jews, God's chosen people, though at the time this story takes place, the two nations are temporarily at peace.

It is important to know that the Moabite people had been cursed by God. Nehemiah 13:1 & 2 says, "On that day they read from the Book of Moses in the hearing of the people. And in it was found written that no Ammonite or Moabite should ever enter the assembly of God, for they did not meet the people of Israel with bread and water but hired Balaam against them to curse them – yet our God turned the curse into a blessing" (ESV). Numbers Chapters 22-24 tells the story of Balak, one of the kings of Moab, hiring Balaam to put a curse on the Israelites, but God did not allow that to happen.

In Deuteronomy 23:3 & 4, God declares His curse on the Moabites:

> "No Ammonite or Moabite may enter the assembly of the LORD. Even to the tenth generation, none of them may enter the assembly of the LORD forever, because they did not meet you with bread and with water on the way, when you came out of Egypt, and because they hired against you Balaam the son of Beor from Pethor of Mesopotamia, to curse you" (ESV).

God had cut off the Moabites from any relationship with Himself for hundreds of years, but years later, Ruth had adopted her mother-in-law's God, Yahweh – the true and living God – as her own God.

In reading the book of Ruth, it is important to remember that Ruth was a Moabitess. Her people had been cursed by the true and living God. But let's see what becomes of Ruth. She had reason to despair, humanly speaking, as we will see as the story unfolds.

To completely understand what God is teaching us in this book, we must know something about the cultural aspect of the kinsman redeemer (or guardian redeemer). The role of the kinsman redeemer is so important in this story. Before we look at the definition of the kinsman redeemer, however, look at the definition of redeem:

redeem[6] –1. to recover ownership of by paying a specified sum 2a. to set free, as from slavery or kidnapping by providing money or other compensation 2b. To save (a person or soul) from a state of sinfulness or its consequences 2c. to restore the honor, worth, or reputation of

kinsman redeemer[7] –male relative who, according to various laws found in the Pentateuch [the first five books of the Hebrew Bible], had the privilege or responsibility to act for a relative who was in trouble, danger, or need of vindication

A kinsman redeemer had to meet the following requirements:

1. He had to be a kinsman (a relative).

2. He had to be free himself.

3. He had to be able to pay the price to redeem.

---

[6] The American Heritage Dictionary of the English Language (Boston: Houghton Mifflin Harcourt Publishing Company, 2016), p. 1472.

[7] Stephen J. Bramer, Baker's Evangelical Dictionary of Biblical Theology (Grand Rapids: Baker Book House Company, 1996), p. 456.

4. He had to be willing to pay the price.

While the concept of redemption is so important in this story, for our purposes, I want to focus primarily on the care that God gave to Ruth, despite her cursed background. Naomi, Ruth's mother-in-law, was also a part of this story of the provisions of Yahweh, the true and living God. She felt cursed because she had lost her husband and two sons – a very difficult position for a woman in those days. But God turned around the story of her life, as well.

Summary of Ruth 1:

The story of Ruth begins when a man, Elimelek, and his wife, Naomi, and their two sons, Mahlon and Kilion, leave their home in Bethlehem in Judah for the country of Moab because there is a famine in the land of Judah. While living in Moab, Naomi's husband dies. Her two sons marry Moabite women, named Orpah and Ruth. They had lived there about ten years when Naomi's two sons also die. So, Naomi now lives in a foreign land without her husband and her two sons. Eventually, the famine in Bethlehem, Judah ends, so Naomi plans to return to her home there. Her two daughters-in-law, Orpah and Ruth, plan to go to Judah with her. On the way there, however, Naomi encourages both of them to go back to their own homes and their families. She blesses them and hopes that all will go well with them, each with a new husband. Both of the women, however, insist upon traveling with Naomi to her native land. In response, Naomi still urges them both to return home, for since she was too old to have another husband, she was surely not going to have any more sons to serve as husbands to the women. Even if she did have more sons, these women would certainly not wait for the boys to grow up so the women could marry them. Naomi continues. "No, my daughters. It is more bitter for me than for you, because the Lord's hand has turned against me!" (Ruth 1:13 NIV).

Orpah then decides to go back to her homeland and her family. Naomi encourages Ruth to go back to her homeland and her gods as Orpah is doing. Tenaciously, Ruth clings to Naomi and insists that she will go wherever Naomi goes, vowing that Naomi's people will be her people, and Naomi's God will be her God. Naomi then relents and allows Ruth to travel with her to Bethlehem.

When they get to Bethlehem, the people cannot believe that this woman is the Naomi that they had known from the past. Naomi insists that the people call her "Mara" rather than Naomi because "the Almighty has made my life very bitter. I went away full, but the LORD has brought me back empty. Why call me Naomi? The LORD has afflicted me; the Almighty has brought misfortune upon me" (Ruth 1:20 & 21 NIV).

Naomi and Ruth arrive in Bethlehem just as the barley harvest is beginning.

Ruth 2:

1 Now Naomi had a relative on her husband's side, a man of standing from the clan of Elimelek, whose name was Boaz.

2 And Ruth the Moabite said to Naomi, "Let me go to the fields and pick up the leftover grain behind anyone in whose eyes I find favor."

Naomi said to her, "Go ahead, my daughter." 3 So she went out, entered a field and began to glean behind the harvesters. As it turned out, she was working in a field belonging to Boaz, who was from the clan of Elimelek.

4 Just then Boaz arrived from Bethlehem and greeted the harvesters, "The Lord be with you!"

"The Lord bless you!" they answered.

5 Boaz asked the overseer of his harvesters, "Who does that young woman belong to?"

6 The overseer replied, "She is the Moabite who came back from Moab with Naomi. **7** She said, 'Please let me glean and gather among the sheaves behind the harvesters.' She came into the field and has remained here from morning till now, except for a short rest in the shelter."

8 So Boaz said to Ruth, "My daughter, listen to me. Don't go and glean in another field and don't go away from here. Stay here with the women who work for me. **9** Watch the field where the men are harvesting, and follow along after the women. I have told the men not to lay a hand on you. And whenever you are thirsty, go and get a drink from the water jars the men have filled."

10 At this, she bowed down with her face to the ground. She asked him, "Why have I found such favor in your eyes that you notice me—a foreigner?"

11 Boaz replied, "I've been told all about what you have done for your mother-in-law since the death of your husband—how you left your father and mother and your homeland and came to live with a people you did not know before. **12** May the Lord repay you for what you have done. May you be richly rewarded by the Lord, the God of Israel, under whose wings you have come to take refuge."

13 "May I continue to find favor in your eyes, my lord," she said. "You have put me at ease by speaking kindly to your servant—though I do not have the standing of one of your servants."

14 At mealtime Boaz said to her, "Come over here. Have some bread and dip it in the wine vinegar."

When she sat down with the harvesters, he offered her some roasted grain. She ate all she wanted and had some left over. **15** As she got up to glean, Boaz gave orders to his men, "Let her gather among the sheaves and don't reprimand her. **16** Even pull out some stalks for her from the bundles and leave them for her to pick up, and don't rebuke her."

17 So Ruth gleaned in the field until evening. Then she threshed the barley she had gathered, and it amounted to about an ephah. **18** She carried it back to town, and her mother-in-law saw how much she had gathered. Ruth also brought out and gave her what she had left over after she had eaten enough.

19 Her mother-in-law asked her, "Where did you glean today? Where did you work? Blessed be the man who took notice of you!" Then Ruth told her mother-in-law about the one at whose place she had been working. "The name of the man I worked with today is Boaz," she said.

20 "The Lord bless him!" Naomi said to her daughter-in-law. "He has not stopped showing his kindness to the living and the dead." She added, "That man is our close relative; he is one of our guardian-redeemers."

21 Then Ruth the Moabite said, "He even said to me, 'Stay with my workers until they finish harvesting all my grain.'"

22 Naomi said to Ruth her daughter-in-law, "It will be good for you, my daughter, to go with the women who work for him, because in someone else's field you might be harmed."

23 So Ruth stayed close to the women of Boaz to glean until the barley and wheat harvests were finished. And she lived with her mother-in-law.

Ruth 3:

1 One day Ruth's mother-in-law Naomi said to her, "My daughter, I must find a home for you, where you will be well provided for. **2** Now Boaz, with whose women you have worked, is a relative of ours. Tonight he will be winnowing barley on the threshing floor. **3** Wash, put on perfume, and get dressed in your best clothes. Then go down to the threshing floor, but don't let him know you are there until he has finished eating and drinking. **4** When he lies down, note the place where he is lying. Then go and uncover his feet and lie down. He will tell you what to do."

5 "I will do whatever you say," Ruth answered. **6** So she went down to the threshing floor and did everything her mother-in-law told her to do.

7 When Boaz had finished eating and drinking and was in good spirits, he went over to lie down at the far end of the grain pile. Ruth approached quietly, uncovered his feet and lay down. **8** In the middle of the night something startled the man; he turned—and there was a woman lying at his feet!

9 "Who are you?" he asked.

"I am your servant Ruth," she said. "Spread the corner of your garment over me, since you are a guardian-redeemer of our family."

10 "The Lord bless you, my daughter," he replied. "This kindness is greater than that which you showed earlier: You have not run after the younger men, whether rich or poor. **11** And now, my daughter, don't be afraid. I will do for you all you ask. All the people of my town know that you are a woman of noble character. **12** Although it is true that I am a guardian-redeemer of our family, there is another who is more closely related than I. **13** Stay here for the night, and in the morning if he wants to do his duty as your guardian-redeemer, good; let him redeem you. But if he is not willing, as surely as the Lord lives I will do it. Lie here until morning."

14 So she lay at his feet until morning, but got up before anyone could be recognized; and he said, "No one must know that a woman came to the threshing floor."

15 He also said, "Bring me the shawl you are wearing and hold it out." When she did so, he poured into it six measures of barley and placed the bundle on her. Then he went back to town.

16 When Ruth came to her mother-in-law, Naomi asked, "How did it go, my daughter?"

Then she told her everything Boaz had done for her **17** and added, "He gave me these six measures of barley, saying, 'Don't go back to your mother-in-law empty-handed.'"

18 Then Naomi said, "Wait, my daughter, until you find out what happens. For the man will not rest until the matter is settled today."

Ruth 4:

1 Meanwhile Boaz went up to the town gate and sat down there just as the guardian-redeemer he had mentioned came along. Boaz said, "Come over here, my friend, and sit down." So he went over and sat down.

2 Boaz took ten of the elders of the town and said, "Sit here," and they did so. **3** Then he said to the guardian-redeemer, "Naomi, who has come back from Moab, is selling the piece of land that belonged to our relative Elimelek. **4** I thought I should bring the matter to your attention and suggest that you buy it in the presence of these seated here and in the presence of the elders of my people. If you will redeem it, do so.

But if you will not, tell me, so I will know. For no one has the right to do it except you, and I am next in line."

"I will redeem it," he said. **5** Then Boaz said, "On the day you buy the land from Naomi, you also acquire Ruth the Moabite, the dead man's widow, in order to maintain the name of the dead with his property."

6 At this, the guardian-redeemer said, "Then I cannot redeem it because I might endanger my own estate. You redeem it yourself. I cannot do it."

7 (Now in earlier times in Israel, for the redemption and transfer of property to become final, one party took off his sandal and gave it to the other. This was the method of legalizing transactions in Israel.)

8 So the guardian-redeemer said to Boaz, "Buy it yourself." And he removed his sandal.

9 Then Boaz announced to the elders and all the people, "Today you are witnesses that I have bought from Naomi all the property of Elimelek, Kilion and Mahlon. **10** I have also acquired Ruth the Moabite, Mahlon's widow, as my wife, in order to maintain the name of the dead with his property, so that his name will not disappear from among his family or from his hometown. Today you are witnesses!"

11 Then the elders and all the people at the gate said, "We are witnesses. May the Lord make the woman who is coming into your home like Rachel and Leah, who together built up the family of Israel. May you have standing in Ephrathah and be famous in Bethlehem. **12** Through the offspring the Lord gives you by this young woman, may your family be like that of Perez, whom Tamar bore to Judah.

13 So Boaz took Ruth and she became his wife. When he made love to her, the Lord enabled her to conceive, and she gave birth to a son. **14** The women said to Naomi: "Praise be to the Lord, who this day has not left you without a guardian-redeemer. May he become famous throughout Israel! **15** He will renew your life and sustain you in your old age. For your daughter-in-law, who loves you and who is better to you than seven sons, has given him birth."

16 Then Naomi took the child in her arms and cared for him. **17** The women living there said, "Naomi has a son!" And they named him Obed. He was the father of Jesse, the father of David.

18 This, then, is the family line of Perez:
    Perez was the father of Hezron,

19 Hezron the father of Ram,
    Ram the father of Amminadab,

20 Amminadab the father of Nahshon,
    Nahshon the father of Salmon,

21 Salmon the father of Boaz,
    Boaz the father of Obed,

22 Obed the father of Jesse,
    and Jesse the father of David. (NIV)

Think about this! **Ruth went from being part of a group of people who were cursed by God to being included in the lineage of Jesus Christ, the Messiah (Matthew 1). She was the great-grandmother of King David, and an ancestor of Jesus Christ. This is redemption! God salvaged Ruth's life!**

Look at the continuing lineage of Jesus Christ:

Matthew 1:5-16:

> **5** Salmon the father of Boaz, whose mother was Rahab,
> Boaz the father of Obed, whose mother was Ruth,
> Obed the father of Jesse,
> **6** and Jesse the father of King David.
>
> David was the father of Solomon, whose mother had been Uriah's wife,
>
> **7** Solomon the father of Rehoboam,
> Rehoboam the father of Abijah,
> Abijah the father of Asa,
> **8** Asa the father of Jehoshaphat,
> Jehoshaphat the father of Jehoram,
> Jehoram the father of Uzziah,
> **9** Uzziah the father of Jotham,
> Jotham the father of Ahaz,
> Ahaz the father of Hezekiah,
> **10** Hezekiah the father of Manasseh,
> Manasseh the father of Amon,
> Amon the father of Josiah,
> **11** and Josiah the father of Jeconiah and
> his brothers at the time of the exile to Babylon.
> **12** After the exile to Babylon:
> Jeconiah was the father of Shealtiel,
> Shealtiel the father of Zerubbabel,
> **13** Zerubbabel the father of Abihud,
> Abihud the father of Eliakim,
> Eliakim the father of Azor,

14 Azor the father of Zadok,
   Zadok the father of Akim,
   Akim the father of Elihud,
15 Elihud the father of Eleazar,
   Eleazar the father of Matthan,
   Matthan the father of Jacob,
16 and Jacob the father of Joseph,
   the husband of Mary, and Mary was the mother
   of Jesus who is called the Messiah (NIV).

It is also noteworthy that the mother of Boaz, the male in the love story in the book of Ruth, was Rahab – a harlot! Boaz himself was part Canaanite (part non-Jew). **This is redemption. The story of Ruth is, in great part, a story of redemption. It is a story of God taking hopeless circumstances and turning them around and bringing forth good.**

We also see a foreshadowing of God's plan to include the Gentiles in His gracious offer of salvation.

That is the big picture.

But can you also see the wonderful providential care of Yahweh, the true and living God in this story? Can you see the hand of God in every event of this story? He undertakes for Ruth and Naomi in such a marvelous way. Naomi went from being a bitter woman without a husband or sons or grandchildren to being blessed by God with a baby boy who was in the lineage of Jesus Christ! Can you imagine her joy when she held her grandson for the first time? Ruth went from being a childless widow to being married to a man who loved her and whose union with her brought forth a baby boy who was in the lineage of Jesus Christ! Doesn't this warm your heart toward the true and living God and produce faith and hope in your heart for your future? If God can provide for Ruth and Naomi in such an abundant way, He can also provide for you! If you are God's child through the shed blood of Jesus Christ on your behalf, then He will take care of you!

Whenever you start to feel disappointed, discouraged, defeated, depressed or in despair, read the story of Ruth. It will help you remember God's story of redemption, not just of Ruth and Naomi, but of a whole host of other people down through the ages. With such a loving, all-knowing, all-powerful God taking care of me, I have no reason to be depressed. If God can provide redemption for the cursed and the lost, such as Ruth (and such as all of us), He can provide whatever we need from day to day. Look to Him to meet your needs.

Philippians 4:19:

> "And my God will meet all your needs according to the riches of his glory in Christ Jesus" (NIV).

Naomi seemed to be blinded by the grief of losing her husband and her two sons. Anyone can understand how difficult that must have been for her. I do not want to minimize the difficulties that this situation brought to Naomi. However, her bitterness seems to have blinded her to what she **had** in spite of what she **lost**.

I will explain. In chapter 1, Naomi urges her two daughters-in-law to go back to Moab, back to their families, and back to their (worthless) gods. After all, there was no way that she could provide husbands again for the two women. So in essence, Naomi was saying that she had nothing else to offer them. They should go back to Moab where they could get the resources necessary to continue living their lives.

But Naomi **did** have something else to offer Ruth and Orpah. Though she could no longer bear sons to offer them, she had something even more valuable that she seems to have overlooked. **She had**

the true and living God, and when a person has Him, that person has the source of everything needed in life. It seems that Naomi's bitterness, due to the loss of the men in her life, caused her to forget this valuable resource. We need to be careful not to make this same mistake!

When we suffer great loss like Naomi did, may we remember to go to our loving Heavenly Father to implore His help. We must trust in His goodness and His ability to help, no matter how desperate our situation is. Let's not forget that He is eager to meet our needs, but He wants us to come and ask and then to remember that He is the source of everything we need. When we are at the end of our human resources, God is able to abundantly provide all that we need. **He is our kinsman-redeemer (guardian-redeemer)!**

Chapter Sixteen

The Study of Joseph

"And now, do not be distressed and do not be angry with yourselves for selling me here, because it was to save lives that God sent me ahead of you. For two years now there has been famine in the land, and for the next five years there will be no plowing and reaping. But God sent me ahead of you to preserve for you a remnant on earth and to save your lives by a great deliverance. So then, it was not you who sent me here, but God. He made me father to Pharaoh, lord of his entire household and ruler of all Egypt."
Genesis 45:5-8 NIV

Sometimes it is our sin that leads to depression, in addition to being offensive to God. To keep from becoming depressed, the child of God should quickly confess and forsake sin rather than hiding or excusing it. Unconfessed sin builds up and can lead to greater sin. The end result can be depression and even devastation. Unconfessed sin also hinders our fellowship with Christ.

There are times, however, when depression can set in not as a result of our having sinned but as a result of being in adverse circumstances which are beyond our control.

The Old Testament story of Joseph is an example of a young man who appeared to love and trust God, despite his adverse circumstances. It is a good lesson for us to trust God even when circumstances do not seem to be in our favor. God is always working behind the scenes, and often what He is doing is not apparent to us. It appears that Joseph trusted God throughout years of unjust treatment. God was working behind the scenes to completely turn around Joseph's circumstances from the pits to great privilege.

As you read the story of Joseph, be mindful of the many ways that God orchestrated events to bring about His plan. All of these events worked together to bring about the final outcome.

The entire passage here of the story of Joseph (Genesis 37-50) comes from the NIV version.

Genesis 37:

> **1** Jacob lived in the land where his father had stayed, the land of Canaan.
>
> **2** This is the account of Jacob's family line.

Joseph, a young man of seventeen, was tending the flocks with his brothers, the sons of Bilhah and the sons of Zilpah, his father's wives, and he brought their father a bad report about them.

3 Now Israel loved Joseph more than any of his other sons, because he had been born to him in his old age; and he made an ornate robe for him. **4** When his brothers saw that their father loved him more than any of them, they hated him and could not speak a kind word to him.

5 Joseph had a dream, and when he told it to his brothers, they hated him all the more. **6** He said to them, "Listen to this dream I had: **7** We were binding sheaves of grain out in the field when suddenly my sheaf rose and stood upright, while your sheaves gathered around mine and bowed down to it."

8 His brothers said to him, "Do you intend to reign over us? Will you actually rule us?" And they hated him all the more because of his dream and what he had said.

9 Then he had another dream, and he told it to his brothers. "Listen," he said, "I had another dream, and this time the sun and moon and eleven stars were bowing down to me."

10 When he told his father as well as his brothers, his father rebuked him and said, "What is this dream you had? Will your mother and I and your brothers actually come and bow down to the ground before you?" **11** His brothers were jealous of him, but his father kept the matter in mind.

12 Now his brothers had gone to graze their father's flocks near Shechem, **13** and Israel said to Joseph, "As you know, your brothers are grazing the flocks near Shechem. Come, I am going to send you to them."

"Very well," he replied.

14 So he said to him, "Go and see if all is well with your brothers and with the flocks, and bring word back to me." Then he sent him off from the Valley of Hebron.

When Joseph arrived at Shechem, **15** a man found him wandering around in the fields and asked him, "What are you looking for?"

16 He replied, "I'm looking for my brothers. Can you tell me where they are grazing their flocks?"

17 "They have moved on from here," the man answered. "I heard them say, 'Let's go to Dothan.'"

So Joseph went after his brothers and found them near Dothan. **18** But they saw him in the distance, and before he reached them, they plotted to kill him.

19 "Here comes that dreamer!" they said to each other. **20** "Come now, let's kill him and throw him into one of these cisterns and say that a ferocious animal devoured him. Then we'll see what comes of his dreams."

21 When Reuben heard this, he tried to rescue him from their hands. "Let's not take his life," he said. **22** "Don't shed any blood. Throw him into this cistern here in the wilderness, but don't lay a hand on him." Reuben said this to rescue him from them and take him back to his father.

23 So when Joseph came to his brothers, they stripped him of his robe—the ornate robe he was wearing— **24** and they took him and threw him into the cistern. The cistern was empty; there was no water in it.

25 As they sat down to eat their meal, they looked up and saw a caravan of Ishmaelites coming from Gilead. Their camels were loaded with spices, balm and myrrh, and they were on their way to take them down to Egypt.

26 Judah said to his brothers, "What will we gain if we kill our brother and cover up his blood? **27** Come, let's sell him to the Ishmaelites and not lay our hands on him; after all, he is our brother, our own flesh and blood." His brothers agreed.

28 So when the Midianite merchants came by, his brothers pulled Joseph up out of the cistern and sold him for twenty shekels of silver to the Ishmaelites, who took him to Egypt.

29 When Reuben returned to the cistern and saw that Joseph was not there, he tore his clothes. **30** He went back to his brothers and said, "The boy isn't there! Where can I turn now?"

31 Then they got Joseph's robe, slaughtered a goat and dipped the robe in the blood. **32** They took the ornate robe back to their father and said, "We found this. Examine it to see whether it is your son's robe."

33 He recognized it and said, "It is my son's robe! Some ferocious animal has devoured him. Joseph has surely been torn to pieces."

34 Then Jacob tore his clothes, put on sackcloth and mourned for his son many days. **35** All his sons and daughters came to comfort him, but he refused to be comforted. "No," he said, "I will continue to mourn until I join my son in the grave." So his father wept for him.

36 Meanwhile, the Midianites sold Joseph in Egypt to Potiphar, one of Pharaoh's officials, the captain of the guard.

Genesis 39:

1 Now Joseph had been taken down to Egypt. Potiphar, an Egyptian who was one of Pharaoh's officials, the captain of the guard, bought him from the Ishmaelites who had taken him there.

2 The Lord was with Joseph so that he prospered, and he lived in the house of his Egyptian master. **3** When his master saw that the Lord was with him and that the Lord gave him success in everything he did, **4** Joseph found favor in his eyes and became his attendant. Potiphar put him in charge of his household, and he entrusted to his care everything he owned. **5** From the time he put him in charge of his household and of all that he owned, the Lord blessed the household of the Egyptian because of Joseph. The blessing of the Lord was on everything Potiphar had, both in the house and in the field. **6** So Potiphar left everything he had in Joseph's care; with Joseph in charge, he did not concern himself with anything except the food he ate.

Now Joseph was well-built and handsome, **7** and after a while his master's wife took notice of Joseph and said, "Come to bed with me!"

8 But he refused. "With me in charge," he told her, "my master does not concern himself with anything in the house; everything he owns he has entrusted to my care. **9** No one is greater in this house than I am. My master has withheld nothing from me except you, because you are his wife. How then could I do such a wicked thing and sin against God?" **10** And though she spoke to Joseph day after day, he refused to go to bed with her or even be with her.

11 One day he went into the house to attend to his duties, and none of the household servants was inside. **12** She caught him by his cloak and said, "Come to bed with me!" But he left his cloak in her hand and ran out of the house.

13 When she saw that he had left his cloak in her hand and had run out of the house, **14** she called her household servants. "Look," she said to them, "this Hebrew has been brought to us to make sport of us! He came in here to sleep with me, but I screamed. **15** When he heard me scream for help, he left his cloak beside me and ran out of the house."

16 She kept his cloak beside her until his master came home. **17** Then she told him this story: "That Hebrew slave you brought us came to me to make sport of me. **18** But as soon as I screamed for help, he left his cloak beside me and ran out of the house."

19 When his master heard the story his wife told him, saying, "This is how your slave treated me," he burned with anger. **20** Joseph's master took him and put him in prison, the place where the king's prisoners were confined.

But while Joseph was there in the prison, **21** the Lord was with him; he showed him kindness and granted him favor in the eyes of the prison warden. **22** So the warden put Joseph in charge of all those held in the prison, and he was made responsible for all that was done there. **23** The warden paid no attention to anything under Joseph's care, because the Lord was with Joseph and gave him success in whatever he did.

Genesis 40:

1 Some time later, the cupbearer and the baker of the king of Egypt offended their master, the king of Egypt. **2** Pharaoh was angry with his two officials, the chief cupbearer and the chief baker, **3** and put them in custody in the house of the captain of the guard, in the same prison where Joseph was confined. **4** The captain of the guard assigned them to Joseph, and he attended them.

After they had been in custody for some time, **5** each of the two men—the cupbearer and the baker of the king of Egypt, who were being held in prison—had a dream the same night, and each dream had a meaning of its own.

6 When Joseph came to them the next morning, he saw that they were dejected. **7** So he asked Pharaoh's officials who were in custody with him in his master's house, "Why do you look so sad today?"

8 "We both had dreams," they answered, "but there is no one to interpret them."

Then Joseph said to them, "Do not interpretations belong to God? Tell me your dreams."

9 So the chief cupbearer told Joseph his dream. He said to him, "In my dream I saw a vine in front of me, **10** and on the vine were three branches. As soon as it budded, it blossomed, and its clusters ripened into grapes. **11** Pharaoh's cup was in my hand, and I took the grapes, squeezed them into Pharaoh's cup and put the cup in his hand."

12 "This is what it means," Joseph said to him. "The three branches are three days. **13** Within three days Pharaoh will lift up your head and restore you to your position, and you will put Pharaoh's cup in his hand, just as you used to do when you were his cupbearer. **14** But when all goes well with you, remember me and show me kindness; mention me to Pharaoh and get me out of this prison. **15** I was forcibly carried off from the land of the Hebrews, and even here I have done nothing to deserve being put in a dungeon."

16 When the chief baker saw that Joseph had given a favorable interpretation, he said to Joseph, "I too had a dream: On my head were three baskets of bread. **17** In the top basket were all kinds of baked goods for Pharaoh, but the birds were eating them out of the basket on my head."

18 "This is what it means," Joseph said. "The three baskets are three days. **19** Within three days Pharaoh will lift off your head and impale your body on a pole. And the birds will eat away your flesh."

20 Now the third day was Pharaoh's birthday, and he gave a feast for all his officials. He lifted up the heads of the chief cupbearer and the chief baker in the presence of his officials: **21** He restored the chief cupbearer to his position, so that he once again put the cup into Pharaoh's hand— **22** but he impaled the chief baker, just as Joseph had said to them in his interpretation.

23 The chief cupbearer, however, did not remember Joseph; he forgot him.

Genesis 41:

1 When two full years had passed, Pharaoh had a dream: He was standing by the Nile, **2** when out of the river there came up seven cows, sleek and fat, and they grazed among the reeds. **3** After them, seven other cows, ugly and gaunt, came up out of the Nile and stood beside those on the riverbank. **4** And the cows that were ugly and gaunt ate up the seven sleek, fat cows. Then Pharaoh woke up.

5 He fell asleep again and had a second dream: Seven heads of grain, healthy and good, were growing on a single stalk. **6** After them, seven other heads of grain sprouted—thin and scorched by the east wind. **7** The thin heads of grain swallowed up the seven healthy, full heads. Then Pharaoh woke up; it had been a dream.

8 In the morning his mind was troubled, so he sent for all the magicians and wise men of Egypt. Pharaoh told them his dreams, but no one could interpret them for him.

9 Then the chief cupbearer said to Pharaoh, "Today I am reminded of my shortcomings. **10** Pharaoh was once angry with his servants, and he imprisoned me and the chief baker in the house of the captain of the guard. **11** Each of us had a dream the same night, and each dream had a meaning of its own. **12** Now a young Hebrew was there with us, a servant of the captain of the guard. We told him our dreams, and he interpreted them for us, giving each man the interpretation of his dream. **13** And things turned out exactly as he interpreted them to us: I was restored to my position, and the other man was impaled."

14 So Pharaoh sent for Joseph, and he was quickly brought from the dungeon. When he had shaved and changed his clothes, he came before Pharaoh.

15 Pharaoh said to Joseph, "I had a dream, and no one can interpret it. But I have heard it said of you that when you hear a dream you can interpret it."

16 "I cannot do it," Joseph replied to Pharaoh, "but God will give Pharaoh the answer he desires."

17 Then Pharaoh said to Joseph, "In my dream I was standing on the bank of the Nile, **18** when out of the river there came up seven cows, fat and sleek, and they grazed among the reeds. **19** After them, seven other cows came up—scrawny and very ugly and lean. I had never seen such ugly cows in all the land of Egypt. **20** The lean, ugly cows ate up the seven fat cows that came up first. **21** But even after they ate them, no one could tell that they had done so; they looked just as ugly as before. Then I woke up.

22 "In my dream I saw seven heads of grain, full and good, growing on a single stalk. **23** After them, seven other heads sprouted—withered and thin and scorched by the east wind. **24** The thin heads of grain swallowed up the seven good heads. I told this to the magicians, but none of them could explain it to me."

25 Then Joseph said to Pharaoh, "The dreams of Pharaoh are one and the same. God has revealed to Pharaoh what he is about to do. **26** The seven good cows are seven years, and the seven good heads of grain are seven years; it is one and the same dream. **27** The seven lean, ugly cows that came up afterward are seven years, and so are the seven worthless heads of grain scorched by the east wind: They are seven years of famine.

28 "It is just as I said to Pharaoh: God has shown Pharaoh what he is about to do. **29** Seven years of great abundance are coming throughout the land of Egypt, **30** but seven years of famine will follow them. Then all the abundance in Egypt will be forgotten, and the famine will ravage the land. **31** The abundance in the land will not be remembered, because the famine that follows it will be so severe. **32** The reason the dream was given to Pharaoh in two forms is that the matter has been firmly decided by God, and God will do it soon.

33 "And now let Pharaoh look for a discerning and wise man and put him in charge of the land of Egypt. **34** Let Pharaoh appoint commissioners over the land to take a fifth of the harvest of Egypt during the seven years of abundance. **35** They should collect all the food of these good years that are coming and store up the grain under the authority of Pharaoh, to be kept in the cities for food. **36** This food should be held in reserve for the country, to be used during the seven years of famine that will come upon Egypt, so that the country may not be ruined by the famine."

37 The plan seemed good to Pharaoh and to all his officials. **38** So Pharaoh asked them, "Can we find anyone like this man, one in whom is the spirit of God?"

39 Then Pharaoh said to Joseph, "Since God has made all this known to you, there is no one so discerning and wise as you. **40** You shall be in charge of my palace, and all my people are to submit to your orders. Only with respect to the throne will I be greater than you."

41 So Pharaoh said to Joseph, "I hereby put you in charge of the whole land of Egypt." **42** Then Pharaoh took his signet ring from his finger and put it on Joseph's finger. He dressed him in robes of fine linen and put a gold chain around his neck. **43** He had him ride in a chariot as his second-in-command, and people shouted before him, "Make way!" Thus he put him in charge of the whole land of Egypt.

44 Then Pharaoh said to Joseph, "I am Pharaoh, but without your word no one will lift hand or foot in all Egypt." **45** Pharaoh gave Joseph the name Zaphenath-Paneah and gave him Asenath daughter of Potiphera, priest of On, to be his wife. And Joseph went throughout the land of Egypt.

46 Joseph was thirty years old when he entered the service of Pharaoh king of Egypt. And Joseph went out from Pharaoh's presence and traveled throughout Egypt. **47** During the seven years of abundance the land produced plentifully. **48** Joseph collected all the food produced in those seven years of abundance in Egypt and stored it in the cities. In each city he put the food grown in the fields surrounding it. **49** Joseph stored up huge quantities of grain, like the sand of the sea; it was so much that he stopped keeping records because it was beyond measure.

50 Before the years of famine came, two sons were born to Joseph by Asenath daughter of Potiphera, priest of On. **51** Joseph named his firstborn Manasseh and said, "It is because God has made me forget all my trouble and all my father's household." **52** The second son he named Ephraim and said, "It is because God has made me fruitful in the land of my suffering."

53 The seven years of abundance in Egypt came to an end, **54** and the seven years of famine began, just as Joseph had said. There was famine in all the other lands, but in the whole land of Egypt there was food. **55** When all Egypt began to feel the famine, the people cried to Pharaoh for food. Then Pharaoh told all the Egyptians, "Go to Joseph and do what he tells you."

56 When the famine had spread over the whole country, Joseph opened all the storehouses and sold grain to the Egyptians, for the famine was severe throughout Egypt. **57** And all the world came to Egypt to buy grain from Joseph, because the famine was severe everywhere.

Genesis 42:

1 When Jacob learned that there was grain in Egypt, he said to his sons, "Why do you just keep looking at each other?" **2** He continued, "I have heard that there is grain in Egypt. Go down there and buy some for us, so that we may live and not die."

3 Then ten of Joseph's brothers went down to buy grain from Egypt. **4** But Jacob did not send Benjamin, Joseph's brother, with the others, because he was afraid that harm might come to him. **5** So Israel's sons were among those who went to buy grain, for there was famine in the land of Canaan also.

6 Now Joseph was the governor of the land, the person who sold grain to all its people. So when Joseph's brothers arrived, they bowed down to him with their faces to the ground. **7** As soon as Joseph saw his brothers, he recognized them, but he pretended to be a stranger and spoke harshly to them. "Where do you come from?" he asked.

"From the land of Canaan," they replied, "to buy food."

8 Although Joseph recognized his brothers, they did not recognize him. **9** Then he remembered his dreams about them and said to them, "You are spies! You have come to see where our land is unprotected."

10 "No, my lord," they answered. "Your servants have come to buy food. **11** We are all the sons of one man. Your servants are honest men, not spies."

12 "No!" he said to them. "You have come to see where our land is unprotected."

13 But they replied, "Your servants were twelve brothers, the sons of one man, who lives in the land of Canaan. The youngest is now with our father, and one is no more."

14 Joseph said to them, "It is just as I told you: You are spies! **15** And this is how you will be tested: As surely as Pharaoh lives, you will not leave this place unless your youngest brother comes here. **16** Send one of your number to get your brother; the rest of you will be kept in prison, so that your words may be tested to see if you are telling the truth. If you are not, then as surely as Pharaoh lives, you are spies!" **17** And he put them all in custody for three days.

18 On the third day, Joseph said to them, "Do this and you will live, for I fear God: **19** If you are honest men, let one of your brothers stay here in prison, while the rest of you go and take grain back for your starving households. **20** But you must bring your youngest brother to me, so that your words may be verified and that you may not die." This they proceeded to do.

21 They said to one another, "Surely we are being punished because of our brother. We saw how distressed he was when he pleaded with us for his life, but we would not listen; that's why this distress has come on us."

22 Reuben replied, "Didn't I tell you not to sin against the boy? But you wouldn't listen! Now we must give an accounting for his blood." **23** They did not realize that Joseph could understand them, since he was using an interpreter.

24 He turned away from them and began to weep, but then came back and spoke to them again. He had Simeon taken from them and bound before their eyes.

25 Joseph gave orders to fill their bags with grain, to put each man's silver back in his sack, and to give them provisions for their journey. After this was done for them, **26** they loaded their grain on their donkeys and left.

27 At the place where they stopped for the night one of them opened his sack to get feed for his donkey, and he saw his silver in the mouth of his sack. **28** "My silver has been returned," he said to his brothers. "Here it is in my sack."

Their hearts sank and they turned to each other trembling and said, "What is this that God has done to us?"

29 When they came to their father Jacob in the land of Canaan, they told him all that had happened to them. They said, **30** "The man who is lord over the land spoke harshly to us and treated us as though we were spying on the land. **31** But we said to him, 'We are honest men; we are not spies. **32** We were twelve brothers, sons of one father. One is no more, and the youngest is now with our father in Canaan.'

33 "Then the man who is lord over the land said to us, 'This is how I will know whether you are honest men: Leave one of your brothers here with me, and take food for your starving households and go. **34** But bring your youngest brother to me so I will know that you are not spies but honest men. Then I will give your brother back to you, and you can trade in the land.'"

35 As they were emptying their sacks, there in each man's sack was his pouch of silver! When they and their father saw the money pouches, they were frightened. **36** Their father Jacob said to them, "You have deprived me of my children. Joseph is no more and Simeon is no more, and now you want to take Benjamin. Everything is against me!"

37 Then Reuben said to his father, "You may put both of my sons to death if I do not bring him back to you. Entrust him to my care, and I will bring him back."

38 But Jacob said, "My son will not go down there with you; his brother is dead and he is the only one left. If harm comes to him on the journey you are taking, you will bring my gray head down to the grave in sorrow."

Genesis 43:

1 Now the famine was still severe in the land. **2** So when they had eaten all the grain they had brought from Egypt, their father said to them, "Go back and buy us a little more food."

3 But Judah said to him, "The man warned us solemnly, 'You will not see my face again unless your brother is with you.' **4** If you will send our brother along with us, we will go down and buy food for you. **5** But if you will not send him, we will not go down, because the man said to us, 'You will not see my face again unless your brother is with you.'"

6 Israel asked, "Why did you bring this trouble on me by telling the man you had another brother?"

7 They replied, "The man questioned us closely about ourselves and our family. 'Is your father still living?' he asked us. 'Do you have another brother?' We simply answered his questions. How were we to know he would say, 'Bring your brother down here'?"

8 Then Judah said to Israel his father, "Send the boy along with me and we will go at once, so that we and you and our children may live and not die. **9** I myself will guarantee his safety; you can hold me personally responsible for him. If I do not bring him back to you and set him here before you, I will bear the blame before you all my life. **10** As it is, if we had not delayed, we could have gone and returned twice."

11 Then their father Israel said to them, "If it must be, then do this: Put some of the best products of the land in your bags and take them down to the man as a gift—a little balm and a little honey, some spices and myrrh, some pistachio nuts and almonds. **12** Take double the amount of silver with you, for you must return the silver that was put back into the mouths of your sacks. Perhaps it was a mistake. **13** Take your brother also and go back to the man at once. **14** And may God Almighty grant you mercy before the man so that he will let your other brother and Benjamin come back with you. As for me, if I am bereaved, I am bereaved."

15 So the men took the gifts and double the amount of silver, and Benjamin also. They hurried down to Egypt and presented themselves to Joseph. **16** When Joseph saw Benjamin with them, he said to the steward of his house, "Take these men to my house, slaughter an animal and prepare a meal; they are to eat with me at noon."

17 The man did as Joseph told him and took the men to Joseph's house. **18** Now the men were frightened when they were taken to his house. They thought, "We were brought here because of the silver that was put back into our sacks the first time. He wants to attack us and overpower us and seize us as slaves and take our donkeys."

19 So they went up to Joseph's steward and spoke to him at the entrance to the house. **20** "We beg your pardon, our lord," they said, "we came down here the first time to buy food. **21** But at the place where we stopped for the night we opened our sacks and each of us found his silver—the exact weight—in the mouth of his sack. So we have brought it back with us. **22** We have also brought additional silver with us to buy food. We don't know who put our silver in our sacks."

23 "It's all right," he said. "Don't be afraid. Your God, the God of your father, has given you treasure in your sacks; I received your silver." Then he brought Simeon out to them.

24 The steward took the men into Joseph's house, gave them water to wash their feet and provided fodder for their donkeys. **25** They prepared their gifts for Joseph's arrival at noon, because they had heard that they were to eat there.

26 When Joseph came home, they presented to him the gifts they had brought into the house, and they bowed down before him to the ground. **27** He asked them how they were, and then he said, "How is your aged father you told me about? Is he still living?"

28 They replied, "Your servant our father is still alive and well." And they bowed down, prostrating themselves before him.

29 As he looked about and saw his brother Benjamin, his own mother's son, he asked, "Is this your youngest brother, the one you told me about?" And he said, "God be gracious to you, my son." **30** Deeply moved at the sight of his brother, Joseph hurried out and looked for a place to weep. He went into his private room and wept there.

31 After he had washed his face, he came out and, controlling himself, said, "Serve the food."

32 They served him by himself, the brothers by themselves, and the Egyptians who ate with him by themselves, because Egyptians could not eat with Hebrews, for that is detestable to Egyptians. **33** The men had been seated before him in the order of their ages, from the firstborn to the youngest; and they looked at each other in astonishment. **34** When portions were served to them from Joseph's table, Benjamin's portion was five times as much as anyone else's. So they feasted and drank freely with him.

Genesis 44:

1 Now Joseph gave these instructions to the steward of his house: "Fill the men's sacks with as much food as they can carry, and put each man's silver in the mouth of his sack. **2** Then put my cup, the silver one, in the mouth of the youngest one's sack, along with the silver for his grain." And he did as Joseph said.

3 As morning dawned, the men were sent on their way with their donkeys. **4** They had not gone far from the city when Joseph said to his steward, "Go after those men at once, and when you catch up with them, say to them, 'Why have you repaid good with evil? **5** Isn't this the cup my master drinks from and also uses for divination? This is a wicked thing you have done.'"

6 When he caught up with them, he repeated these words to them. **7** But they said to him, "Why does my lord say such things? Far be it from your servants to do anything like that! **8** We even brought back to you from the land of Canaan the silver we found inside the mouths of our sacks. So why would we steal silver or gold from your master's house? **9** If any of your servants is found to have it, he will die; and the rest of us will become my lord's slaves."

10 "Very well, then," he said, "let it be as you say. Whoever is found to have it will become my slave; the rest of you will be free from blame."

11 Each of them quickly lowered his sack to the ground and opened it. **12** Then the steward proceeded to search, beginning with the oldest and ending with the youngest. And the cup was found in Benjamin's sack. **13** At this, they tore their clothes. Then they all loaded their donkeys and returned to the city.

14 Joseph was still in the house when Judah and his brothers came in, and they threw themselves to the ground before him. **15** Joseph said to them, "What is this you have done? Don't you know that a man like me can find things out by divination?"

16 "What can we say to my lord?" Judah replied. "What can we say? How can we prove our innocence? God has uncovered your servants' guilt. We are now my lord's slaves—we ourselves and the one who was found to have the cup."

17 But Joseph said, "Far be it from me to do such a thing! Only the man who was found to have the cup will become my slave. The rest of you, go back to your father in peace."

18 Then Judah went up to him and said: "Pardon your servant, my lord, let me speak a word to my lord. Do not be angry with your servant, though you are equal to Pharaoh himself. **19** My lord asked his servants, 'Do you have a father or a brother?' **20** And we answered, 'We have an aged father, and there is a young son born to him in his old age. His brother is dead, and he is the only one of his mother's sons left, and his father loves him.'

21 "Then you said to your servants, 'Bring him down to me so I can see him for myself.' **22** And we said to my lord, 'The boy cannot leave his father; if he leaves him, his father will die.' **23** But you told your servants, 'Unless your youngest brother comes down with you, you will not see my face again.' **24** When we went back to your servant my father, we told him what my lord had said.

25 "Then our father said, 'Go back and buy a little more food.' **26** But we said, 'We cannot go down. Only if our youngest brother is with us will we go. We cannot see the man's face unless our youngest brother is with us.'

27 "Your servant my father said to us, 'You know that my wife bore me two sons. **28** One of them went away from me, and I said, "He has surely been torn to pieces." And I have not seen him since. **29** If you take this one from me too and harm comes to him, you will bring my gray head down to the grave in misery.'

30 "So now, if the boy is not with us when I go back to your servant my father, and if my father, whose life is closely bound up with the boy's life, **31** sees that the boy isn't there, he will die. Your servants will bring the gray head of our father down to the grave in sorrow. **32** Your servant guaranteed the boy's safety to my father. I said, 'If I do not bring him back to you, I will bear the blame before you, my father, all my life!'

33 "Now then, please let your servant remain here as my lord's slave in place of the boy, and let the boy return with his brothers. **34** How can I go back to my father if the boy is not with me? No! Do not let me see the misery that would come on my father."

Genesis 45:

1 Then Joseph could no longer control himself before all his attendants, and he cried out, "Have everyone leave my presence!" So there was no one with Joseph when he made himself known to his brothers. **2** And he wept so loudly that the Egyptians heard him, and Pharaoh's household heard about it.

3 Joseph said to his brothers, "I am Joseph! Is my father still living?" But his brothers were not able to answer him, because they were terrified at his presence.

4 Then Joseph said to his brothers, "Come close to me." When they had done so, he said, "I am your brother Joseph, the one you sold into Egypt! **5 And now, do not be distressed and do not be angry with yourselves for selling me here, because it was to save lives that God sent me ahead of you. 6 For two years now there has been famine in the land, and for the next five years there will be no plowing and reaping. 7 But God sent me ahead of you to preserve for you a remnant on earth and to save your lives by a great deliverance** [emphasis added].

8 "So then, it was not you who sent me here, but God. He made me father to Pharaoh, lord of his entire household and ruler of all Egypt. **9** Now hurry back to my father and say to him, 'This is what your son Joseph says: God has made me lord of all Egypt. Come down to me; don't delay. **10** You shall live in the region of Goshen and be near me—you, your children and grandchildren, your flocks and herds, and all you have. **11** I will provide for you there, because five years of famine are still to come. Otherwise you and your household and all who belong to you will become destitute.'

12 "You can see for yourselves, and so can my brother Benjamin, that it is really I who am speaking to you. **13** Tell my father about all the honor accorded me in Egypt and about everything you have seen. And bring my father down here quickly."

14 Then he threw his arms around his brother Benjamin and wept, and Benjamin embraced him, weeping. **15** And he kissed all his brothers and wept over them. Afterward his brothers talked with him.

16 When the news reached Pharaoh's palace that Joseph's brothers had come, Pharaoh and all his officials were pleased. **17** Pharaoh said to Joseph, "Tell your brothers, 'Do this: Load your animals and return to the land of Canaan, **18** and bring your father and your families back to me. I will give you the best of the land of Egypt and you can enjoy the fat of the land.'

19 "You are also directed to tell them, 'Do this: Take some carts from Egypt for your children and your wives, and get your father and come. **20** Never mind about your belongings, because the best of all Egypt will be yours.'"

21 So the sons of Israel did this. Joseph gave them carts, as Pharaoh had commanded, and he also gave them provisions for their journey. **22** To each of them he gave new clothing, but to Benjamin he gave three hundred shekels of silver and five sets of clothes. **23** And this is what he sent to his father: ten donkeys loaded with the best things of Egypt, and ten female donkeys loaded with grain and bread and other provisions for his journey. **24** Then he sent his brothers away, and as they were leaving he said to them, "Don't quarrel on the way!"

25 So they went up out of Egypt and came to their father Jacob in the land of Canaan. **26** They told him, "Joseph is still alive! In fact, he is ruler of all Egypt." Jacob was stunned; he did not believe them. **27**

But when they told him everything Joseph had said to them, and when he saw the carts Joseph had sent to carry him back, the spirit of their father Jacob revived. **28** And Israel said, "I'm convinced! My son Joseph is still alive. I will go and see him before I die."

Genesis 46:

1 So Israel set out with all that was his, and when he reached Beersheba, he offered sacrifices to the God of his father Isaac.

2 And God spoke to Israel in a vision at night and said, "Jacob! Jacob!"

"Here I am," he replied.

3 "I am God, the God of your father," he said. "Do not be afraid to go down to Egypt, for I will make you into a great nation there. **4** I will go down to Egypt with you, and I will surely bring you back again. And Joseph's own hand will close your eyes."

5 Then Jacob left Beersheba, and Israel's sons took their father Jacob and their children and their wives in the carts that Pharaoh had sent to transport him. **6** So Jacob and all his offspring went to Egypt, taking with them their livestock and the possessions they had acquired in Canaan. **7** Jacob brought with him to Egypt his sons and grandsons and his daughters and granddaughters—all his offspring.

8 These are the names of the sons of Israel (Jacob and his descendants) who went to Egypt:

Reuben the firstborn of Jacob.

9 The sons of Reuben:
   Hanok, Pallu, Hezron and Karmi.

10 The sons of Simeon:

Jemuel, Jamin, Ohad, Jakin, Zohar and Shaul the son of a Canaanite woman.

11 The sons of Levi:
Gershon, Kohath and Merari.

12 The sons of Judah:
Er, Onan, Shelah, Perez and Zerah (but Er and Onan had died in the land of Canaan).

The sons of Perez:
Hezron and Hamul.

13 The sons of Issachar:
Tola, Puah, Jashub and Shimron.

14 The sons of Zebulun:
Sered, Elon and Jahleel.

15 These were the sons Leah bore to Jacob in Paddan Aram, besides his daughter Dinah. These sons and daughters of his were thirty-three in all.

16 The sons of Gad:
Zephon, Haggi, Shuni, Ezbon, Eri, Arodi and Areli.

17 The sons of Asher:
Imnah, Ishvah, Ishvi and Beriah.

Their sister was Serah.

The sons of Beriah:
Heber and Malkiel.

18 These were the children born to Jacob by Zilpah, whom Laban had given to his daughter Leah—sixteen in all.

19 The sons of Jacob's wife Rachel:

Joseph and Benjamin. **20** In Egypt, Manasseh and Ephraim were born to Joseph by Asenath daughter of Potiphera, priest of On.

21 The sons of Benjamin:
   Bela, Beker, Ashbel, Gera, Naaman, Ehi, Rosh, Muppim, Huppim and Ard.

22 These were the sons of Rachel who were born to Jacob—fourteen in all.

23 The son of Dan:
   Hushim.

24 The sons of Naphtali:
   Jahziel, Guni, Jezer and Shillem.

25 These were the sons born to Jacob by Bilhah, whom Laban had given to his daughter Rachel—seven in all.

26 All those who went to Egypt with Jacob—those who were his direct descendants, not counting his sons' wives—numbered sixty-six persons. **27** With the two sons who had been born to Joseph in Egypt, the members of Jacob's family, which went to Egypt, were seventy in all.

28 Now Jacob sent Judah ahead of him to Joseph to get directions to Goshen. When they arrived in the region of Goshen, **29** Joseph had his chariot made ready and went to Goshen to meet his father Israel. As soon as Joseph appeared before him, he threw his arms around his father and wept for a long time.

30 Israel said to Joseph, "Now I am ready to die, since I have seen for myself that you are still alive."

31 Then Joseph said to his brothers and to his father's household, "I will go up and speak to Pharaoh and will say to him, 'My brothers and my father's household, who were living in the land of Canaan, have come to me. **32** The men are shepherds; they tend livestock, and they have brought along their flocks and herds and everything they own.' **33** When Pharaoh calls you in and asks, 'What is your occupation?' **34** you should answer, 'Your servants have tended livestock from our boyhood on, just as our fathers did.' Then you will be allowed to settle in the region of Goshen, for all shepherds are detestable to the Egyptians."

Genesis 47:

1 Joseph went and told Pharaoh, "My father and brothers, with their flocks and herds and everything they own, have come from the land of Canaan and are now in Goshen." **2** He chose five of his brothers and presented them before Pharaoh.

3 Pharaoh asked the brothers, "What is your occupation?"

"Your servants are shepherds," they replied to Pharaoh, "just as our fathers were." **4** They also said to him, "We have come to live here for a while, because the famine is severe in Canaan and your servants' flocks have no pasture. So now, please let your servants settle in Goshen."

5 Pharaoh said to Joseph, "Your father and your brothers have come to you, **6** and the land of Egypt is before you; settle your father and your brothers in the best part of the land. Let them live in Goshen. And if you know of any among them with special ability, put them in charge of my own livestock."

7 Then Joseph brought his father Jacob in and presented him before Pharaoh. After Jacob blessed Pharaoh, **8** Pharaoh asked him, "How old are you?"

9 And Jacob said to Pharaoh, "The years of my pilgrimage are a hundred and thirty. My years have been few and difficult, and they do not equal the years of the pilgrimage of my fathers." **10** Then Jacob blessed Pharaoh and went out from his presence.

11 So Joseph settled his father and his brothers in Egypt and gave them property in the best part of the land, the district of Rameses, as Pharaoh directed. **12** Joseph also provided his father and his brothers and all his father's household with food, according to the number of their children.

13 There was no food, however, in the whole region because the famine was severe; both Egypt and Canaan wasted away because of the famine. **14** Joseph collected all the money that was to be found in Egypt and Canaan in payment for the grain they were buying, and he brought it to Pharaoh's palace. **15** When the money of the people of Egypt and Canaan was gone, all Egypt came to Joseph and said, "Give us food. Why should we die before your eyes? Our money is all gone."

16 "Then bring your livestock," said Joseph. "I will sell you food in exchange for your livestock, since your money is gone." **17** So they brought their livestock to Joseph, and he gave them food in exchange for their horses, their sheep and goats, their cattle and donkeys. And he brought them through that year with food in exchange for all their livestock.

18 When that year was over, they came to him the following year and said, "We cannot hide from our lord the fact that since our money is gone and our livestock belongs to you, there is nothing left for our lord except our bodies and our land. **19** Why should we perish before your eyes—we and our land as well? Buy us and our land in exchange for food, and we with our land will be in bondage to Pharaoh. Give us seed so that we may live and not die, and that the land may not become desolate."

20 So Joseph bought all the land in Egypt for Pharaoh. The Egyptians, one and all, sold their fields, because the famine was too severe for them. The land became Pharaoh's, **21** and Joseph reduced the people to servitude, from one end of Egypt to the other. **22** However, he did not buy the land of the priests, because they received a regular allotment from Pharaoh and had food enough from the allotment Pharaoh gave them. That is why they did not sell their land.

23 Joseph said to the people, "Now that I have bought you and your land today for Pharaoh, here is seed for you so you can plant the ground. **24** But when the crop comes in, give a fifth of it to Pharaoh. The other four-fifths you may keep as seed for the fields and as food for yourselves and your households and your children."

25 "You have saved our lives," they said. "May we find favor in the eyes of our lord; we will be in bondage to Pharaoh."

26 So Joseph established it as a law concerning land in Egypt—still in force today—that a fifth of the produce belongs to Pharaoh. It was only the land of the priests that did not become Pharaoh's.

27 Now the Israelites settled in Egypt in the region of Goshen. They acquired property there and were fruitful and increased greatly in number.

28 Jacob lived in Egypt seventeen years, and the years of his life were a hundred and forty-seven. **29** When the time drew near for Israel to die, he called for his son Joseph and said to him, "If I have found favor in your eyes, put your hand under my thigh and promise that you will show me kindness and faithfulness. Do not bury me in Egypt, **30** but when I rest with my fathers, carry me out of Egypt and bury me where they are buried."

"I will do as you say," he said.

31 "Swear to me," he said. Then Joseph swore to him, and Israel worshiped as he leaned on the top of his staff.

Genesis 50:

1 Joseph threw himself on his father and wept over him and kissed him. **2** Then Joseph directed the physicians in his service to embalm his father Israel. So the physicians embalmed him, **3** taking a full forty days, for that was the time required for embalming. And the Egyptians mourned for him seventy days.

4 When the days of mourning had passed, Joseph said to Pharaoh's court, "If I have found favor in your eyes, speak to Pharaoh for me. Tell him, **5** 'My father made me swear an oath and said, "I am about to die; bury me in the tomb I dug for myself in the land of Canaan." Now let me go up and bury my father; then I will return.'"

6 Pharaoh said, "Go up and bury your father, as he made you swear to do."

7 So Joseph went up to bury his father. All Pharaoh's officials accompanied him—the dignitaries of his court and all the dignitaries of Egypt— **8** besides all the members of Joseph's household and his brothers and those belonging to his father's household. Only their children and their flocks and herds were left in Goshen. **9** Chariots and horsemen also went up with him. It was a very large company.

10 When they reached the threshing floor of Atad, near the Jordan, they lamented loudly and bitterly; and there Joseph observed a seven-day period of mourning for his father. **11** When the Canaanites who lived there saw the mourning at the threshing floor of Atad, they said, "The Egyptians are holding a solemn ceremony of mourning." That is why that place near the Jordan is called Abel Mizraim.

12 So Jacob's sons did as he had commanded them: **13** They carried him to the land of Canaan and buried him in the cave in the field of Machpelah, near Mamre, which Abraham had bought along with the field as a burial place from Ephron the Hittite. **14** After burying his father, Joseph returned to Egypt, together with his brothers and all the others who had gone with him to bury his father.

15 When Joseph's brothers saw that their father was dead, they said, "What if Joseph holds a grudge against us and pays us back for all the wrongs we did to him?" **16** So they sent word to Joseph, saying, "Your father left these instructions before he died: **17** 'This is what you are to say to Joseph: I ask you to forgive your brothers the sins and the wrongs they committed in treating you so badly.' Now please forgive the sins of the servants of the God of your father." When their message came to him, Joseph wept.

18 His brothers then came and threw themselves down before him. "We are your slaves," they said.

19 But Joseph said to them, "Don't be afraid. Am I in the place of God? **20** You intended to harm me, but God intended it for good to accomplish what is now being done, the saving of many lives. **21** So then, don't be afraid. I will provide for you and your children." **And he reassured them and spoke kindly to them** [emphasis added].

22 Joseph stayed in Egypt, along with all his father's family. He lived a hundred and ten years **23** and saw the third generation of Ephraim's children. Also the children of Makir son of Manasseh were placed at birth on Joseph's knees.

24 Then Joseph said to his brothers, "I am about to die. But God will surely come to your aid and take you up out of this land to the land he promised on oath to Abraham, Isaac and Jacob." **25** And Joseph made the Israelites swear an oath and said, "God will surely come to your aid, and then you must carry my bones up from this place."

26 So Joseph died at the age of a hundred and ten. And after they embalmed him, he was placed in a coffin in Egypt.

Observations of the providence of God working out His plan:

1. At the age of seventeen, Joseph has a couple of strange, fantastical dreams that eventually come true.

2. There is no water in the cistern where Joseph is thrown by his brothers. If there had been water in the cistern, would Joseph have drowned? Was this God's protection of Joseph?

3. The caravan of Ishmaelites travels by just as the brothers are eating after they had put Joseph in the cistern.

4. The Ishmaelites are going to Egypt.

5. The Ishmaelites are willing to buy Joseph.

6. In Egypt, Potiphar, Pharaoh's official – the captain of the guard – buys Joseph.

7. The Lord is with Joseph, and he prospers in Potiphar's house.

8. Joseph becomes Potiphar's attendant.

9. God blesses Potiphar's household because of Joseph.

10. Joseph is put in prison after Potiphar's wife tries to seduce him. She claims that he had tried to take advantage of her. He is innocent, however. Indeed, he fled from her advances, knowing that giving in to her would be sinful.

11. God is with Joseph while he is in prison, and he is elevated to a place of responsibility.

12. Due to offending Pharaoh, the chief cupbearer and the chief baker are both imprisoned at the same prison where Joseph is confined.

13. They are both assigned to Joseph, and he attends them.

14. They both have dreams – on the same night.

15. Joseph is able to correctly interpret the dreams of the cupbearer and the baker.

16. Both dreams come to pass.

17. The cupbearer forgets his promise to help Joseph get out of prison.

18. Pharaoh has a couple of dreams that none of the wise men can interpret.

19. The cupbearer tells Pharaoh that he should go to Joseph for the interpretation of his dream.

20. Joseph is brought out of prison and asked to interpret Pharaoh's dreams. God gives Joseph the ability to correctly interpret Pharaoh's dreams and to devise a plan to deal with the famine that God reveals, through Pharaoh's dreams, is coming to the land of Egypt.

21. Pharaoh puts Joseph in charge of the palace. The people are to submit to his orders. Only Pharaoh will be greater than Joseph.

22. There is a famine throughout the world, and people of other countries go to Egypt for food.

23. Joseph's father Israel (Jacob) hears that there is food in Egypt, and so he sends his sons there to buy food.

24. Joseph's brothers bow down to him, just as they did in the dream he had before he was taken captive to Egypt.

25. Joseph is able to help his family by giving them food.

26. Joseph knows that God had sent him to Egypt. He says, "And now, do not be distressed and do not be angry with yourselves for selling me here, because it was to save lives that God sent me ahead of you. For two years now there has been famine in the land, and for the next five years there will be no plowing and reaping. But God sent me ahead of you to preserve for you a remnant on earth and to save your lives by a great deliverance. So then, it was not you who sent me here, but God.

He made me father to Pharaoh, lord of his entire household and ruler of all Egypt" (Genesis 45:5-8 NIV).

27. God says to Jacob, "Do not be afraid to go down to Egypt, for I will make you into a great nation there" (Genesis 46:3 NIV). We can conclude from this one verse alone that God is involved not just in the life of Joseph but his family as well. His plan is to make a great nation from this one family. Remember God's covenant with Abraham? In Genesis 12:2 & 3, the Lord says to Abraham, "I will make you into a great nation, and I will bless you; I will make your name great, and you will be a blessing. I will bless those who bless you, and whoever curses you I will curse; and all peoples on earth will be blessed through you" (NIV). The Lord also tells Abraham, "I will surely bless you and make your descendants as numerous as the stars in the sky and as the sand on the seashore. Your descendants will take possession of the cities of their enemies, and through your offspring all nations on earth will be blessed, because you have obeyed me" (Genesis 22:17 & 18 NIV). God is continuing to fulfill His great plan, and He is using Joseph and his family at this particular time in history to accomplish that plan.

28. Joseph says to his brothers, "Don't be afraid. Am I in the place of God? You intended to harm me, but God intended it for good to accomplish what is now being done, the saving of many lives" (Genesis 50:19 & 20 NIV). Again, we see that Joseph acknowledges that it was God's plan all along to bring him to Egypt. Though his brothers intended to harm him back in Canaan when he was seventeen, and they sold him to the Ishmaelites, it was God's way of getting Joseph to Egypt where God would eventually use him to save many lives.

So now that you have finished the story of Joseph, the question is, "What can we learn from this story that will help us to biblically handle disappointment, discouragement, defeat, depression, and despair?"

Joseph is a good example of how to biblically handle these emotions, even though, humanly speaking, he had reason to despair. He was taken from his homeland, from his family, from his security, and sold into slavery in a foreign and hostile country when he was just seventeen years old! Can you imagine his fear and anguish as he was being transported to Egypt? He likely did not even know where he was headed or what would happen to him when he got there. No doubt he was treated with contempt, for he was a slave. How terrifying and humiliating! The Ishmaelites hated the Israelites. Joseph was from the part of Abraham's family that came from his promised son, Isaac. Remember the prophecy about Ishmael, Abraham's son from Hagar, given by the angel of the Lord to Hagar in Genesis 16:11 & 12? The angel of the LORD also said to her: "You are now pregnant and you will give birth to a son. You shall name him Ishmael, for the LORD has heard of your misery. He will be a wild donkey of a man; his hand will be against everyone and everyone's hand against him, and he will live in hostility toward all his brothers" (NIV). These were the descendants of Ishmael, Abraham's son from Hagar, who was born of the flesh and not of the power of the Spirit (Galatians 4:29), who were carrying Joseph off to Egypt. If anyone had reason to despair, it was Joseph!

We do not, however, see any evidence that young Joseph did despair. We are given limited details about how he responded to what happened to him, but certainly Joseph made the best of his circumstances. His attitude and behavior won him the favor of everyone who was in authority over him. He must have been a good worker with a good attitude, or he would not have been elevated to positions of authority over others. Those in authority over him would certainly not have trusted him so thoroughly if he had not been a man of integrity and a good worker with a good attitude.

In Joseph's life, we see no hint of bitterness or resentment toward others or toward God. He did not seek to get even with his brothers for their mistreatment. He did not give up on life. He did not cease doing right even after being wrongly imprisoned for doing the right thing by fleeing from Potiphar's wife's advances. He did not sit around feeling sorry for himself. He apparently made the best of his circumstances, knowing that God was in control of every event of his life and of the whole world. Apparently, he did not despair, even while he waited to be released from prison where he was unjustly confined. I wonder if he even imagined to what heights he would be raised once he was released from prison. Without God's intervention, he could have spent the rest of his life languishing there. The dreams he had while living in his homeland were a clue as to his future, but I wonder if he realized that. Regardless, he must have trusted God for his welfare.

How could this be? Is it not human nature to despair over our adverse circumstances and to become enraged over personal injustices and to seek revenge? Don't many humans sometimes allow their trials and difficulties to paralyze them and rob them of joy and productivity? Don't they tend to focus on what they don't have, what isn't pleasant, and how other people have wronged them, so that they sometimes can barely get by, much less soar to heights of greatness? So what about Joseph was different than many other humans? Even in prison, he excelled. He rose to the top.

We are told that God was with Joseph, granting him success and giving him favor in the eyes of his superiors. But is it feasible that Joseph was successful in all he did and that he gained favor by sitting around feeling sorry for himself? It is much more likely that Joseph was successful and gained favor by having a good attitude and doing a good job at his tasks rather than becoming angry and difficult. Bitterness and resentment did not rule his heart and life. He apparently trusted God through all his trials. God does His part, and He expects us also to do our part. We cannot expect God to bless our lives if we are not doing our part by fulfilling our tasks with a cheerful attitude, submitting to those in authority over us, and trusting God for our welfare. Joseph must have done all of these things, and even though he experienced great troubles in his young life, he did not seem to despair. He recognized the sovereignty of God over everything, and he recognized the goodness of God. Though others tried to harm him, God used those circumstances to bring about His plan. It is possible that Joseph had to wrestle with his feelings and work hard at having a good attitude. If so, it appears that he at least eventually got control of his feelings. We do not really know how much Joseph did or did not struggle with his emotions, but his behavior indicates that he did not allow negative emotions to rule himself.

We do know that while Joseph was in prison, God was refining him. Joseph apparently had some character flaws that needed to be purged from his life. (Don't we all?!) Evidence for this view is found in Psalm 105:16-19: "When he [God] summoned a famine on the land and broke all supply of bread, he had sent a man ahead of them, Joseph, who was sold as a slave. **His feet were hurt with fetters; his neck was put in a collar of iron; until what he had said came to pass, the word of the LORD tested him**" [emphasis added] (ESV). The same Hebrew word that is translated as "tested" is used in Psalm 12:6 and Psalm 66:10, where **the testing process is likened to the refining process of silver or gold**. Psalm 12:6 says, "The words of the Lord are pure words, like silver refined in a furnace on the ground, purified seven times" (ESV). Psalm 66:10 says, "For you, O God, have tested us; you have tried us as silver is tried" (ESV). So while in prison, Joseph was being refined by God. I think we can conclude that Joseph must have cooperated with God in this refining process, for he did not come out of prison bitter or doubting the goodness of God. He had a humble attitude, recognizing that he could not interpret Pharaoh's dream, but God could. God gave to Joseph the interpretation of Pharaoh's dream.

The story of Joseph is one of the greatest examples of the truth that God's plans are always greater than our plans. Perhaps if Joseph had had his way when he was seventeen, he would have continued in the tradition of his family by being a shepherd. There was dignity in being a shepherd, just as there is dignity in all legitimate work. However, instead of becoming a shepherd, Joseph had much more influence by ruling all of Egypt! He saved the lives of many people through implementing God's plan to prepare for the famine! God's plans are always greater than our plans, even though His plans may involve hardship.

I became aware of an example of this recently, in 2022. I still have contact with a family in Ukraine in whose home I stayed while I was on a short-term mission trip in 1999. The Russian invasion of Ukraine began in February of 2022. This couple, a pastor and his wife, lived in Kharkiv, the second largest city in Ukraine and a region where the Russian army was doing a lot of bombing, very close to their home. Rather than fleeing to the United States where their three married daughters live, they chose to continue with their work spreading the Gospel in their native Ukraine.

At first, they hid in the cellar of their church. Vitaliy, the pastor, would go out every day to buy food to share with people in his congregation. Eventually, this proved to be too dangerous, and he and his wife realized that it was imperative that they flee to the western side of the country where there was less Russian occupation.

This was very difficult for Nadia to accept. She was devastated about having to flee, and she questioned God about why this was happening. A pastor friend of theirs told her that she would not be able to help anybody if she were dead. Disappointed, yet conceding to the inevitable, the couple relocated to Zakarpattia, close to the Hungarian border. They continued to work for God's kingdom by Vitaliy preaching and Nadia speaking to women in this new location.

It soon became apparent why God had led them from Kharkiv to this different area of Ukraine. In the western region of Ukraine, few people speak Russian. They speak Hungarian, so there was no one to teach those displaced Ukrainian people the Gospel in a language they could understand. God sent Vitaly and Nadia to that area so that they could share the Gospel with the people who might not have heard it otherwise. What a privilege it was for them to lead others to Christ! And how rewarding! God's plans are always better than our own plans!

When we find ourselves in a situation that is difficult, we tend to focus on the situation and yearn for the day when we will be released from it, when things will get better for us. We may see the situation as a waste of time because we think we have better things to do with our time. In a sense, we count down the time until our discomfort will be over. We think that when our circumstances improve, then we can really be happy and start living.

This is a mistake, though. I relish comfort as much as anybody else, but I have come to realize that this attitude of "biding my time" is a waste of God-given time and opportunity. God has either put me in this uncomfortable situation or allowed me to be here for some good reason. I should look at it as an opportunity to serve God in some way and not simply waste the time. Also, I should seek to learn something from the situation.

When I taught these lessons at a women's prison several years ago, I could understand the temptation of the incarcerated women in the class to count down the days until they would be released. Oh, how I can identify with that attitude! I know I would savor the thought of finally being free and would probably daydream about life after prison.

As I taught these lessons, however, I realized that the women in the prison had opportunities right then and there to serve God, right where they were in prison. I encouraged them to make the most of the opportunities they had right then and there to live for Christ. They could help other women in the prison. They could have a cheerful, caring attitude in the midst of much darkness and drudgery. They could pray for others while they were waiting to be released. Biding one's time does not make the time go by any faster, so they might as well use their time wisely for the benefit of others, rather than dwelling only on their own interests.

I don't know about you, but after reading the story of Joseph, I cannot help but praise God for His greatness. This story is a marvelous demonstration of how He holds history in His hands. He is in control of everything, and He works out human events for His own purposes.

The psalmist confirms this in Psalm 105:16-19:

"When he [God] summoned a famine on the land and broke all supply of bread, he had sent a man ahead of them, Joseph, who was sold as a slave. His feet were hurt with fetters; his neck was put in a collar of iron; until what he had said came to pass, the word of the LORD tested him" (ESV).

This is the God to whom I look when I am faced with disappointment, discouragement, defeat, depression, and despair!

Will you remember during the times of trials and troubles that God rules over all people and all events and can change your circumstances and position? Will you commit to trusting Him, remembering that He is with you in the midst of your troubling circumstances, and that His plan is to use your circumstances to teach you something and perhaps use you in a way beyond your imagination? Will you let go of anger, bitterness, and resentment against those who have wronged you and rise up and do your tasks to the best of your ability, even in the prison of your circumstance as Joseph did? Will you, like Joseph, choose to excel where you are, even if it is not where you want to be? Will you believe that God has a good purpose for you to fulfill and that He is working all things out for your good and His glory? Joseph had reason to be angry with his brothers, with Potiphar's wife, with Potiphar himself, and with the cupbearer, but he had an even greater reason to let go of the anger and live for God. That reason was God Himself, and Joseph chose to focus on Him rather than his difficulties. God help us all to do the same!

Chapter Seventeen

The Study of Saul

> "'But now your kingdom will not endure; the LORD has sought out a man after his own heart and appointed him ruler of his people, because you have not kept the LORD's command.'"
> 1 Samuel 13:14 NIV

Sometimes we suffer difficulties as a natural consequence of sins we have committed. Our sins have gotten us into trouble, and now we are suffering the consequences of those sins. We eventually suffer when we refuse to follow God's ways in a matter and choose to go our own way instead. Unlike the story of Job who suffered trials even though he was upright and followed God (though he was not sinless), we sometimes suffer trials because we have sinned.

This lesson is about a man in the Old Testament who sinned and failed to make things right. Instead of turning away from his sin, he compounded his sin by sinning even more so as to get out of the trouble he was in because of his sin. What was the end result of his life of sin? Dethronement, depression, and suicide! His name was Saul.

Saul was the first king of Israel. Prior to Saul, Israel was ruled by judges. Samuel was a good judge who served God well in that capacity. When he got old, he appointed his sons Joel and Abijah as judges to replace himself. But they did not judge righteously as their father Samuel had. They were dishonest; they accepted bribes and perverted justice.

Upset about this, the elders of Israel insisted that Samuel appoint a king to rule over them instead of his dishonest sons. Samuel was displeased with this request and went to the Lord about it. The Lord told Samuel that the people were rejecting Him, not Samuel. God told Samuel to listen to the people and to give them a king but told him also to tell the people that a king will take advantage of them. The people refused to listen and continued to insist upon a king to rule over them – like the nations around them. Sounds like they thought they knew better than God what would be good for them.

When Samuel informed Saul that God had appointed him to rule over Israel, he said that the Spirit of the Lord would come upon Saul in power and that God was with him. When Saul started to leave Samuel, God changed Saul's heart and all that was prophesied by Samuel was fulfilled that day.

1 Samuel 9:

1 There was a Benjamite, a man of standing, whose name was Kish son of Abiel, the son of Zeror, the son of Bekorath, the son of Aphiah of Benjamin. **2** Kish had a son named Saul, as handsome a young man as could be found anywhere in Israel, and he was a head taller than anyone else.

3 Now the donkeys belonging to Saul's father Kish were lost, and Kish said to his son Saul, "Take one of the servants with you and go and look for the donkeys." **4** So he passed through the hill country of Ephraim and through the area around Shalisha, but they did not find them. They went on into the district of Shaalim, but the donkeys were not there. Then he passed through the territory of Benjamin, but they did not find them.

5 When they reached the district of Zuph, Saul said to the servant who was with him, "Come, let's go back, or my father will stop thinking about the donkeys and start worrying about us."

6 But the servant replied, "Look, in this town there is a man of God; he is highly respected, and everything he says comes true. Let's go there now. Perhaps he will tell us what way to take."

7 Saul said to his servant, "If we go, what can we give the man? The food in our sacks is gone. We have no gift to take to the man of God. What do we have?"

8 The servant answered him again. "Look," he said, "I have a quarter of a shekel of silver. I will give it to the man of God so that he will tell us what way to take." **9** (Formerly in Israel, if someone went to inquire of God, they would say, "Come, let us go to the seer," because the prophet of today used to be called a seer.)

10 "Good," Saul said to his servant. "Come, let's go." So they set out for the town where the man of God was.

11 As they were going up the hill to the town, they met some young women coming out to draw water, and they asked them, "Is the seer here?"

12 "He is," they answered. "He's ahead of you. Hurry now; he has just come to our town today, for the people have a sacrifice at the high place. **13** As soon as you enter the town, you will find him before he goes up to the high place to eat. The people will not begin eating until he comes, because he must bless the sacrifice; afterward, those who are invited will eat. Go up now; you should find him about this time."

14 They went up to the town, and as they were entering it, there was Samuel, coming toward them on his way up to the high place.

15 Now the day before Saul came, the Lord had revealed this to Samuel: **16** "About this time tomorrow I will send you a man from the land of Benjamin. Anoint him ruler over my people Israel; he will deliver them from the hand of the Philistines. I have looked on my people, for their cry has reached me."

17 When Samuel caught sight of Saul, the Lord said to him, "This is the man I spoke to you about; he will govern my people."

18 Saul approached Samuel in the gateway and asked, "Would you please tell me where the seer's house is?"

19 "I am the seer," Samuel replied. "Go up ahead of me to the high place, for today you are to eat with me, and in the morning I will send you on your way and will tell you all that is in your heart. **20** As for the donkeys you lost three days ago, do not worry about them; they have been found. And to whom is all the desire of Israel turned, if not to you and your whole family line?"

21 Saul answered, "But am I not a Benjamite, from the smallest tribe of Israel, and is not my clan the least of all the clans of the tribe of Benjamin? Why do you say such a thing to me?"

22 Then Samuel brought Saul and his servant into the hall and seated them at the head of those who were invited—about thirty in number. **23** Samuel said to the cook, "Bring the piece of meat I gave you, the one I told you to lay aside."

24 So the cook took up the thigh with what was on it and set it in front of Saul. Samuel said, "Here is what has been kept for you. Eat, because it was set aside for you for this occasion from the time I said, 'I have invited guests.'" And Saul dined with Samuel that day.

25 After they came down from the high place to the town, Samuel talked with Saul on the roof of his house. **26** They rose about daybreak, and Samuel called to Saul on the roof, "Get ready, and I will send you on your way." When Saul got ready, he and Samuel went outside together. **27** As they were going down to the edge of the town, Samuel said to Saul, "Tell the servant to go on ahead of us"—and the servant did so—"but you stay here for a while, so that I may give you a message from God."

1 Samuel 10:

1 Then Samuel took a flask of olive oil and poured it on Saul's head and kissed him, saying, "Has not the Lord anointed you ruler over his inheritance? **2** When you leave me today, you will meet two men near Rachel's tomb, at Zelzah on the border of Benjamin. They will say to you, 'The donkeys you set out to look for have been found. And now your father has stopped thinking about them and is worried about you. He is asking, 'What shall I do about my son?'"

3 "Then you will go on from there until you reach the great tree of Tabor. Three men going up to worship God at Bethel will meet you there. One will be carrying three young goats, another three loaves of bread, and another a skin of wine. **4** They will greet you and offer you two loaves of bread, which you will accept from them.

5 "After that you will go to Gibeah of God, where there is a Philistine outpost. As you approach the town, you will meet a procession of prophets coming down from the high place with lyres, timbrels, pipes and harps being played before them, and they will be prophesying. **6**

The Spirit of the Lord will come powerfully upon you, and you will prophesy with them; and you will be changed into a different person. **7** Once these signs are fulfilled, do whatever your hand finds to do, for God is with you.

8 "Go down ahead of me to Gilgal. I will surely come down to you to sacrifice burnt offerings and fellowship offerings, but you must wait seven days until I come to you and tell you what you are to do."

9 As Saul turned to leave Samuel, God changed Saul's heart, and all these signs were fulfilled that day. **10** When he and his servant arrived at Gibeah, a procession of prophets met him; the Spirit of God came powerfully upon him, and he joined in their prophesying. **11** When all those who had formerly known him saw him prophesying with the prophets, they asked each other, "What is this that has happened to the son of Kish? Is Saul also among the prophets?"

12 A man who lived there answered, "And who is their father?" So it became a saying: "Is Saul also among the prophets?" **13** After Saul stopped prophesying, he went to the high place.

14 Now Saul's uncle asked him and his servant, "Where have you been?"

"Looking for the donkeys," he said. "But when we saw they were not to be found, we went to Samuel."

15 Saul's uncle said, "Tell me what Samuel said to you."

16 Saul replied, "He assured us that the donkeys had been found." But he did not tell his uncle what Samuel had said about the kingship.

17 Samuel summoned the people of Israel to the Lord at Mizpah **18** and said to them, "This is what the Lord, the God of Israel, says: 'I brought Israel up out of Egypt, and I delivered you from the power of Egypt and all the kingdoms that oppressed you.' **19** But you have now rejected your God, who saves you out of all your disasters and calamities. And you have said, 'No, appoint a king over us.' So now present yourselves before the Lord by your tribes and clans."

20 When Samuel had all Israel come forward by tribes, the tribe of Benjamin was taken by lot. **21** Then he brought forward the tribe of Benjamin, clan by clan, and Matri's clan was taken. Finally Saul son of Kish was taken. But when they looked for him, he was not to be found. **22** So they inquired further of the Lord, "Has the man come here yet?"

And the Lord said, "Yes, he has hidden himself among the supplies."

23 They ran and brought him out, and as he stood among the people he was a head taller than any of the others. **24** Samuel said to all the people, "Do you see the man the Lord has chosen? There is no one like him among all the people."

Then the people shouted, "Long live the king!"

25 Samuel explained to the people the rights and duties of kingship. He wrote them down on a scroll and deposited it before the Lord. Then Samuel dismissed the people to go to their own homes.

26 Saul also went to his home in Gibeah, accompanied by valiant men whose hearts God had touched. **27** But some scoundrels said, "How can this fellow save us?" They despised him and brought him no gifts. But Saul kept silent (NIV).

Saul starts out his kingship well, but he ends in disaster. The following is a list of his actions and God's response to those actions.

1. The Spirit of God comes upon Saul in power, and he burns with anger against Nahash, who besieged the city of Jabesh. Saul rescues the city. Saul gives credit to God for rescuing Israel (1 Samuel 11:1-13). Good job, Saul!

2. Saul offers the burnt offering when he sees his men scatter at Gilgal. Samuel has not yet arrived. By offering the burnt offering, Saul does not keep the command that the Lord had given him. Saul enters into the realm of the priest, which no one but a priest was allowed to do. Saul takes matters into his own hands rather than obeying God and trusting Him with the results. Therefore, his kingdom is going to come to an end, and he will be replaced by "a man after God's own heart" (1 Samuel 13:1-14).

3. God tells Saul to attack the Amalekites because they mistreated the Israelites. He tells Saul to totally destroy everything that belongs to the Amalekites: men, women, children, infants, cattle, sheep, camels, and donkeys. Instead of following these instructions, Saul only destroys what is "despised and weak." He spares Agag, king of the Amalekites, and the best of the sheep and cattle, the fat calves and lambs – everything that is good (1 Samuel 15:1-35). Therefore, Saul disobeys God.

4. After he is confronted by Samuel, Saul acknowledges his sin. Saul worships God with Samuel (1 Samuel 15:13-31).

5. The Lord rejects Saul as king because he did not follow His ways (1 Samuel 15:26-29).

6. Saul becomes very jealous of David. After David kills Goliath, the Philistine giant who taunts and defies the God of Israel, the Israelite

women sing this song: "Saul has slain his thousands, and David his tens of thousands" (1 Samuel 18:7 NIV). Saul is angry and jealous that David received more credit than he did (1 Samuel 18:6-9).

7. The Spirit of the Lord departs from Saul, and an evil spirit from the Lord torments him (1 Samuel 18:10).

8. Saul tries to kill David several times (1 Samuel 18:10 & 11; 1 Samuel 19:1-20).

9. Saul has the priests of the Lord, eighty-five men, killed because they sided with David. "He also put to the sword Nob, the town of the priests, with its men and women, its children and infants, and its cattle, donkeys and sheep" (1 Samuel 22:19 NIV).

10. Desperate for answers because the Lord no longer answers him by the established means of dreams or Urim or prophets, Saul consults a medium who calls up Samuel from the dead. Saul asks Samuel what he should do about the Philistines who are fighting against him (1 Samuel 28:3-25). God had already warned the Israelites to not allow mediums or spiritists to practice in Israel (Leviticus 19:31; Leviticus 20:6, 27; Deuteronomy 18:9-11), and Saul had, therefore, outlawed the practice.

11. Saul kills himself (1 Samuel 31:1-6).

What can we learn from the tragic life of Saul? What went wrong? He went from being the anointed king of Israel with the Spirit of God upon him to being dethroned, being replaced by a better man than himself, and eventually ending his own life.

Saul's first mistake was disobeying the Lord by not waiting for Samuel to come and offer the sacrifices. He was afraid of his enemies, so he did not wait for Samuel. He offered the sacrifices himself. Samuel had told Saul that he had a message from God for him. Part of that message was this: "Go down ahead of me to Gilgal. I will surely come down to you to sacrifice burnt offerings and fellowship offerings, but you must wait seven days until I come to you and tell you what you are to do" (1 Samuel 10:8 NIV). But Saul did not wait for Samuel; he made the offerings himself.

Saul also disobeyed the Lord by not carrying out "his fierce wrath against the Amalekites" (1 Samuel 28:18). He did not completely destroy the Amalekites like God had told him to do. "This is what the LORD Almighty says: 'I will punish the Amalekites for what they did to Israel when they waylaid them as they came up from Egypt. **Now go, attack the Amalekites and totally destroy all that belongs to them. Do not spare them; put to death men and women, children and infants, cattle and sheep, camels and donkeys'"** [emphasis added] (1 Samuel 15:2 & 3 NIV).

So, because of Saul's disobedience, his throne was taken away from him and given to David, a man after God's own heart. **But even though Saul lost his kingdom, he still could have lived out the rest of his life better than he did.**

He became intensely jealous of David and tried to have him killed several times. He killed the priests of Nob along with every other human being there because the priests sided with David. Rather than confronting his own sin of jealousy, he allowed this sin to fester and overtake his heart, allowing the jealousy to turn into rage. He then wanted to kill David, and he followed through with this desire by attempting several times to kill him. Then he consulted a medium, something which God had prohibited. (See below, "Definitions and Scripture Passages Concerning the Occult".)

Instead of confessing and rejecting his sin along the way and making things right, he continued in his sin. We see the progression of Saul's sin: disobedience to God's specified commands, jealousy of the man who would replace him, attempting to kill that man, looking to the evil spirit world rather than to God, the taking of his own life. Had Saul taken care of his sin way back when he became so jealous of David, he might not have continued down the slippery slope of his sin. See how the unchecked jealousy that burned within Saul's heart caused him to sin further? The end of Saul's slippery slope was despair, and he completed the progression of his sin by taking his own life. Unchecked sin in our lives can cause us to go down that slippery slope.

How can we apply this lesson to our lives today? We do not want to make the same mistakes that Saul made!

The application of this lesson is this:

When you have sinned, confess it to the Lord and forsake the sin so that you can receive His forgiveness. Thus, you will put a check on your heart, keeping it pure.

Do not allow any sin to interfere with your fellowship with the Lord and His hand upon your life.

Keep confessing and forsaking sin.

Do not allow any sin to overtake you, like Saul did with his jealousy over David. Saul's lust for recognition caused him to do some desperate, sinful things. Rather than looking to God for his identity, he sought to have David killed so that he would not be outdone by him. When he did not receive answers from the Lord, he sought answers by a means prohibited – calling up a dead man from the grave.

When you realize you have sinned, confess it to the Lord and seek to obey Him in every area of your life. Do not resort to sinful measures to get what you want. Look to the Lord for your fulfillment.

Nothing will banish depression better than intimacy with the true and living God!

Definitions and Scripture Passages Concerning the Occult

Dictionary definitions:

divination[8] – the art or act of foretelling future events or revealing occult knowledge by means of augury or an alleged supernatural agency

fortune teller[9] – one who professes to predict future events

medium[10] – a person thought to have the power to communicate with the spirits of the dead or with agents of another world or dimension

occult[11] – of, relating to, or dealing with supernatural or magical influences, agencies, or occurrences

sorcery[12] – use of supernatural power over others through the assistance of spirits; witchcraft

---

[8] The American Heritage Dictionary of the English Language (Boston: Houghton Mifflin Harcourt Publishing Company, 2016), p. 527.

[9] Ibid., p. 691.

[10] Ibid., p. 1093.

[11] Ibid., p. 1218.

[12] Ibid., p. 1671.

spiritualism[13] – the belief that the dead communicate with the living, as through a medium

witch[14] – a person, especially a woman, claiming or popularly believed to possess magical powers and practicing sorcery

God prohibited the Israelites from engaging in any of these practices of the occult.

Exodus 22:18 (NIV):

> "Do not allow a sorceress to live."

Leviticus 19:26 (NIV):

> "Do not practice divination or seek omens."

Leviticus 19:31 (NIV):

> "Do not turn to mediums or seek out spiritists, for you will be defiled by them. I am the LORD your God."

Leviticus 20:6 (NIV):

> "I will set my face against anyone who turns to mediums and spiritists to prostitute themselves by following them, and I will cut them off from their people."

---

[13] Ibid., p. 1689.
[14] Ibid., p. 1989.

Leviticus 20:27 (NIV):

"A man or woman who is a medium or spiritist among you must be put to death. You are to stone them; their blood will be on their own heads."

Deuteronomy 18:9-13 (NIV):

"When you enter the land the LORD your God is giving you, do not learn to imitate the detestable ways of the nations there. Let no one be found among you who sacrifices their son or daughter in the fire, who practices divination or sorcery, interprets omens, engages in witchcraft, or casts spells, or who is a medium or spiritist or who consults the dead. Anyone who does these things is detestable to the LORD; because of these same detestable practices the LORD your God will drive out those nations before you. You must be blameless before the LORD your God."

1 Samuel 15:22 & 23 (NIV):

"But Samuel replied [to Saul]: 'Does the LORD delight in burnt offerings and sacrifices as much as in obeying the LORD? To obey is better than sacrifice, and to heed is better than the fat of rams. For rebellion is like the sin of divination, and arrogance like the evil of idolatry. Because you have rejected the word of the LORD, he has rejected you as king.'"

2 Kings 17:16 & 17 (NIV):

"They [the Israelites] forsook all the commands of the LORD their God and made for themselves two idols cast in the shape of calves, and an Asherah pole. They bowed down to all the starry hosts, and they worshiped Baal. They sacrificed their sons and daughters in the fire. They practiced divination and sought omens and sold themselves to do evil in the eyes of the LORD, arousing his anger."

2 Chronicles 33:6 (NIV):

"He [Manasseh, king of Judah] sacrificed his children in the fire in the Valley of Ben Hinnom, practiced divination and witchcraft, sought omens, and consulted mediums and spiritists. He did much evil in the eyes of the LORD, arousing his anger."

Galatians 5:19-21 (NIV):

"The acts of the flesh are obvious: sexual immorality, impurity and debauchery; idolatry and witchcraft; hatred, discord, jealousy, fits of rage, selfish ambition, dissensions, factions and envy; drunkenness, orgies, and the like. I warn you, as I did before, that those who live like this will not inherit the kingdom of God."

*****WARNING!***WARNING!***WARNING!***WARNING!*****

It is fitting and wise, I think, at this point to put forth a strong admonition against dabbling in the supernatural world of the occult. Anyone who does this is inviting Satan to enter his or her life. It is opening up the door to the demonic world, and once you open the door, you set yourself up for stalking by demons! This is a sure recipe for depression and even despair. Stay away from anything that promotes or even merely flirts with the evil spirit world of Satan: music, games, movies, and literature that promote Satan and the underworld, calling up the dead, astrology, tarot cards, palm reading, mediums, fortune tellers, ouija boards, horoscopes, and the like. These are not fun and innocent; they are evil and dangerous! Stay away from them!

Chapter Eighteen

The Study of David

> "Search me, God, and know my heart; test me and know my anxious thoughts. See if there is any offensive way in me, and lead me in the way everlasting."
> Psalm 139:23 & 24 NIV

Throughout our study on handling disappointment, discouragement, defeat, depression, and despair, we have studied various causes for these emotional hijackers: our own faulty thinking, satanic influences, and our sinful attitudes or practices.

It is sobering to think that some of our struggles with these emotions are due to our own sinful attitudes and practices, but if we stop and examine ourselves, we might learn that there is a connection between our sin and our discouragement, depression, or despair.

Like the lesson about King Saul, this lesson centers around a man who sinned, and he attempted to cover up his sin by committing another serious sin. And like Saul, his sin cost him something very precious. Had he not sinned like he did, he would not have suffered the emotional trauma that followed.

After Saul lost his kingdom, he was replaced by David. King David was a very powerful man, and at times he used his power for his own sinful purposes.

2 Samuel 11:

1 In the spring, at the time when kings go off to war, David sent Joab out with the king's men and the whole Israelite army. They destroyed the Ammonites and besieged Rabbah. But David remained in Jerusalem.

2 One evening, David got up from his bed and walked around on the roof of the palace. From the roof he saw a woman bathing. The woman was very beautiful, **3** and David sent someone to find out about her. The man said, "She is Bathsheba, the daughter of Eliam and the wife of Uriah the Hittite." **4** Then David sent messengers to get her. She came to him, and he slept with her. (Now she was purifying herself from her monthly uncleanness.) Then she went back home. **5** The woman conceived and sent word to David, saying, "I am pregnant."

6 So David sent this word to Joab: "Send me Uriah the Hittite." And Joab sent him to David. **7** When Uriah came to him, David asked him how Joab was, how the soldiers were and how the war was going. **8** Then David said to Uriah, "Go down to your house and wash your feet." So Uriah left the palace, and a gift from the king was sent after him. **9** But Uriah slept at the entrance to the palace with all his master's servants and did not go down to his house.

10 David was told, "Uriah did not go home." So he asked Uriah, "Haven't you just come from a military campaign? Why didn't you go home?"

11 Uriah said to David, "The ark and Israel and Judah are staying in tents, and my commander Joab and my lord's men are camped in the open country. How could I go to my house to eat and drink and make love to my wife? As surely as you live, I will not do such a thing!"

12 Then David said to him, "Stay here one more day, and tomorrow I will send you back." So Uriah remained in Jerusalem that day and the next. **13** At David's invitation, he ate and drank with him, and David made him drunk. But in the evening Uriah went out to sleep on his mat among his master's servants; he did not go home.

14 In the morning David wrote a letter to Joab and sent it with Uriah. **15** In it he wrote, "Put Uriah out in front where the fighting is fiercest. Then withdraw from him so he will be struck down and die."

16 So while Joab had the city under siege, he put Uriah at a place where he knew the strongest defenders were. **17** When the men of the city came out and fought against Joab, some of the men in David's army fell; moreover, Uriah the Hittite died.

18 Joab sent David a full account of the battle. **19** He instructed the messenger: "When you have finished giving the king this account of the battle, **20** the king's anger may flare up, and he may ask you, 'Why did you get so close to the city to fight? Didn't you know they would shoot arrows from the wall? **21** Who killed Abimelek son of Jerub-Besheth? Didn't a woman drop an upper millstone on him from the wall, so that he died in Thebez? Why did you get so close to the wall?' If he asks you this, then say to him, 'Moreover, your servant Uriah the Hittite is dead.'"

22 The messenger set out, and when he arrived he told David everything Joab had sent him to say. **23** The messenger said to David, "The men overpowered us and came out against us in the open, but we drove them back to the entrance of the city gate. **24** Then the archers shot arrows at your servants from the wall, and some of the king's men died. Moreover, your servant Uriah the Hittite is dead."

25 David told the messenger, "Say this to Joab: 'Don't let this upset you; the sword devours one as well as another. Press the attack against the city and destroy it.' Say this to encourage Joab."

26 When Uriah's wife heard that her husband was dead, she mourned for him. **27** After the time of mourning was over, David had her brought to his house, and she became his wife and bore him a son. But the thing David had done displeased the LORD.

2 Samuel 12:

1 The Lord sent Nathan to David. When he came to him, he said, "There were two men in a certain town, one rich and the other poor. **2** The rich man had a very large number of sheep and cattle, **3** but the poor man had nothing except one little ewe lamb he had bought. He raised it, and it grew up with him and his children. It shared his food, drank from his cup and even slept in his arms. It was like a daughter to him.

4 "Now a traveler came to the rich man, but the rich man refrained from taking one of his own sheep or cattle to prepare a meal for the traveler who had come to him. Instead, he took the ewe lamb that belonged to the poor man and prepared it for the one who had come to him."

5 David burned with anger against the man and said to Nathan, "As surely as the Lord lives, the man who did this must die! **6** He must pay for that lamb four times over, because he did such a thing and had no pity."

7 Then Nathan said to David, "You are the man! This is what the Lord, the God of Israel, says: 'I anointed you king over Israel, and I delivered you from the hand of Saul. **8** I gave your master's house to you, and your master's wives into your arms. I gave you all Israel and Judah. And if all this had been too little, I would have given you even more. **9** Why did you despise the word of the Lord by doing what is evil in his eyes? You struck down Uriah the Hittite with the sword and took his wife to be your own. You killed him with the sword of the Ammonites. **10** Now, therefore, the sword will never depart from your house, because you despised me and took the wife of Uriah the Hittite to be your own.'

11 "This is what the Lord says: 'Out of your own household I am going to bring calamity on you. Before your very eyes I will take your wives and give them to one who is close to you, and he will sleep with your wives in broad daylight. **12** You did it in secret, but I will do this thing in broad daylight before all Israel.'"

13 Then David said to Nathan, "I have sinned against the Lord."

Nathan replied, "The Lord has taken away your sin. You are not going to die. **14** But because by doing this you have shown utter contempt for the Lord, the son born to you will die."

15 After Nathan had gone home, the Lord struck the child that Uriah's wife had borne to David, and he became ill. **16** David pleaded with God for the child. He fasted and spent the nights lying in sackcloth on the ground. **17** The elders of his household stood beside him to get him up from the ground, but he refused, and he would not eat any food with them.

18 On the seventh day the child died. David's attendants were afraid to tell him that the child was dead, for they thought, "While the child was still living, he wouldn't listen to us when we spoke to him. How can we now tell him the child is dead? He may do something desperate."

19 David noticed that his attendants were whispering among themselves, and he realized the child was dead. "Is the child dead?" he asked.

"Yes," they replied, "he is dead."

20 Then David got up from the ground. After he had washed, put on lotions and changed his clothes, he went into the house of the Lord and worshiped. Then he went to his own house, and at his request they served him food, and he ate.

21 His attendants asked him, "Why are you acting this way? While the child was alive, you fasted and wept, but now that the child is dead, you get up and eat!"

22 He answered, "While the child was still alive, I fasted and wept. I thought, 'Who knows? The Lord may be gracious to me and let the child live.' **23** But now that he is dead, why should I go on fasting? Can I bring him back again? I will go to him, but he will not return to me."

24 Then David comforted his wife Bathsheba, and he went to her and made love to her. She gave birth to a son, and they named him Solomon. The Lord loved him; **25** and because the Lord loved him, he sent word through Nathan the prophet to name him Jedidiah.

26 Meanwhile Joab fought against Rabbah of the Ammonites and captured the royal citadel. **27** Joab then sent messengers to David, saying, "I have fought against Rabbah and taken its water supply. **28** Now muster the rest of the troops and besiege the city and capture it. Otherwise I will take the city, and it will be named after me."

29 So David mustered the entire army and went to Rabbah, and attacked and captured it. **30** David took the crown from their king's head, and it was placed on his own head. It weighed a talent of gold, and it was set with precious stones. David took a great quantity of plunder from the city **31** and brought out the people who were there, consigning them to labor with saws and with iron picks and axes, and he made them work at brickmaking. David did this to all the Ammonite towns. Then he and his entire army returned to Jerusalem (NIV).

So, both Saul and David sinned, but one lost his kingdom because of his sin, and the other did not. What was the difference between these two men that accounts for this? The answer is somewhat conjecture, since we are not told outright in Scripture. But I think we have enough clues to come to a confident conclusion.

First, though David did not lose his kingdom, he did lose his son. So, he did suffer because of his sin of committing adultery with Bathsheba and having her husband killed (2 Samuel 12:11-14). Losing his infant son and seeing his calamity come from his own household was God's chastisement for David's sin.

Consider God's words concerning adultery in Proverbs 6:27-33:

> "Can a man carry fire next to his chest and his clothes not be burned? Or can one walk on hot coals and his feet not be scorched? So is he who goes in to his neighbor's wife; none who touches her will go unpunished. People do not despise a thief if he steals to satisfy his appetite when he is hungry, but if he is caught, he will pay sevenfold; he will give all the goods of his house. **He who commits adultery lacks sense; he who does it destroys himself** [emphasis added]. He will get wounds and dishonor, and his disgrace will not be wiped away" (ESV).

There is another admonition in Proverbs which pertains to David's sins in this historical account: "Whoever conceals his transgressions will not prosper, but he who confesses and forsakes them will obtain mercy" (Proverbs 28:13 ESV).

Though David confessed his sins of adultery and murder after he was confronted by Nathan, he first covered up his sin of adultery by having Bathsheba's husband killed. It is human nature to try to hide our sin rather than honestly admitting that we have sinned and confessing and forsaking our sin. Proverbs warns us that it is foolish to conceal our sin because we will not prosper. The wise thing to do is to confess and forsake our sin.

Also, though both Saul (1 Samuel 15:24) and David (2 Samuel 12:13) **said "I have sinned,"** the rest of the story gives us insight into the heart condition of both men. After admitting to Samuel that he sinned by offering the sacrifices rather than waiting for Samuel to do it, Saul continued to sin time after time. He did not totally wipe out the Amalekites, as God had instructed. Out of jealous rage, he tried to kill David several times. Then he consulted a witch to call up dead Samuel! From the picture we are given of Saul, he did not have a heart for God like David did. God describes David as "a man after God's own heart." Though David grievously sinned, he truly repented and attempted to follow the Lord. It appears that though both men **said words of confession of sin, Saul did not really repent, as David did.**

Not only did Saul try several times to kill David, but Samuel feared that Saul would try to kill him if he went up to Jesse's house to anoint one of his sons as the new king (1 Samuel 16:2).

In contrast, David refused to kill Saul when he had the opportunity more than once. One time when Saul was relieving himself in a cave, David and his men were also in the cave. Upon seeing Saul in this vulnerable situation, David's men encouraged him to take advantage of this opportunity and kill Saul. They told David that this opportunity was provided by God. So, David got up and cut off a piece of Saul's robe. David immediately felt remorse for doing that to Saul, because Saul was God's "anointed." David did not allow his men to attack Saul. David had respect for King Saul because he was "the LORD's anointed" (1 Samuel 24:3-21; 1 Samuel 26:1-25).

David killed Goliath because he "defied the armies of the living God" and defied the living God Himself (1 Samuel 17:26, 45-47). David did not kill out of jealousy or fear of losing something; he killed Goliath out of honor and respect for the true and living God.

David inquired of the Lord about what he should do as a warrior in the army of Israel, and the Lord gave him instructions. The Lord was with David (1 Samuel 23:1-4; 1 Samuel 30:7 & 8).

When Saul killed himself after being injured in battle, David mourned his death (2 Samuel 1). This again shows us that David had a good heart while Saul had a bad heart.

The following verses give us insight into how God viewed David's heart:

1 Samuel 13:14: "But now your kingdom [Saul] will not endure; the LORD has sought out a man [David] after his own heart and appointed him ruler of his people, because you have not kept the LORD's command" (NIV).

1 Samuel 15:28: "Samuel said to him [Saul], 'The LORD has torn the kingdom of Israel from you today and has given it to one of your neighbors – to one better than you [David]" (NIV).

1 Samuel 16:7: "But the LORD said to Samuel, 'Do not consider his [Eliab – David's brother] appearance or his height, for I have rejected him. The LORD does not look at the things people look at. People look at the outward appearance, but the LORD looks at the heart'" (NIV). God chose David to replace Saul as king.

1 Kings 11:6: "So Solomon did what was evil in the sight of the Lord and did not wholly follow the Lord, as David his father had done" (ESV).

1 Kings 15:3-5 contrasts the heart of Jeroboam, one of Israel's kings, with King David. "And he walked in all the sins that his father did before him, and his heart was not wholly true to the Lord his God, as the heart of David his father. Nevertheless, for David's sake the Lord his God gave him a lamp in Jerusalem, setting up his son after him, and establishing Jerusalem, because David did what was right in the eyes of the Lord and did not turn aside from anything that he commanded him all the days of his life, except in the matter of Uriah the Hittite" (ESV).

So we can conclude that, though David grievously sinned by committing adultery with Bathsheba and having her husband Uriah murdered, the overall heart and behavior of David throughout his life was that he attempted to follow the Lord. He had some temporary failures, just like the rest of us, but he quickly got back on track. He acknowledged his sin and repented – turned away from that sin. He kept his heart free from idolatry; his heart was wholly devoted to God.

Of course, it was prophesied by the prophet Nathan that David's kingdom would be established forever (2 Samuel 7:16; 1 Chronicles 17:14; Psalm 132:11 & 12). David appears in the lineage of Jesus Christ. David's father was Jesse whose father was Obed whose father was Boaz and whose mother was Ruth. There were twenty-eight generations from David to Jesus Christ.

David wrote the following psalm. It also gives us a look into his heart.

Psalm 139 (written by David):

"1 You have searched me, LORD,

and you know me.
2 You know when I sit and when I rise;
  you perceive my thoughts from afar.
3 You discern my going out and my lying down;
  you are familiar with all my ways.
4 Before a word is on my tongue
  you, LORD, know it completely.
5 You hem me in behind and before,
  and you lay your hand upon me.
6 Such knowledge is too wonderful for me,
  too lofty for me to attain.
7 Where can I go from your Spirit?
  Where can I flee from your presence?
8 If I go up to the heavens, you are there;
  if I make my bed in the depths, you are there.
9 If I rise on the wings of the dawn,
  if I settle on the far side of the sea,
10 even there your hand will guide me,
  your right hand will hold me fast.
11 If I say, 'Surely the darkness will hide me
  and the light become night around me,'
12 even the darkness will not be dark to you;
  the night will shine like the day, for darkness is as light to you.
13 For you created my inmost being;
  you knit me together in my mother's womb.
14 I praise you because I am fearfully and
  wonderfully made;
  your works are wonderful,
  I know that full well.
15 My frame was not hidden from you
  when I was made in the secret place,
  when I was woven together in the depths of the earth.
16 Your eyes saw my unformed body;

all the days ordained for me were written
   in your book before one of them came to be.
17 How precious to me are your thoughts, God!
   How vast is the sum of them!
18 Were I to count them,
   they would outnumber the grains of sand –
   when I awake, I am still with you.
19 If only you, God, would slay the wicked!
   Away from me, you who are bloodthirsty!
20 They speak of you with evil intent;
   your adversaries misuse your name.
21 Do I not hate those who hate you, LORD,
   and abhor those who are in rebellion against you?
22 I have nothing but hatred for them;
   I count them my enemies.
23 **Search me, God, and know my heart;**
   test me and know my anxious thoughts.
24 **See if there is any offensive way in me,**
   and lead me in the way everlasting" [emphasis added] (NIV).

In these last two verses, David asks God to search his heart and to reveal any sin there. Consider also Psalm 51, written by David after he was confronted by Nathan about his adultery with Bathsheba and the murder of her husband:

"1 Have mercy on me, O God,
   according to your unfailing love;
   according to your great compassion
   blot out my transgressions.
 2 Wash away all my iniquity
   and cleanse me from my sin.
 3 For I know my transgressions,
   and my sin is always before me.

4 Against you, you only, have I sinned
   and done what is evil in your sight;
   so you are right in your verdict
   and justified when you judge.
5 Surely I was sinful at birth,
   sinful from the time my mother conceived me.
6 Yet you desired faithfulness even in the womb;
   you taught me wisdom in that secret place.
7 Cleanse me with hyssop, and I will be clean;
   wash me, and I will be whiter than snow.
8 Let me hear joy and gladness;
   let the bones you have crushed rejoice.
9 Hide your face from my sins
   and blot out all my iniquity.
10 Create in me a pure heart, O God,
    and renew a steadfast spirit within me.
11 Do not cast me from your presence
    or take your Holy Spirit from me.
12 Restore to me the joy of your salvation
    and grant me a willing spirit, to sustain me.
13 Then I will teach transgressors your ways,
    so that sinners will turn back to you.
14 Deliver me from the guilt of bloodshed, O God,
    you who are God my Savior,
    and my tongue will sing of your righteousness.
15 Open my lips, Lord,
    and my mouth will declare your praise.
16 You do not delight in sacrifice, or I would bring it;
    you do not take pleasure in burnt offerings.
17 My sacrifice, O God, is a broken spirit;
    a broken and contrite heart
    you, God, will not despise.
18 May it please you to prosper Zion,

> to build up the walls of Jerusalem.
> 19 Then you will delight in the sacrifices of the righteous,
> in burnt offerings offered whole;
> then bulls will be offered on your altar" (NIV).

So, now that we have studied these two men who were contemporaries, who lived at the same time in history, who made choices about how they were going to live their lives, what can we learn in our study of biblically handling disappointment, discouragement, defeat, depression, and despair?

As we have compared and contrasted these two men, we have seen that both grievously sinned, but Saul continued to make sinful, selfish choices while David attempted to live for the living God and respected and valued others.

Our lesson is this: after sinning, confess your sin to the Lord and repent, which means to turn away from the sin. Start going in the opposite direction. Turn from your sin and start doing those things that please God. It is certain that while on the path of sin a true believer will battle depression. Unconfessed, persistent sin leads to strained fellowship with the true and living God, for whom we were created to live. That causes our perspective to be skewed. We do not see things as they really are. We can start to distrust the Lord, who cares more about our welfare than anyone else does. We can become discontent and start to seek pleasure outside of God's will. We might even rationalize or try to justify our sin. All of this ultimately leads to depression. The Lord's rebuke to David shows us that David had everything he needed and more. He already had plenty, but he still sought what belonged to someone else – someone who had far less than David did. May we learn from this story about David that the pleasures of sin for a season are not worth the damage done by our sin. Trying to satisfy our longings without God is a vain pursuit guaranteed to end in emptiness.

The answer to this depression is to turn away – even run away – from your sin and radically take steps to get it out of your life. After having done so, take the next step and start implementing in your life those attitudes and behaviors that God calls believers to possess. Intimacy with the true and living God and joyful service to Him is one cure for depression!

Chapter Nineteen

The Study of Solomon

"The end of the matter; all has been heard. Fear God
and keep his commandments, for this is the whole duty of man.
For God will bring every deed into judgment,
with every secret thing, whether good or evil."
Ecclesiastes 12:13 & 14 ESV

In this lesson, we turn to one of the wisest men who has ever lived. Scholars tend to think that Solomon wrote the book of Ecclesiastes, which is our text for this lesson. God gave Solomon, king of Israel, unrivaled wisdom because he desired the ability to rule his people wisely more than he desired great wealth. In addition to unrivaled wisdom, God gave him unrivaled wealth.

We must remember as we read the book of Ecclesiastes that what the writer says is not necessarily objective truth but his opinion as he experiments with various aspects of life. This part of the Bible, just like every other part, is inspired by God; it is God-breathed. Therefore, it comes from God and is profitable for us. But just like the inspired, perfect Word of God records the foolish counsel of Job's three friends, the Bible also accurately records the thinking of the writer of the book of Ecclesiastes as he analyzes earthly life.

Ecclesiastes 1:

1 The words of the Teacher, son of David, king in Jerusalem:
2 "Meaningless! Meaningless!"
   says the Teacher.
   "Utterly meaningless!
   Everything is meaningless."
3 What do people gain from all their labors
   at which they toil under the sun?
4 Generations come and generations go,
   but the earth remains forever.
5 The sun rises and the sun sets,
   and hurries back to where it rises.
6 The wind blows to the south
   and turns to the north;
   round and round it goes,
   ever returning on its course.
7 All streams flow into the sea,
   yet the sea is never full.
   To the place the streams come from,
   there they return again.
8 All things are wearisome,
   more than one can say.
   The eye never has enough of seeing,
   nor the ear its fill of hearing.
9 What has been will be again,
   what has been done will be done again;
   there is nothing new under the sun.
10 Is there anything of which one can say,
   "Look! This is something new"?
   It was here already, long ago;
   it was here before our time.
11 No one remembers the former generations,

and even those yet to come
will not be remembered
by those who follow them.

12 I, the Teacher, was king over Israel in Jerusalem. **13** I applied my mind to study and to explore by wisdom all that is done under the heavens. What a heavy burden God has laid on mankind! **14** I have seen all the things that are done under the sun; all of them are meaningless, a chasing after the wind.

15 What is crooked cannot be straightened;
what is lacking cannot be counted.

16 I said to myself, "Look, I have increased in wisdom more than anyone who has ruled over Jerusalem before me; I have experienced much of wisdom and knowledge." **17** Then I applied myself to the understanding of wisdom, and also of madness and folly, but I learned that this, too, is a chasing after the wind.

18 For with much wisdom comes much sorrow;
the more knowledge, the more grief.

Ecclesiastes 2:

1 I said to myself, "Come now, I will test you with pleasure to find out what is good." But that also proved to be meaningless. **2** "Laughter," I said, "is madness. And what does pleasure accomplish?" **3** I tried cheering myself with wine, and embracing folly—my mind still guiding me with wisdom. I wanted to see what was good for people to do under the heavens during the few days of their lives.

4 I undertook great projects: I built houses for myself and planted vineyards. **5** I made gardens and parks and planted all kinds of fruit trees in them. **6** I made reservoirs to water groves of flourishing trees. **7** I bought male and female slaves and had other slaves who were born in my house. I also owned more herds and flocks than anyone in Jerusalem before me. **8** I amassed silver and gold for myself, and the treasure of kings and provinces. I acquired male and female singers, and a harem as well—the delights of a man's heart. **9** I became greater by far than anyone in Jerusalem before me. In all this my wisdom stayed with me.

> **10** I denied myself nothing my eyes desired;
> I refused my heart no pleasure.
> My heart took delight in all my labor,
> and this was the reward for all my toil.
> **11** Yet when I surveyed all that my hands had done
> and what I had toiled to achieve,
> everything was meaningless, a chasing after the wind;
> nothing was gained under the sun.
> **12** Then I turned my thoughts to consider wisdom,
> and also madness and folly.
> What more can the king's successor do
> than what has already been done?
> **13** I saw that wisdom is better than folly,
> just as light is better than darkness.
> **14** The wise have eyes in their heads,
> while the fool walks in the darkness;
> but I came to realize
> that the same fate overtakes them both.
> **15** Then I said to myself,
> "The fate of the fool will overtake me also.
> What then do I gain by being wise?"
> I said to myself,
> "This too is meaningless."
> **16** For the wise, like the fool, will not be long remembered;
> the days have already come when both have been forgotten.

Like the fool, the wise too must die!

17 So I hated life, because the work that is done under the sun was grievous to me. All of it is meaningless, a chasing after the wind. **18** I hated all the things I had toiled for under the sun, because I must leave them to the one who comes after me. **19** And who knows whether that person will be wise or foolish? Yet they will have control over all the fruit of my toil into which I have poured my effort and skill under the sun. This too is meaningless. **20** So my heart began to despair over all my toilsome labor under the sun. **21** For a person may labor with wisdom, knowledge and skill, and then they must leave all they own to another who has not toiled for it. This too is meaningless and a great misfortune. **22** What do people get for all the toil and anxious striving with which they labor under the sun? **23** All their days their work is grief and pain; even at night their minds do not rest. This too is meaningless.

24 A person can do nothing better than to eat and drink and find satisfaction in their own toil. This too, I see, is from the hand of God, **25** for without him, who can eat or find enjoyment? **26** To the person who pleases him, God gives wisdom, knowledge and happiness, but to the sinner he gives the task of gathering and storing up wealth to hand it over to the one who pleases God. This too is meaningless, a chasing after the wind (NIV).

The above verses are dripping with despair! Solomon cannot see anything that makes life worth living! He surmises that everything that man can experience on Earth is futile, useless, inconsequential. Solomon tries everything to find meaning; he has access to limitless wealth that could purchase all kinds of possessions and experiences. But in the end, he does not find any of these things satisfying. He compares the pursuit of them to chasing the wind. We all realize that we can never catch the wind, no matter how hard we try. It is futile to try because it cannot be done. So even though Solomon has vast riches and abundant experiences, he feels like he never really catches what he was chasing.

So vexing is all of this, the writer of Ecclesiastes says, that he hates life. This is despair! We can almost see him wrestling with these thoughts to the point of exhaustion. His is a very negative commentary of life on Earth.

Solomon experiments with several pursuits to find out what in life on Earth would bring purpose to man's existence:

- pleasure
- laughter
- wine and folly
- great projects (houses, vineyards, gardens, parks, reservoirs, etc.)
- slaves
- herds and flocks
- silver and gold
- treasures
- singers
- a harem
- wisdom

This is the conclusion he comes to regarding all of these pursuits:

1. They are utterly meaningless (1:2).

2. Nothing is gained by them (1:3).

3. There is never an end to the need for these things (1:7).

4. They never completely satisfy (1:8).

5. They have no lasting value (1:8).

6. They are like chasing the wind (1:14).

7. Some of these things bring sorrow (1:18).

8. They accomplish nothing (2:2).

9. The same fate overtakes both the fool and the wise man (2:14).

10. Both the fool and the wise man will be forgotten after they die (2:16).

11. Solomon hates life because of these observations (2:17).

12. The rewards of a man's life are left to others who have not worked to get them (2:18).

13. There is nothing gained by a man's "toil and anxious striving" but pain and grief (2:22).

14. There is nothing better for a man than to enjoy his work (3:22).

The last chapter of Ecclesiastes gives the conclusion to Solomon's experiment that he comes to about life on Earth.

Ecclesiastes 12:

9 Not only was the Teacher wise, but he also imparted knowledge to the people. He pondered and searched out and set in order many proverbs. **10** The Teacher searched to find just the right words, and what he wrote was upright and true.

> **11** The words of the wise are like goads, their collected sayings like firmly embedded nails—given by one shepherd. **12** Be warned, my son, of anything in addition to them.
>
> Of making many books there is no end, and much study wearies the body.
>
> **13** Now all has been heard;
> here is the conclusion of the matter:
> Fear God and keep his commandments,
> for this is the duty of all mankind.
> **14** For God will bring every deed into judgment,
> including every hidden thing,
> whether it is good or evil (NIV).

Solomon's conclusion to his experiment is simple. He concludes that the only thing that amounts to anything in this life ("under the sun") is to fear God and keep His commandments. All the other stuff – riches, possessions, status, experiences, and such – is as futile as chasing the wind! These things mean nothing if one does not fear God and keep His commandments. That is what gives life meaning.

People who try to fill up their lives with riches, possessions, status, experiences, and the like, hoping that these things will satisfy and bring fulfillment, are eventually disappointed because the pursuit of these things without God is futile. No matter how much money, possessions, status, or experiences you have, it is never enough. You always need to chase after more, for none of these things, in and of themselves, ultimately brings satisfaction or happiness. Chasing after these things is as futile as chasing the wind.

One sure way to get depressed and to slip into despair is to try to live life without God – the true and living God as He has revealed

Himself to be in Scripture. God gives us good gifts to enjoy, but depression comes from valuing the gifts more than the Giver. The gifts, in and of themselves, will never ultimately satisfy. Long-lasting satisfaction comes from worshiping and enjoying the One who gives the good gifts and enjoying the gifts that come from Him who deserves to be worshiped. Solomon reminds us that eventually God will judge every deed and every thought of man, so it is important in this life to fear God and obey His commandments.

Genuine worship of the true and living God and thankfulness for His gifts will keep us from long-term depression and despair.

Chapter Twenty

The Study of Elijah

> "'Yet I will leave seven thousand in Israel, all the knees that have not bowed to Baal, and every mouth that has not kissed him.'"
> 1 Kings 19:18 ESV

Even God's most faithful servants can get depressed and overtaken with despair. In previous lessons, you read about some godly people recorded in Scripture who struggled with these emotions. This lesson is about another godly man who was so overtaken with depression and despair that he wanted to die.

Of course, God had these real-life events recorded for us to teach us what He is like and how we are to live so as to please Him and bring Him glory. I think there are some lessons in the recorded events of the life of Elijah that will help us know how to biblically handle depression and despair.

1 Kings 18:

1 After a long time, in the third year, the word of the Lord came to Elijah: "Go and present yourself to Ahab, and I will send rain on the land." **2** So Elijah went to present himself to Ahab.

Now the famine was severe in Samaria, **3** and Ahab had summoned Obadiah, his palace administrator. (Obadiah was a devout believer in the Lord. **4** While Jezebel was killing off the Lord's prophets, Obadiah had taken a hundred prophets and hidden them in two caves, fifty in each, and had supplied them with food and water.) **5** Ahab had said to Obadiah, "Go through the land to all the springs and valleys. Maybe we can find some grass to keep the horses and mules alive so we will not have to kill any of our animals." **6** So they divided the land they were to cover, Ahab going in one direction and Obadiah in another.

7 As Obadiah was walking along, Elijah met him. Obadiah recognized him, bowed down to the ground, and said, "Is it really you, my lord Elijah?"

8 "Yes," he replied. "Go tell your master, 'Elijah is here.'"

9 "What have I done wrong," asked Obadiah, "that you are handing your servant over to Ahab to be put to death? **10** As surely as the Lord your God lives, there is not a nation or kingdom where my master has not sent someone to look for you. And whenever a nation or kingdom claimed you were not there, he made them swear they could not find you. **11** But now you tell me to go to my master and say, 'Elijah is here.' **12** I don't know where the Spirit of the Lord may carry you when I leave you. If I go and tell Ahab and he doesn't find you, he will kill me. Yet I your servant have worshiped the Lord since my youth. **13** Haven't you heard, my lord, what I did while Jezebel was killing the prophets of the Lord? I hid a hundred of the Lord's prophets in two caves, fifty in each, and supplied them with food and water. **14** And now you tell me to go to my master and say, 'Elijah is here.' He will kill me!"

15 Elijah said, "As the Lord Almighty lives, whom I serve, I will surely present myself to Ahab today."

16 So Obadiah went to meet Ahab and told him, and Ahab went to meet Elijah. **17** When he saw Elijah, he said to him, "Is that you, you troubler of Israel?"

18 "I have not made trouble for Israel," Elijah replied. "But you and your father's family have. You have abandoned the Lord's commands and have followed the Baals. **19** Now summon the people from all over Israel to meet me on Mount Carmel. And bring the four hundred and fifty prophets of Baal and the four hundred prophets of Asherah, who eat at Jezebel's table."

20 So Ahab sent word throughout all Israel and assembled the prophets on Mount Carmel. **21** Elijah went before the people and said, "How long will you waver between two opinions? If the Lord is God, follow him; but if Baal is God, follow him."

But the people said nothing.

22 Then Elijah said to them, "I am the only one of the Lord's prophets left, but Baal has four hundred and fifty prophets. **23** Get two bulls for us. Let Baal's prophets choose one for themselves, and let them cut it into pieces and put it on the wood but not set fire to it. I will prepare the other bull and put it on the wood but not set fire to it. **24** Then you call on the name of your god, and I will call on the name of the Lord. The god who answers by fire—he is God."

Then all the people said, "What you say is good."

25 Elijah said to the prophets of Baal, "Choose one of the bulls and prepare it first, since there are so many of you. Call on the name of your god, but do not light the fire." **26** So they took the bull given them and prepared it.

Then they called on the name of Baal from morning till noon. "Baal, answer us!" they shouted. But there was no response; no one answered. And they danced around the altar they had made.

27 At noon Elijah began to taunt them. "Shout louder!" he said. "Surely he is a god! Perhaps he is deep in thought, or busy, or traveling. Maybe he is sleeping and must be awakened." **28** So they shouted louder and slashed themselves with swords and spears, as was their custom, until their blood flowed. **29** Midday passed, and they continued their frantic prophesying until the time for the evening sacrifice. But there was no response, no one answered, no one paid attention.

30 Then Elijah said to all the people, "Come here to me." They came to him, and he repaired the altar of the Lord, which had been torn down. **31** Elijah took twelve stones, one for each of the tribes descended from Jacob, to whom the word of the Lord had come, saying, "Your name shall be Israel." **32** With the stones he built an altar in the name of the Lord, and he dug a trench around it large enough to hold two seahs of seed. **33** He arranged the wood, cut the bull into pieces and laid it on the wood. Then he said to them, "Fill four large jars with water and pour it on the offering and on the wood."

34 "Do it again," he said, and they did it again.

"Do it a third time," he ordered, and they did it the third time. **35** The water ran down around the altar and even filled the trench.

36 At the time of sacrifice, the prophet Elijah stepped forward and prayed: "Lord, the God of Abraham, Isaac and Israel, let it be known today that you are God in Israel and that I am your servant and have done all these things at your command. **37** Answer me, Lord, answer me, so these people will know that you, Lord, are God, and that you are turning their hearts back again."

38 Then the fire of the Lord fell and burned up the sacrifice, the wood, the stones and the soil, and also licked up the water in the trench.

39 When all the people saw this, they fell prostrate and cried, "The Lord—he is God! The Lord—he is God!"

40 Then Elijah commanded them, "Seize the prophets of Baal. Don't let anyone get away!" They seized them, and Elijah had them brought down to the Kishon Valley and slaughtered there.

41 And Elijah said to Ahab, "Go, eat and drink, for there is the sound of a heavy rain." **42** So Ahab went off to eat and drink, but Elijah climbed to the top of Carmel, bent down to the ground and put his face between his knees.

43 "Go and look toward the sea," he told his servant. And he went up and looked.

"There is nothing there," he said.

Seven times Elijah said, "Go back."

44 The seventh time the servant reported, "A cloud as small as a man's hand is rising from the sea."

So Elijah said, "Go and tell Ahab, 'Hitch up your chariot and go down before the rain stops you.'"

45 Meanwhile, the sky grew black with clouds, the wind rose, a heavy rain started falling and Ahab rode off to Jezreel. **46** The power of the Lord came on Elijah and, tucking his cloak into his belt, he ran ahead of Ahab all the way to Jezreel.

1 Kings 19:

1 Now Ahab told Jezebel everything Elijah had done and how he had killed all the prophets with the sword. **2** So Jezebel sent a messenger to Elijah to say, "May the gods deal with me, be it ever so severely, if by this time tomorrow I do not make your life like that of one of them."

3 Elijah was afraid and ran for his life. When he came to Beersheba in Judah, he left his servant there, **4** while he himself went a day's journey into the wilderness. He came to a broom bush, sat down under it and prayed that he might die. "I have had enough, Lord," he said. "Take my life; I am no better than my ancestors." **5** Then he lay down under the bush and fell asleep.

All at once an angel touched him and said, "Get up and eat." **6** He looked around, and there by his head was some bread baked over hot coals, and a jar of water. He ate and drank and then lay down again.

7 The angel of the Lord came back a second time and touched him and said, "Get up and eat, for the journey is too much for you." **8** So he got up and ate and drank. Strengthened by that food, he traveled forty days and forty nights until he reached Horeb, the mountain of God. **9** There he went into a cave and spent the night.

And the word of the Lord came to him: "What are you doing here, Elijah?"

10 He replied, "I have been very zealous for the Lord God Almighty. The Israelites have rejected your covenant, torn down your altars, and put your prophets to death with the sword. I am the only one left, and now they are trying to kill me too."

11 The Lord said, "Go out and stand on the mountain in the presence of the Lord, for the Lord is about to pass by."

Then a great and powerful wind tore the mountains apart and shattered the rocks before the Lord, but the Lord was not in the wind. After the wind there was an earthquake, but the Lord was not in the earthquake. **12** After the earthquake came a fire, but the Lord was not in the fire. And after the fire came a gentle whisper. **13** When Elijah heard it, he pulled his cloak over his face and went out and stood at the mouth of the cave.

Then a voice said to him, "What are you doing here, Elijah?"

14 He replied, "I have been very zealous for the Lord God Almighty. The Israelites have rejected your covenant, torn down your altars, and put your prophets to death with the sword. I am the only one left, and now they are trying to kill me too."

15 The Lord said to him, "Go back the way you came, and go to the Desert of Damascus. When you get there, anoint Hazael king over Aram. **16** Also, anoint Jehu son of Nimshi king over Israel, and anoint Elisha son of Shaphat from Abel Meholah to succeed you as prophet. **17** Jehu will put to death any who escape the sword of Hazael, and Elisha will put to death any who escape the sword of Jehu. **18** Yet I reserve seven thousand in Israel—all whose knees have not bowed down to Baal and whose mouths have not kissed him."

19 So Elijah went from there and found Elisha son of Shaphat. He was plowing with twelve yoke of oxen, and he himself was driving the twelfth pair. Elijah went up to him and threw his cloak around him. **20** Elisha then left his oxen and ran after Elijah. "Let me kiss my father and mother goodbye," he said, "and then I will come with you."

"Go back," Elijah replied. "What have I done to you?"

21 So Elisha left him and went back. He took his yoke of oxen and slaughtered them. He burned the plowing equipment to cook the meat and gave it to the people, and they ate. Then he set out to follow Elijah and became his servant (NIV).

What problems led to Elijah's depression?

1. Elijah was hungry, thirsty, and exhausted. Think about the physical energy Elijah had exerted throughout this passage. He repaired the altar to the true and living God, dug a trench around it, and cut the bull into pieces. After the contest was completed, he killed the 450 prophets of Baal. Then he ran ahead of Ahab to Jezreel, a trip of about seventeen miles. When Jezebel found out about the slaughter of her prophets of Baal and she threatened Elijah's life, he fled. He traveled a day and stayed in the desert. There he was given food and water. Then he traveled another forty days to another spot.

I know that people in that day generally were far more used to physical exercise than we are today, but this was still a lot of physical exertion! Elijah was undoubtedly tired, hungry, and thirsty, and God knew this. God provided the rest and the food and the water that Elijah needed.

2. Elijah was running away from people who were trying to kill him. Jezebel had sworn to him that within twenty-four hours, she was going to have him killed, and she was in a position to make good on that threat. Can you imagine her fury? Elijah had killed all of her false prophets of Baal and had publicly made fun of that false god. This was no doubt humiliating to Jezebel. Elijah was in fear of Jezebel's threat. She had killed the other prophets of the true and living God, and so he had good reason to believe that she would attempt to have him killed

as well, especially after the spectacle on Mount Carmel! Elijah's fear of being killed was obviously emotionally draining.

3. He had just experienced a great victory of the true and living God over the false god Baal, and he had probably been on a spiritual "high." He had just seen a great display of God's power in answer to his prayer, thus showing to all that the God of Abraham, Isaac and Israel (Jacob) is the one true God! And now all the false prophets of Baal were dead! What a great spiritual experience! But after it was over, his emotions might have come crashing down.

4. He thought he was the only prophet left in Israel who had remained loyal to the true and living God and who was willing to take a stand against Baal worship. This thought apparently discouraged Elijah. It was sickening, no doubt, to see so many of God's chosen people worship a false god rather than, or in addition to, the true and living God! He probably felt alone, as well.

5. He also thought that he was no better than his ancestors. I am not certain what he meant by this. Did he mean that he had not been any more successful in his undertakings than his ancestors were in theirs? Or did he mean that his life's circumstances, such as his life being threatened, were not any better than the circumstances of his ancestors? Or perhaps he meant that his spiritual condition was no better than that of his ancestors. Whatever the cause for his feeling this way, his assessment caused him to want to die.

What were the solutions to the problems?

1. The first solution was to eat and rest. Sometimes we can get depressed because our physical bodies need attention. I know that when I rest and eat a nutritious meal, I feel far better able to handle the tasks I have before me. When I think about the laundry, the dirty

kitchen floor, the preparation of a meal, and the running here and there, I can become overwhelmed by the thought of it. But after I have rested and received nourishment, I feel that I can tackle all that and more.

I think the lesson here is to take care of my physical body with rest and with nutritious food and water. Dehydration alone can cause my body to feel drained. God has created us as whole beings – physical, mental, emotional, and spiritual. One aspect affects all the other aspects of my well-being.

2. The solution to Jezebel's death threat was to trust God. I know this sounds simplistic, and it is easy to say when I am sitting in the safety of my home. I am not belittling Elijah's fear. But think about Elijah's options in this situation. He could either trust God or not trust God. God had sent him to go before Ahab in the first place. And at the contest between Baal and the true and living God, Elijah had prayed before God: "O LORD, God of Abraham, Isaac and Israel, let it be known this day that you are God in Israel, and that I am your servant, and that I have done all these things at your word" (1 Kings 18:36 ESV). God answered him as he requested. I think that as fear started to swell up in Elijah after Jezebel threatened him, he should have remembered his prayer and God's marvelous answer to his prayer, thus showing him that God was with him. He should also have taken encouragement in the fact that he was serving the true and living God, and that God knew how to take care of him and preserve his life. I mean, if God can send down fire from Heaven to lap up all that water and meat, no doubt He can watch over Elijah, right? This is not to say that Elijah should not have taken precautions to protect his life, however.

I certainly understand human fear. I have never received a death threat, but I assure you that if I ever do, I will take it very seriously! I will no doubt be afraid. I will try to protect and preserve my own life.

However, fear is a powerful emotion that can be a relentless, paralyzing master. If I focus on the object of my fear to the exclusion of the other realities of life and to the exclusion of communion with God, fear becomes my master; it will dictate my attitudes and behavior. Elijah had reason to fear and to take precautions, but it appears that his fear drove him a little crazy! He had just stood up to 450 prophets of Baal, but now the threat of one woman caused him to cower in fear. The absurdity is rather humorous! Of course, Jezebel was no ordinary woman, as a lady in one of my Sunday school classes aptly observed. Very true, but Jezebel was no match for the true and living God who was on Elijah's side!

We do not know very much about Elijah's thoughts while he was fleeing from Jezebel, but we do know that he wanted to die. Again, I can understand this human feeling, but the question is, "Is this a biblical response?" It seems to me that had Elijah thought more about it and prayed to God as he had at the contest between Baal and the true and living God, he might have not been in such despair. Elijah had experienced the presence of the Lord while he was there in the desert feeling sorry for himself. But rather than focusing on the presence of his powerful God and the triumph over Baal at Mount Carmel, he dwelled on his fear of Jezebel, his feelings of failure because of the idolatry of the people of Israel, on his loneliness due to his faulty thinking he was the lone true prophet, and his own exhaustion. In other words, in those moments, he was controlled by his own feelings rather than the presence of the all-powerful God!

As for Elijah wanting to die, we must remember this: he had reason to live as long as God gave him breath. When God is finished with us, He will take us home. Until then, God has some reason for us to live – something to do in service to Him. We do not get to decide when our lives are over; only God does. In time, our depression can lift if we forget about wanting to die and just get busy living for the true and living God.

3. Have you ever been on a spiritual high for a little while and then come down from that high later? Perhaps you spent a week or weekend at camp where you experienced closeness with God in a fresh way and others around you were also excited about living for God. Then you came home from camp to the harsh realities of life. Maybe you went back to work or school where most of those around you obviously do not live for the true and living God, and it kind of put a damper on your enthusiasm. Or maybe God used you to lead someone else to Christ. You were elated, and then life returned to normal. The reality is that when we come down from a spiritual high, it is difficult! Doesn't that sometimes happen to you when you go from corporate worship with other believers on Sunday to work or school on Monday where there are no other believers around you?

But God has promised to be with us always, even when we do not sense His presence and we do not observe Him doing any mighty works, such as sending down fire on the altar dedicated to Him. We are promised that if we are led by the Holy Spirit, we will have the fruit of love, joy, peace, patience, kindness, goodness, faithfulness, gentleness and self-control (Galatians 5:22 & 23). God is in control of our Mondays just as much as He is our Sundays. He is present with us on Monday just as much as He is on Sunday. It is hard to come down from a spiritual high, but I think it is a rather normal phenomenon in the life of a believer who has experienced God doing something spectacular – something that he does not witness every day. This may be what Elijah experienced, and again, the solution to this problem is to trust the true and living God during times of spiritual struggle as well as times of spiritual victory. It is also essential to keep moving forward in the midst of emotional pain (as long as physical health is not an issue) and not allow our low spirits to immobilize us.

4. Elijah was deluded into thinking that he was the only person in Israel who had not bowed down to Baal. We do not know how Elijah had come to this conclusion, but God told him that actually there were seven thousand others in Israel who had been faithful to the true and living God and had not bowed down to Baal. What a colossal miscalculation! Elijah's perception of reality was more than a little off!

The solution to incorrect thinking and perception is correct thinking and perception. God gave reality to Elijah – that his concern about being the only person in Israel loyal to God was unfounded. I do not know if Elijah should have done anything differently – if he should have known that truth. But the point is, a person can become depressed on the basis of a faulty picture he has in his mind about reality. I have experienced this phenomenon many times. I think the only solution to this problem is to ask God to reveal to us the true picture of the way things are. He could do this in many ways. Sometimes He does this for me through my husband who occasionally views differently than I do the events that are disturbing me. As we discuss the troubling issues, I can see that I have a distorted or exaggerated view of how things are. God can use others to help us see reality, if we ask Him to show us the true picture of how things really are.

There is a saying that perception is reality, meaning that one's perception of something defines how he sees that something, and that perception dictates his actions, regardless of the truth. I think, in a sense, this is true. In most cases, the way a person perceives something will dictate the way he will act. For him, that perception is what is reality – in his mind. But of course, we know that this is a crazy, sometimes dangerous way to live. Proverbs 14:12 says, "There is a way which seemeth right unto a man, but the end thereof are the ways of death" (KJV). Some misconceptions are far more consequential than others. If you think that your friend is mad at you, and you act according to that perception only to find out later that she is really not mad at you after all, it is not as consequential as if you think that you do not have cancer and, therefore, receive no treatment for the cancer that is actually spreading throughout your body. It would be even worse if one worships a false god rather than the true and living God because he thinks that the false god is real.

Elijah's distorted perception caused him unnecessary grief.

5. Comparing himself to his ancestors does not seem like a wise, productive thing to do; it only caused him to want to die. I would say he must have felt defeated. From God's perspective, we are defeated only if we fail to do what God wants us to do in the way He wants us to do it. When we have obeyed what He has told us to do, we should not feel defeated, no matter the outcome. We need to simply obey Him and leave the results to Him. When we do that, we are victorious, not defeated.

Jeremiah obediently prophesied the eventual destruction of Jerusalem by the wicked Babylonians if the people did not repent. They did not repent, so the Babylonians destroyed Jerusalem and took many people captive. Does this mean that Jeremiah was defeated because the people did not do what he told them they should do? No, Jeremiah was not defeated. He obeyed what God told him to do. Therefore, he was successful.

Obedience to God should be our standard for assessing our success or defeat, not comparing ourselves to others. I do not think that Elijah should have felt defeated. The one thing he did which appears to have been wrong was to wildly run away in response to Jezebel's threat. After Elijah fled to the desert, God asked him two times, "What are you doing here, Elijah?" This seems to imply that Elijah had not been directed by God to flee to the desert. Up to this point, God had directed Elijah what to do and where to go.

Remember that though there are many causes of depression and despair, the solution is to handle these emotions biblically!

Chapter Twenty-One

The Study of Jonah

"But the Lord said, 'You have been concerned about this plant,
though you did not tend it or make it grow.
It sprang up overnight and died overnight.
And should I not have concern for the great city of Nineveh,
in which there are more than a hundred and twenty thousand
people who cannot tell their right hand from their left—
and also many animals?'"
Jonah 4:10 & 11 NIV

Sometimes depression comes from being selfish and myopically focused on our own perspective, preferences, desires, and plans. When our focus is on ourselves like this, we can easily miss what God wants to do in our midst. **His plans are always greater than our plans**. Many times, our goals are meant to please ourselves with temporary pleasure, but God's plans have the eternal welfare of many people in mind. Though He realizes, of course, that people have physical needs, His primary concern is their spiritual welfare.

This lesson is about a man who was given a wonderful opportunity to be of service to God and to help others, but he ran the other way! He was primarily focused on his own perspective, and he did not want to help the people God had called him to help. He did not want God to help them either! He was so focused on his hatred of these Gentile "dogs" that at first, he missed God's plan for him. However, since God is long-suffering and patient, He gave this man another chance. But Jonah was resistant to God's plan, and he was one depressed person! Even after he relented and half-heartedly did what God had called him to do, he was miserable. He even wanted to die. Why?

I am sure that as you read these passages in the book of Jonah, you will easily see how selfish Jonah's perspective was. His view was really limited.

Jonah 1:

1 The word of the Lord came to Jonah son of Amittai: **2** "Go to the great city of Nineveh and preach against it, because its wickedness has come up before me."

3 But Jonah ran away from the Lord and headed for Tarshish. He went down to Joppa, where he found a ship bound for that port. After paying the fare, he went aboard and sailed for Tarshish to flee from the Lord.

4 Then the Lord sent a great wind on the sea, and such a violent storm arose that the ship threatened to break up. **5** All the sailors were afraid and each cried out to his own god. And they threw the cargo into the sea to lighten the ship.

But Jonah had gone below deck, where he lay down and fell into a deep sleep. **6** The captain went to him and said, "How can you sleep? Get up and call on your god! Maybe he will take notice of us so that we will not perish."

7 Then the sailors said to each other, "Come, let us cast lots to find out who is responsible for this calamity." They cast lots and the lot fell on Jonah. **8** So they asked him, "Tell us, who is responsible for making all this trouble for us? What kind of work do you do? Where do you come from? What is your country? From what people are you?"

9 He answered, "I am a Hebrew and I worship the Lord, the God of heaven, who made the sea and the dry land."

10 This terrified them and they asked, "What have you done?" (They knew he was running away from the Lord, because he had already told them so.)

11 The sea was getting rougher and rougher. So they asked him, "What should we do to you to make the sea calm down for us?"

12 "Pick me up and throw me into the sea," he replied, "and it will become calm. I know that it is my fault that this great storm has come upon you."

13 Instead, the men did their best to row back to land. But they could not, for the sea grew even wilder than before. **14** Then they cried out to the Lord, "Please, Lord, do not let us die for taking this man's life. Do not hold us accountable for killing an innocent man, for you, Lord, have done as you pleased." **15** Then they took Jonah and threw him overboard, and the raging sea grew calm. **16** At this the men greatly feared the Lord, and they offered a sacrifice to the Lord and made vows to him.

17 Now the Lord provided a huge fish to swallow Jonah, and Jonah was in the belly of the fish three days and three nights.

Jonah 2:

Marti Scott

1 From inside the fish Jonah prayed to the Lord his God. **2** He said:
"In my distress I called to the Lord,
and he answered me.
From deep in the realm of the dead I called for help,
and you listened to my cry.
3 You hurled me into the depths,
into the very heart of the seas,
and the currents swirled about me;
all your waves and breakers
swept over me.
4 I said, 'I have been banished
from your sight;
yet I will look again
toward your holy temple.'
5 The engulfing waters threatened me,
the deep surrounded me;
seaweed was wrapped around my head.
6 To the roots of the mountains I sank down;
the earth beneath barred me in forever.
But you, Lord my God,
brought my life up from the pit.
7 "When my life was ebbing away,
I remembered you, Lord,
and my prayer rose to you,
to your holy temple.
8 "Those who cling to worthless idols
turn away from God's love for them.
9 But I, with shouts of grateful praise,
will sacrifice to you.
What I have vowed I will make good.
I will say, 'Salvation comes from the Lord.'"

10 And the Lord commanded the fish, and it vomited Jonah onto dry land (NIV).

Summary of Jonah 3:

God again told Jonah to go to Nineveh and preach God's message of repentance. This time, Jonah went to that great city proclaiming the simple message that in forty days Nineveh would be overthrown. The people of Nineveh believed God and showed their repentance by fasting and putting on sackcloth. Even the king replaced his royal robe with sackcloth, and he sat in ashes, a sign of humility and remorse. He issued a decree stating that no human or animal should eat or drink but instead be covered in sackcloth, call out to God, and turn from their wicked ways in hopes that God would withhold judgment and spare their lives. God saw the actions of the people and spared them from the calamity He had vowed to inflict upon the city.

Jonah 4:

1 But to Jonah this seemed very wrong, and he became angry. **2** He prayed to the Lord, "Isn't this what I said, Lord, when I was still at home? That is what I tried to forestall by fleeing to Tarshish. I knew that you are a gracious and compassionate God, slow to anger and abounding in love, a God who relents from sending calamity. **3** Now, Lord, take away my life, for it is better for me to die than to live."

4 But the Lord replied, "Is it right for you to be angry?"

5 Jonah had gone out and sat down at a place east of the city. There he made himself a shelter, sat in its shade and waited to see what would happen to the city. **6** Then the Lord God provided a leafy plant and made it grow up over Jonah to give shade for his head to ease his discomfort, and Jonah was very happy about the plant. **7** But at dawn the next day God provided a worm, which chewed the plant so that it withered. **8** When the sun rose, God provided a scorching east wind, and the sun blazed on Jonah's head so that he grew faint. He wanted to die, and said, "It would be better for me to die than to live."

9 But God said to Jonah, "Is it right for you to be angry about the plant?"

"It is," he said. "And I'm so angry I wish I were dead."

10 But the Lord said, "You have been concerned about this plant, though you did not tend it or make it grow. It sprang up overnight and died overnight. **11** And should I not have concern for the great city of Nineveh, in which there are more than a hundred and twenty thousand people who cannot tell their right hand from their left—and also many animals?" (NIV).

What lessons does this real-life story of Jonah teach us about the true and living God?

1. God often uses people to accomplish His purposes. He wanted Jonah to preach to the people of Nineveh to bring God's message to them. God could have reached the people of Nineveh without help from any human, but He chose to use Jonah. What a privilege it is to be used by God to help build His kingdom!

2. God is aware of the wickedness of nations. God calls these nations to repentance, or His judgment will fall upon them (Jonah 1:1; Jonah 3:1-4; Jeremiah 18:7-10; Joel 3:12).

3. God controls the weather, and He sometimes uses weather to accomplish His purposes. God caused rain to fall for forty days and forty nights while Noah and his family sheltered in the ark Noah built

(Genesis 7:4 & 12). Then God gave rise to a wind which caused the waters to subside (Genesis 8:1). In the story of Jonah in Nineveh, God sent a great wind on the sea which caused a violent storm (Jonah 1:4), He calmed the raging sea (Jonah 1:15), and He provided a scorching east wind (Jonah 4:8).

4. God also controls animals, and He sometimes uses animals to accomplish His purposes. God caused Balaam's donkey to speak sense to him (Numbers 22:28-30). God used the great fish to swallow Jonah and then to vomit Jonah onto dry land (Jonah 1:17 & Jonah 2:10).

5. No one can ever really run away from the Lord! He is everywhere. Psalm 139:7-10 says:

> "Where shall I go from your Spirit? Or where shall I flee from your presence? If I ascend to heaven, you are there! If I make my bed in Sheol, you are there! If I take the wings of the morning and dwell in the uttermost parts of the sea, even there your hand shall lead me, and your right hand shall hold me" (ESV).

6. God is not limited by any circumstance. He can use any means He wants to accomplish His will. He prepared a huge fish to swallow Jonah in order to accomplish His will.

7. God heard Jonah's cry for help from inside the great fish. He responded to Jonah's cries for help and caused the great fish to spew Jonah out onto dry land.

8. God was patient with Jonah. He did not give up on Jonah when Jonah tried to run away from Him. He pursued Jonah.

9. When God saw that the Ninevites turned from their sin, He had compassion on them and did not bring upon them the destruction that He had threatened.

10. God is gracious and compassionate, slow to anger and abounding in love, a God who relents from sending calamity.

11. God used an object lesson to teach Jonah a truth that he needed to learn. This shows again God's patience with a rebellious man and God's control of all nature. God made the vine (gourd) to quickly spring up and then quickly die.

12. God cares about the souls of people!

13. God loves and wants to save Gentiles as well as Jews.

So, how does the story of Jonah apply to our lives today? What lessons can we learn about how to biblically handle disappointment, discouragement, defeat, depression, and despair?

Jonah was certainly in distress when God told him to go to Nineveh and preach to the people there. He remained in that condition even after he finally preached to the people of Nineveh and they repented. He did not want them to repent because then God would forgive them rather than punishing them. I would say he wanted his own will over God's will. What short-sightedness! But alas, we all can be short-sighted at times, just like Jonah.

There are probably a couple of reasons why Jonah wanted God to punish the people of Nineveh rather than to forgive them. First, Nineveh was a great city in Assyria, an enemy of Jonah's native Israel, and Jonah was a patriot! Nineveh was set upon destroying the northern kingdom of Israel, and that would naturally put the people of Israel at odds with the people of Nineveh. Second, it is possible that Jonah was proud of his heritage as an Israelite, God's chosen people. He might have wanted God to restrict His favor to Israel only. (This is only my conjecture.)

So how should Jonah have biblically responded to his depression over this situation? What was wrong about Jonah's attitude?

Do you see Jonah's selfishness? Rather than rejoicing that the people of Nineveh might favorably respond to his preaching and repent, he was fearful that this was exactly what was going to happen. He did not want the people of Nineveh to repent and be spared. He might have even relished the prospect of seeing them punished. And after the people of Nineveh repented, he should have been glad that God used his preaching to bring about a spiritual victory! Instead, he felt sorry for himself and wanted to die.

Also, Jonah did not seem to be concerned about how his running away from the Lord would reflect upon the other passengers' view of God, whom he professed to serve. The other passengers did not know the true and living God, and they could have gotten a negative view of Him from what was happening to the boat due to Jonah's flight from the Lord. Again, Jonah was so focused on his own feelings that he did not seem to be thinking about how he was representing God.

After the city of Nineveh repented before the Lord, Jonah felt sorry for himself because God spared that city from destruction. God points out that Jonah mourned the death of the vine he was using for protection from the sun, even though he neither tended it nor made it grow. So, God asked Jonah, should God not be concerned about people He created who do not know right from wrong? Do we ever have some of the same selfish attitudes that Jonah had? Do we want to see God punish our enemies rather than saving them?

As I am writing this paragraph in the year 2020 as an addition to this lesson, our country has experienced some troubling times. The year started with the impeachment of President Trump, which seemed to further divide the country. Then in March of this year, COVID-19, a coronavirus, hit the United States, killing thousands of people. Quickly, the country went into lockdown, closing many businesses and putting many people out of work. This sent our booming economy into a tailspin. Fearful of running out of necessities, some people hoarded toilet paper and hand sanitizer, leaving the store shelves empty for other shoppers who did not get there soon enough. There were fights over whether or not people should wear masks. Some people thought the masks were useless in preventing the spread of the virus, while others insisted that masks should be worn by everyone. Those who refused to wear masks were killing other people, the mask wearers claimed. Then in May, due to a black man dying apparently at the hands of a white police officer, the country quickly diverted its attention to race relations. Black Lives Matter and other groups called for social justice and an end to "white privilege", "white supremacy", "systemic racism", and "police brutality." Demonstrations took place every day around the country. Some were peaceful, but many were not. Riots broke out in many cities, and rioters burned and looted many businesses and set fire to some police stations and police cars. Many statues were viciously removed from their place of prominence and defaced or destroyed. The extreme protesters called for the defunding of the police. The weather got hot and tempers flared. The whole country was in unrest and turmoil. The air was thick with hate. People took sides very quickly.

I found myself looking with contempt upon people who had a different outlook than mine. I eventually realized that I should pray for them and not let hate reign in my heart. The COVID-19 virus allegedly began in China, and apparently the leaders there did not do what they should have done to contain it, therefore allowing it to spread throughout the whole world. I believe that China should be held accountable for their lack of responsibility concerning the virus; however, it is unbiblical for me to hate the Chinese and shut up my heart from compassion for their souls. (I do not blame the Chinese people but the government of China, if the virus did indeed begin in China.) God wants to save some of the Chinese people – maybe even some of the leaders who made the decision to cover up the fact that a deadly virus had escaped from a laboratory or market or wherever in China and threatened to spread to other countries. Also, I should examine my heart to see if I have an attitude of ethnic superiority. Do I really care if God saves people from other ethnic groups? If not, then my heart is as guilty as Jonah's. He was upset that God had forgiven the people of Nineveh after they repented of their sin. We should all examine our own hearts to see if we lack compassion for lost people – perhaps people who have even tried to injure us.

My question is this: While crimes and injustices were rampant during this time and most people thought the perpetrators should be held accountable, did we delight at the thought of God condemning these people eternally to Hell, or did we desire to see God save them? Their crimes should be punished on Earth, but are we compassionate about their eternal souls?

Being inside the belly of the great fish with seaweed wrapped around his head must have brought Jonah to his senses. His prayer gives us good words of advice if we seek to ward off discouragement, depression, and despair. Jonah says:

> "When my life was ebbing away, I remembered you, LORD, and my prayer rose to you, to your holy temple. Those who cling to worthless idols turn away from God's love for them" (Jonah 2:7 & 8 NIV).

During times of discouragement, depression, and despair, call out to God for His grace rather than turning to worthless idols! Then open your eyes to what is around you. Look for what God is seeking to do in your midst. Do not think just about yourself and your small world; think about the world around you. There are more people God wants to save, and maybe He wants to use you to accomplish that purpose. He is probably not calling you to preach a sermon, but maybe He wants you to share the good news of the Gospel to people you know. Though it may cost you something to do that, think about the blessing of it, and do not run the other way. Are you figuratively running from God by resisting following any of His commands? It is certain that you will struggle with depression if you, as a believer, are out of fellowship with God because of disobedience and unbelief. Whatever God is calling you to do, He will give you the grace to do it, if you ask for His help.

God accomplishes His purposes despite the sin of mankind. As was said before, God's plans are always greater than our plans!

Chapter Twenty-Two

The Study of Jeremiah

"'Get yourself ready! Stand up and say to them whatever I command you. Do not be terrified by them, or I will terrify you before them. Today I have made you a fortified city, an iron pillar and a bronze wall to stand against the whole land – against the kings of Judah, its officials, its priests and the people of the land. They will fight against you but will not overcome you, for I am with you and will rescue you,' declares the LORD." Jeremiah 1:17-19 NIV

This lesson is about another man from the Old Testament who cursed the day he was born. Sounds like he must have been a little discouraged. He was a great, faithful servant of the true and living God, but he was severely persecuted for speaking out against the sins of the people of Judah, so he was distressed.

God called Jeremiah to speak His message of repentance to the southern kingdom of Judah, but the people did not accept His message. God's message to the people was to repent of their sins – specifically idol worship – or He would raise up a nation from the north, Babylon, to besiege Jerusalem.

In an attempt to squelch God's unpopular, distasteful message, some of Jeremiah's enemies mocked him, beat him, put him into stocks, threatened his life, imprisoned him, and threw him into a cistern. One of the kings of Judah, Jehoiakim, burned the scroll on which God had commanded Jeremiah to record His message to the people.

True to God's message, Jerusalem was taken over by the Babylonians in 586 BC. Jerusalem was burned and the walls torn down. Most of the healthy, prosperous people were taken into captivity. God had warned the people through His faithful prophet Jeremiah, but the people did not turn from their evil ways; therefore, God sent the judgment that He had threatened.

Jeremiah unwaveringly proclaimed God's unpopular message of repentance for forty years, during the reign of five kings: Josiah, Jehoahaz, Jehoiakim, Jehoiachin, and Zedekiah.

Jeremiah 1:

1 The words of Jeremiah son of Hilkiah, one of the priests at Anathoth in the territory of Benjamin. **2** The word of the Lord came to him in the thirteenth year of the reign of Josiah son of Amon king of Judah, **3** and through the reign of Jehoiakim son of Josiah king of Judah, down to the fifth month of the eleventh year of Zedekiah son of Josiah king of Judah, when the people of Jerusalem went into exile.

4 The word of the Lord came to me, saying,
5 "Before I formed you in the womb I knew you,
   before you were born I set you apart;
   I appointed you as a prophet to the nations."

6 "Alas, Sovereign Lord," I said, "I do not know how to speak; I am too young."

7 But the Lord said to me, "Do not say, 'I am too young.' You must go to everyone I send you to and say whatever I command you. 8 Do not be afraid of them, for I am with you and will rescue you," declares the Lord.

9 Then the Lord reached out his hand and touched my mouth and said to me, "I have put my words in your mouth. 10 See, today I appoint you over nations and kingdoms to uproot and tear down, to destroy and overthrow, to build and to plant."

11 The word of the Lord came to me: "What do you see, Jeremiah?"
"I see the branch of an almond tree," I replied.

12 The Lord said to me, "You have seen correctly, for I am watching to see that my word is fulfilled."

13 The word of the Lord came to me again: "What do you see?"

"I see a pot that is boiling," I answered. "It is tilting toward us from the north."

14 The Lord said to me, "From the north disaster will be poured out on all who live in the land. 15 I am about to summon all the peoples of the northern kingdoms," declares the Lord.

> "Their kings will come and set up their thrones
> in the entrance of the gates of Jerusalem;
> they will come against all her surrounding walls
> and against all the towns of Judah.
> 16 I will pronounce my judgments on my people
> because of their wickedness in forsaking me,
> in burning incense to other gods
> and in worshiping what their hands have made.

17 "Get yourself ready! Stand up and say to them whatever I command you. Do not be terrified by them, or I will terrify you before them. **18** Today I have made you a fortified city, an iron pillar and a bronze wall to stand against the whole land—against the kings of Judah, its officials, its priests and the people of the land. **19** They will fight against you but will not overcome you, for I am with you and will rescue you," declares the Lord.

Jeremiah 12:

Jeremiah's complaint

    1 You are always righteous, Lord,
      when I bring a case before you.
      Yet I would speak with you about your justice:
      Why does the way of the wicked prosper?
      Why do all the faithless live at ease?
    2 You have planted them, and they have taken root;
      they grow and bear fruit.
      You are always on their lips
      but far from their hearts.
    3 Yet you know me, Lord;
      you see me and test my thoughts about you.
      Drag them off like sheep to be butchered!
      Set them apart for the day of slaughter!
    4 How long will the land lie parched
      and the grass in every field be withered?
      Because those who live in it are wicked,
      the animals and birds have perished.
      Moreover, the people are saying,
      "He will not see what happens to us."

God's Answer

5 "If you have raced with men on foot
   and they have worn you out,
   how can you compete with horses?
   If you stumble in safe country,
   how will you manage in the thickets by the Jordan?
6 Your relatives, members of your own family—
   even they have betrayed you;
   they have raised a loud cry against you.
   Do not trust them,
   though they speak well of you.
7 "I will forsake my house,
   abandon my inheritance;
   I will give the one I love
   into the hands of her enemies.
8 My inheritance has become to me
   like a lion in the forest.
   She roars at me;
   therefore I hate her.
9 Has not my inheritance become to me
   like a speckled bird of prey
   that other birds of prey surround and attack?
   Go and gather all the wild beasts;
   bring them to devour.
10 Many shepherds will ruin my vineyard
   and trample down my field;
   they will turn my pleasant field
   into a desolate wasteland.
11 It will be made a wasteland,
   parched and desolate before me;
   the whole land will be laid waste
   because there is no one who cares.
12 Over all the barren heights in the desert
   destroyers will swarm,

> for the sword of the Lord will devour
> from one end of the land to the other;
> no one will be safe.
> **13** They will sow wheat but reap thorns;
> they will wear themselves out but gain nothing.
> They will bear the shame of their harvest
> because of the Lord's fierce anger."

14 This is what the Lord says: "As for all my wicked neighbors who seize the inheritance I gave my people Israel, I will uproot them from their lands and I will uproot the people of Judah from among them. **15** But after I uproot them, I will again have compassion and will bring each of them back to their own inheritance and their own country. **16** And if they learn well the ways of my people and swear by my name, saying, 'As surely as the Lord lives'—even as they once taught my people to swear by Baal—then they will be established among my people. **17** But if any nation does not listen, I will completely uproot and destroy it," declares the Lord.

Jeremiah 20:

> **7** You deceived me, Lord, and I was deceived;
> you overpowered me and prevailed.
> I am ridiculed all day long;
> everyone mocks me.
> **8** Whenever I speak, I cry out
> proclaiming violence and destruction.
> So the word of the Lord has brought me
> insult and reproach all day long.
> **9** But if I say, "I will not mention his word
> or speak anymore in his name,"
> his word is in my heart like a fire,
> a fire shut up in my bones.
> I am weary of holding it in;

indeed, I cannot.
10 I hear many whispering,
 "Terror on every side!
 Denounce him! Let's denounce him!"
 All my friends
 are waiting for me to slip, saying,
 "Perhaps he will be deceived;
 then we will prevail over him
 and take our revenge on him."
11 But the Lord is with me like a mighty warrior;
 so my persecutors will stumble and not prevail.
 They will fail and be thoroughly disgraced;
 their dishonor will never be forgotten.
12 Lord Almighty, you who examine the righteous
 and probe the heart and mind,
 let me see your vengeance on them,
 for to you I have committed my cause.
13 Sing to the Lord!
 Give praise to the Lord!
 He rescues the life of the needy
 from the hands of the wicked.
14 Cursed be the day I was born!
 May the day my mother bore me not be blessed!
15 Cursed be the man who brought my father the news,
 who made him very glad, saying,
 "A child is born to you—a son!"
16 May that man be like the towns
 the Lord overthrew without pity.
 May he hear wailing in the morning,
 a battle cry at noon.
17 For he did not kill me in the womb,
 with my mother as my grave,
 her womb enlarged forever.

18 Why did I ever come out of the womb
to see trouble and sorrow
and to end my days in shame?

Jeremiah 32:

17 "Ah, Sovereign LORD, you have made the heavens and the earth by your great power and outstretched arm. Nothing is too hard for you. **18** You show love to thousands but bring the punishment for the parents' sins into the laps of their children after them. Great and mighty God, whose name is the LORD Almighty, **19** great are your purposes and mighty are your deeds. Your eyes are open to the ways of all mankind; you reward each person according to their conduct and as their deeds deserve. **20** You performed signs and wonders in Egypt and have continued them to this day, in Israel and among all mankind, and have gained the renown that is still yours. **21** You brought your people Israel out of Egypt with signs and wonders, by a mighty hand and an outstretched arm and with great terror. **22** You gave them this land you had sworn to give their ancestors, a land flowing with milk and honey. **23** They came in and took possession of it, but they did not obey you or follow your law; they did not do what you commanded them to do. So you brought all this disaster on them.

24 "See how the siege ramps are built up to take the city. Because of the sword, famine and plague, the city will be given into the hands of the Babylonians who are attacking it. What you said has happened, as you now see. **25** And though the city will be given into the hands of the Babylonians, you, Sovereign LORD, say to me, 'Buy the field with silver and have the transaction witnessed'" (NIV).

The problems that led to Jeremiah's despondency are obvious; he was greatly mistreated, though all he was trying to do was dutifully carry out what God had called him to do. If it were not bad enough that the people refused to listen to his message, they compounded their sin by trying to kill him! Anybody can understand Jeremiah's feelings.

But how should Jeremiah have responded to these events biblically? For the most part, I think he did respond biblically.

1. He continued to proclaim the message, even though many people tried to stop him. Actually, his worst enemies were the priests and the prophets – other religious people! And Jeremiah's own family turned against him. But it appears that he feared God more than he feared men.

2. He did not take revenge on those who mistreated him.

3. He kept his own life free from idolatry and other sins.

So, he basically did handle his situation biblically. And this is a great lesson for us.

But what was it about Jeremiah's thinking that caused him to say that he should never have been born?

It appears to me that at times, he was more focused on circumstances for his well-being than he was focused on God's approval for his well-being, at least momentarily. I understand the discouragement that would come from seeing very little response to the message he brought to the people. Jeremiah spent forty years of his life proclaiming God's message of repentance, but for the most part, the message was shunned. It would be so easy to become discouraged and to quit if one focuses primarily on circumstances! Rejection is not pleasant because it is normal to desire acceptance from others. **God's call on Jeremiah's life was to keep proclaiming God's message, even though the message would be ignored**. Remember that early in God's conversation with Jeremiah, He told Jeremiah that even while he was developing in his mother's womb, God had appointed him the task of being a prophet. This was the primary reason for Jeremiah's existence. Obviously, Jeremiah needed God's grace to carry out this challenging task. Though admittedly hard to do, Jeremiah should have kept his focus on the joy that comes from faithfulness to God rather than on circumstances of being mistreated. This is what Jesus did. Though Jesus greatly despised the shame of the cross, He looked forward to the joy of completing His mission from the Father! Hebrews 12:2 & 3 says:

> "Fixing our eyes on Jesus, the pioneer and perfecter of faith. For the joy set before him he endured the cross, scorning its shame, and sat down at the right hand of the throne of God. Consider him who endured such opposition from sinners, so that you will not grow weary and lose heart" (NIV).

As followers of Christ, we must also keep our focus not on circumstances but on the smile of our God as we faithfully pursue Him and faithfully serve Him! Let that be our reward, our bread, our sustenance.

In addition, Jeremiah could have focused more on God's promises to him. What promises? Jeremiah 1:8 says, "'Do not be afraid of them, for I am with you and will rescue you,' declares the LORD" (NIV). God also promised to give Jeremiah the words to say to the inhabitants of Judah. He told Jeremiah that He had **given him power to do the job** of warning the people. Jeremiah 1:18 & 19 says, "Today I have made you a fortified city, an iron pillar and a bronze wall to stand against the whole land – against the kings of Judah, its officials, its priests and the people of the land. They will fight against you but will not overcome you, for I am with you and will rescue you,' declares the LORD" (NIV). What a promise for Jeremiah to cling to when the job got difficult! God also promised to restore the land. The first hint of this is in Jeremiah 12:15 & 16: "But after I uproot them, I will again have compassion and will bring each of them back to their own inheritance and their own country. And if they learn well the ways of my people and swear by my name, saying, 'As surely as the LORD lives' – even as they once taught my people to swear by Baal – then they will be established among my people" (NIV). In addition, think about this amazing promise to the people of Judah in Jeremiah 29:11: "For I know the plans I have for you,' declares the LORD, 'plans to prosper you and not to harm you, plans to give you hope and a future'" (NIV). Then, foreshadowing events to come, in chapter 32, God tells Jeremiah to "buy the field with silver and have the transaction witnessed." Jeremiah wonders why he should buy some property when it was inevitable that the country would be conquered by the Babylonians. It was because God planned, in time, to restore the land! Of course, the good things to come would follow judgment, devastation, and loss, but good things were promised!

Jeremiah's prayers are a strange mixture of distrust and trust in God. The following is a list of Jeremiah's "complaints":

1. The wicked prosper. That's not fair (Jeremiah 12:1)! In an upcoming lesson, we will see God's answer to the universal question pondered by many throughout the ages: "Why does the way of the wicked prosper?"

2. The people are hypocrites (Jeremiah 12:2).

3. The famine is the fault of the wicked. How long will God allow that to happen (Jeremiah 12:4)?

4. I am ridiculed, mocked, insulted, and reproached because of my message to the people (Jeremiah 20:7).

5. I hear people saying that they want to kill me (Jeremiah 20:10).

6. I should never have been born. That would have spared me this trouble, sorrow, and shame (Jeremiah 20:14).

See how much he is focusing on himself and his circumstances?

Now let's look at the praise that Jeremiah gives in his prayers to the true and living God:

1. He is always righteous (Jeremiah 12:1).

2. He is with me like a mighty warrior (Jeremiah 20:11).

3. He examines the hearts and minds of the righteous (Jeremiah 20:12).

4. He rescues the life of the needy from the hands of the wicked (Jeremiah 20:13).

5. He is sovereign (Jeremiah 32:17).

6. He is the creator of everything (Jeremiah 32:17).

7. Nothing is too hard for Him (Jeremiah 32:17).

8. He shows love and mercy to many people (Jeremiah 32:18).

9. He brings the punishment of the fathers' sins upon their children (Jeremiah 32:18).

10. He is great and powerful (Jeremiah 32:18).

11. His purposes are great (Jeremiah 32:19).

12. Mighty are His deeds (Jeremiah 32:19).

13. He sees the deeds of all men (Jeremiah 32:19).

14. He rewards men according to their conduct and their deeds (Jeremiah 32:19).

15. He performed miraculous signs and wonders in Egypt and still does today – the time that the book of Jeremiah was written (Jeremiah 32:20).

16. He brought His people out of Egypt (Jeremiah 32:21).

17. He gave the Jews the Promised Land (Jeremiah 32:22).

18. What He said would happen has happened. He keeps His word (Jeremiah 32:24).

19. He is the God of hope and renewal (Jeremiah 32:25).

I think all that Jeremiah needed to do was to focus more intensely on these things rather than on his circumstances. Sure, his circumstances were extremely unpleasant. The righteous never like to see the wicked prosper while they suffer. And that is the way it often is during this life. **But that is not the end of the story, and that is what we must remember!** God did eventually bring about the disaster that Jeremiah warned about for forty years. God, who is long-suffering, withheld His judgment for over forty years; yet, He eventually allowed the Babylonians to besiege the walls of Jerusalem, destroy the city and take captive most of the people. **If not in this life, we can be sure that God will bring about His justice in the next life!**

Though Jeremiah probably would have chosen to do something else with his life, what he did was glorious because he faithfully carried out what God called him to do. He played a great part in history, and his work is forever recorded in the pages of Scripture. Jeremiah has been in Heaven for more than 2,600 years, and I can assure you that once he got to Heaven, all his suffering seemed like nothing (2 Corinthians

4:17). He will be greatly rewarded by God at the Great White Throne Judgment some day. **It takes an eternal perspective to praise God and obey Him, despite unpleasant circumstances. Our lives on Earth are really very short, compared to eternity.**

Has God called you to do some difficult, thankless task? Are you sometimes discouraged because you see wicked people doing better in life than you are doing, though you strive to live for Christ? If so, you must remember to **keep your eyes focused on the Lord and His call upon your life.** Know with confidence the promise of 2 Corinthians 4:17:

> "For our light and momentary troubles are achieving for us an eternal glory that far outweighs them all. So we fix our eyes not on what is seen, but on what is unseen, since what is seen is temporary, but what is unseen is eternal" (NIV).

Circumstances are temporary, but serving God with a pure heart is eternal!

Chapter Twenty-Three

The Study of Esther

> "'And who knows but that you have come to your
> royal position for such a time as this?'"
> Esther 4:14 NIV

God may sometimes put us in a severe situation where the right thing to do is to take action. Rather than sitting by, watching injustice take place and becoming depressed about it, God sometimes calls us to do something to change the situation.

This lesson is about a Jewish man and his young cousin who took action against injustice despite great personal risk. Esther (Hadassah) was a young woman when she replaced Vashti as queen of a vast Persian kingdom of 127 provinces. She found herself in a dire situation. She chose to act, despite the possibility of losing her life, rather than wallowing in self-pity, fear, and depression.

The historical events that this book records probably took place between 486 and 465 BC. The Babylonian Captivity, which Jeremiah prophesied, took place in 586 BC, and the Jews were captive in Babylon for 70 years. Around 516 BC, some of the Jews returned to Israel to rebuild what the Babylonians had destroyed. The historical events that the book of Esther records took place after some of the Jews had already returned to Israel. Many of the Jews did not return to Israel at the end of the captivity. That is why Mordecai, Esther's cousin, and Esther herself were Jews in a foreign land when the events in the book of Esther took place. As you read part of this book, notice how God was still involved in the events of those Jews who remained in the foreign land.

Most of the historical events that are recorded in the book of Esther took place at the palace of King Xerxes (Ahasuerus), whose vast Persian empire covered 127 provinces. The following is a summary of the events that take place in Chapters 1-6. Carefully observe how these events, though seemingly isolated, actually do influence other events which culminate in the final big picture.

Summary of Esther 1-6:

King Xerxes summons Queen Vashti to display her beauty before his many guests at a banquet he is hosting. Vashti refuses to appear, and so she is deposed as queen. The king sets out to replace Vashti, and many young virgins are brought to the palace so that the king can select the one girl he prefers to become the new queen. Xerxes favors Esther, the young Jewish girl, over all the others, and so she becomes the new queen. (At this point, the king does not realize that Esther is a Jew.)

Mordecai, Esther's older cousin and adopted father, is sitting at the king's gate when he hears about a plot by two of the king's officials to kill the king. He reports this to Esther who informs the king. The traitors are executed.

Another official of the king, Haman, is given a prominent position in the kingdom. Therefore, it is required of everyone to pay respect to Haman by bowing down to him. Mordecai refuses to bow down to Haman, who is a descendent of Agag, king of Amalek, Israel's bitter enemy. Haman becomes very angry and despondent, and another plot emerges.

This plot involves not only the murder of Mordecai but the annihilation of every Jew – men, women, and children. (The slaughter of over six million Jews in the 1940s by Hitler was not the first time that Satan attempted to completely wipe out the Jewish population.) When Haman learns that Mordecai is a Jew, he sees the perfect way to punish Mordecai for refusing to pay him the homage he seeks.

It is obvious that Haman hates the Jews. He informs the king about this group of people who are different from all the other people of the kingdom. He explains to the king that it is really not in his best interest to allow these people to be a part of his kingdom. He proposes a plan to rid the kingdom of these foreigners forever!

The king blindly agrees with this wicked plan, and an edict with the king's stamp of approval is sent out to every province in the kingdom. A date is set for the killing of every Jew in this vast kingdom.

Mordecai finds out about the edict, and he knows this situation is dire; in a short time, the Jews will be facing mass murder unless someone intervenes! He urges Queen Esther, through a message to her eunuch, to go before the king and plead for her people, the Jews. In his message to Esther, Mordecai implies that it is probable that Esther was put into her royal position for this very reason. Esther is also distressed about the news of this plot to kill all the Jews, but she knows that if she appears before the king without being summoned, she could be put to death. Esther decides that she must risk her life and go before the king to plead for the lives of her fellow Jews. She asks all the Jews in the kingdom to fast and pray for her night and day for three days. Esther then says, "When this is done, I will go to the king, even though it is against the law. And if I perish, I perish" (Esther 4:16 NIV).

Queen Esther does go before the king without being summoned, but he welcomes her into his presence anyway! He asks her about her request, and she says that she wants to have a banquet the next day for the king and Haman. The next day at the banquet where the king and Haman are present, the king again asks Esther what he can do for her. She wants the king and Haman to come to another banquet the next day.

Haman is so proud and excited about being asked to the queen's banquet, but he cannot get over the fact that Mordecai still refuses to bow down to him. He broods over this until his friends and his wife advise him to quickly resolve this situation that is causing him so much unhappiness. To them the answer is simple: Haman should have a pole erected and ask the king to impale Mordecai on the pole! So Haman has the pole built.

That night, because the king cannot sleep, he calls for the record book of his reign to be brought and read to him. When he is reminded by the book about the foiled plot by two of his officials to kill him, he wonders what has been done for Mordecai, who had exposed the plot. His attendants inform him that nothing had been done to honor Mordecai. The king thinks that something should be done belatedly. As he is contemplating this, Haman appears in the king's outer court to speak to him about having Mordecai impaled on the pole he had built. But the king's mind is focused on honoring the man who saved his life. He then asks Haman what he thinks should be done for the man that the king seeks to honor. Of course, the king means Mordecai, but prideful Haman assumes the king must be thinking of honoring him. With this in mind, Haman says that the king should place one of his royal robes on that man and provide him with one of his horses and that he should be led on horseback throughout the city with shouts of honor for that man. The king likes Haman's idea, so he commands Haman to get the robe and horse and do unto Mordecai just as he suggested. Haman is the one who has to put the robe on Mordecai and lead him on horseback throughout the city, proclaiming honor to him! Wow! What humiliation!

Shortly after this, Haman appears at the second banquet that Esther has prepared for him and the king. That is where the story starts in chapter 7.

Esther 7:

1 So the king and Haman went to Queen Esther's banquet, **2** and as they were drinking wine on the second day, the king again asked, "Queen Esther, what is your petition? It will be given you. What is your request? Even up to half the kingdom, it will be granted."

3 Then Queen Esther answered, "If I have found favor with you, Your Majesty, and if it pleases you, grant me my life—this is my petition. And spare my people—this is my request. **4** For I and my people have been sold to be destroyed, killed and annihilated. If we had merely been sold as male and female slaves, I would have kept quiet, because no such distress would justify disturbing the king."

5 King Xerxes asked Queen Esther, "Who is he? Where is he—the man who has dared to do such a thing?"

6 Esther said, "An adversary and enemy! This vile Haman!"

Then Haman was terrified before the king and queen. **7** The king got up in a rage, left his wine and went out into the palace garden. But Haman, realizing that the king had already decided his fate, stayed behind to beg Queen Esther for his life.

8 Just as the king returned from the palace garden to the banquet hall, Haman was falling on the couch where Esther was reclining.

The king exclaimed, "Will he even molest the queen while she is with me in the house?"

As soon as the word left the king's mouth, they covered Haman's face. **9** Then Harbona, one of the eunuchs attending the king, said, "A pole reaching to a height of fifty cubits stands by Haman's house. He had it set up for Mordecai, who spoke up to help the king."

The king said, "Impale him on it!" **10** So they impaled Haman on the pole he had set up for Mordecai. Then the king's fury subsided.

Esther 8:

1 That same day King Xerxes gave Queen Esther the estate of Haman, the enemy of the Jews. And Mordecai came into the presence of the king, for Esther had told how he was related to her. **2** The king took off his signet ring, which he had reclaimed from Haman, and presented it to Mordecai. And Esther appointed him over Haman's estate.

3 Esther again pleaded with the king, falling at his feet and weeping. She begged him to put an end to the evil plan of Haman the Agagite, which he had devised against the Jews. **4** Then the king extended the gold scepter to Esther and she arose and stood before him.

5 "If it pleases the king," she said, "and if he regards me with favor and thinks it the right thing to do, and if he is pleased with me, let an order be written overruling the dispatches that Haman son of Hammedatha, the Agagite, devised and wrote to destroy the Jews in all the king's provinces. **6** For how can I bear to see disaster fall on my people? How can I bear to see the destruction of my family?"

7 King Xerxes replied to Queen Esther and to Mordecai the Jew, "Because Haman attacked the Jews, I have given his estate to Esther, and they have impaled him on the pole he set up. **8** Now write another decree in the king's name in behalf of the Jews as seems best to you, and seal it with the king's signet ring—for no document written in the king's name and sealed with his ring can be revoked."

9 At once the royal secretaries were summoned—on the twenty-third day of the third month, the month of Sivan. They wrote out all Mordecai's orders to the Jews, and to the satraps, governors and nobles of the 127 provinces stretching from India to Cush. These orders were written in the script of each province and the language of each people and also to the Jews in their own script and language. **10** Mordecai wrote in the name of King Xerxes, sealed the dispatches with the king's signet ring, and sent them by mounted couriers, who rode fast horses especially bred for the king.

11 The king's edict granted the Jews in every city the right to assemble and protect themselves; to destroy, kill and annihilate the armed men of any nationality or province who might attack them and their women and children, and to plunder the property of their enemies. **12** The day appointed for the Jews to do this in all the provinces of King Xerxes was the thirteenth day of the twelfth month, the month of Adar. **13** A copy of the text of the edict was to be issued as law in every province and made known to the people of every nationality so that the Jews would be ready on that day to avenge themselves on their enemies.

14 The couriers, riding the royal horses, went out, spurred on by the king's command, and the edict was issued in the citadel of Susa.

15 When Mordecai left the king's presence, he was wearing royal garments of blue and white, a large crown of gold and a purple robe of fine linen. And the city of Susa held a joyous celebration. **16** For the Jews it was a time of happiness and joy, gladness and honor. **17** In every province and in every city to which the edict of the king came, there was joy and gladness among the Jews, with feasting and celebrating. And many people of other nationalities became Jews because fear of the Jews had seized them.

Esther 9:

1 On the thirteenth day of the twelfth month, the month of Adar, the edict commanded by the king was to be carried out. On this day the enemies of the Jews had hoped to overpower them, but now the tables were turned and the Jews got the upper hand over those who hated them. **2** The Jews assembled in their cities in all the provinces of King Xerxes to attack those determined to destroy them. No one could stand against them, because the people of all the other nationalities were afraid of them. **3** And all the nobles of the provinces, the satraps, the governors and the king's administrators helped the Jews, because fear of Mordecai had seized them. **4** Mordecai was prominent in the palace; his reputation spread throughout the provinces, and he became more and more powerful.

5 The Jews struck down all their enemies with the sword, killing and destroying them, and they did what they pleased to those who hated them. **6** In the citadel of Susa, the Jews killed and destroyed five hundred men. **7** They also killed Parshandatha, Dalphon, Aspatha, **8** Poratha, Adalia, Aridatha, **9** Parmashta, Arisai, Aridai and Vaizatha, **10** the ten sons of Haman son of Hammedatha, the enemy of the Jews. But they did not lay their hands on the plunder.

11 The number of those killed in the citadel of Susa was reported to the king that same day. **12** The king said to Queen Esther, "The Jews have killed and destroyed five hundred men and the ten sons of Haman in the citadel of Susa. What have they done in the rest of the king's provinces? Now what is your petition? It will be given you. What is your request? It will also be granted."

13 "If it pleases the king," Esther answered, "give the Jews in Susa permission to carry out this day's edict tomorrow also, and let Haman's ten sons be impaled on poles."

14 So the king commanded that this be done. An edict was issued in Susa, and they impaled the ten sons of Haman. **15** The Jews in Susa came together on the fourteenth day of the month of Adar, and they put to death in Susa three hundred men, but they did not lay their hands on the plunder.

16 Meanwhile, the remainder of the Jews who were in the king's provinces also assembled to protect themselves and get relief from their enemies. They killed seventy-five thousand of them but did not lay their hands on the plunder. **17** This happened on the thirteenth day of the month of Adar, and on the fourteenth, they rested and made it a day of feasting and joy.

18 The Jews in Susa, however, had assembled on the thirteenth and fourteenth, and then on the fifteenth they rested and made it a day of feasting and joy.

19 That is why rural Jews—those living in villages—observe the fourteenth of the month of Adar as a day of joy and feasting, a day for giving presents to each other.

20 Mordecai recorded these events, and he sent letters to all the Jews throughout the provinces of King Xerxes, near and far, **21** to have them celebrate annually the fourteenth and fifteenth days of the month of Adar **22** as the time when the Jews got relief from their enemies, and as the month when their sorrow was turned into joy and their mourning into a day of celebration. He wrote them to observe the days as days of feasting and joy and giving presents of food to one another and gifts to the poor.

23 So the Jews agreed to continue the celebration they had begun, doing what Mordecai had written to them. **24** For Haman son of Hammedatha, the Agagite, the enemy of all the Jews, had plotted against the Jews to destroy them and had cast the *pur* (that is, the lot) for their ruin and destruction. **25** But when the plot came to the king's attention, he issued written orders that the evil scheme Haman had devised against the Jews should come back onto his own head, and that he and his sons should be impaled on poles. **26** (Therefore these days were called Purim, from the word *pur*.) Because of everything written in this letter and because of what they had seen and what had happened to them, **27** the Jews took it on themselves to establish the custom that they and their descendants and all who join them should without fail observe these two days every year, in the way prescribed and at the time appointed. **28** These days should be remembered and observed in every generation by every family, and in every province and in every city. And these days of Purim should never fail to be celebrated by the Jews—nor should the memory of these days die out among their descendants.

29 So Queen Esther, daughter of Abihail, along with Mordecai the Jew, wrote with full authority to confirm this second letter concerning Purim. **30** And Mordecai sent letters to all the Jews in the 127 provinces of Xerxes' kingdom—words of goodwill and assurance— **31** to establish these days of Purim at their designated times, as Mordecai the Jew and Queen Esther had decreed for them, and as they had established for themselves and their descendants in regard to their times of fasting and lamentation. **32** Esther's decree confirmed these regulations about Purim, and it was written down in the records.

Esther 10:

1 King Xerxes imposed tribute throughout the empire, to its distant shores. **2** And all his acts of power and might, together with a full account of the greatness of Mordecai, whom the king had promoted, are they not written in the book of the annals of the kings of Media and Persia? **3** Mordecai the Jew was second in rank to King Xerxes, pre-eminent among the Jews, and held in high esteem by his many fellow Jews, because he worked for the good of his people and spoke up for the welfare of all the Jews" (NIV).

What does the book of Esther teach us about how to biblically handle disappointment, discouragement, defeat, depression, and despair? What are the biblical principles from this book that can be applied to our subject at hand? Though the big picture in this book is God's providential preservation of the Jews in fulfillment of His plan for His chosen people, there are some other lessons we can learn as well.

1. Remember that God is ultimately in control of every person and every event. This is clearly demonstrated in the book of Esther. Other passages in the Old and the New Testaments also bear out this fact. Remember the life of Joseph? We see the sovereignty of God throughout the story of Joseph. And what about Job? God was obviously in control; Satan had to get God's permission to bring destruction to Job's life. And after the testing was over, God gave Job even more than he had before he lost everything except for his own life and that of his wife. Nothing dissipates my depression faster than looking at how God has operated throughout history, displaying His sovereignty over all people and all events! This attribute of God brings me great comfort! I am so thankful that the all-knowing, all-powerful, just, righteous, loving Creator-God is in control of all events in this year 2023!

Ponder these verses declaring God's sovereign rule over everything. (Sovereignty means supreme power or authority.)

Psalm 22:28: "...for dominion belongs to the LORD and he rules over the nations" (NIV). (Dominion means sovereignty or control.)

Psalm 115:3: "Our God is in heaven; he does whatever pleases him" (NIV).

Psalm 135:6: "The LORD does whatever pleases him, in the heavens and on the earth, in the seas and all their depths" (NIV).

Proverbs 20:24: "A person's steps are directed by the LORD. How then can anyone understand their own way?" (NIV).

Isaiah 46:10: "I make known the end from the beginning, from ancient times, what is still to come. I say, 'My purpose will stand, and I will do all that I please'" (NIV).

Ephesians 1:11 & 12: "In him we were also chosen, having been predestined according to the plan of him who works out everything in conformity with the purpose of his will, in order that we, who were the first to put our hope in Christ, might be for the praise of his glory" (NIV).

Consider all the events that take place in this story. God engineered all of them! All of these events come together to bring about the final outcome. Although God is never mentioned in the book of Esther, we know that it is God who worked behind the scenes because we know from other places in the Bible that God is in control of all things.

A. Queen Vashti is deposed.

B. Esther wins the favor of Hegai, the king's eunuch, who cares for the girls who are candidates for the queenship. Because she has won his favor, Hegai treats her as special. He immediately provides her with her beauty treatments, with special food, and with seven special maids. He moves Esther and her maids into the best place in the harem.

C. Esther wins the favor of everyone who sees her.

D. Of all the girls who are previewed by King Xerxes (Ahasuerus) to replace Vashti as queen, it is a Jewish girl, Esther (Hadassah) who wins his favor. He is more pleased with her than any of the others who appear before him.

E. Mordecai finds out about the plot of Bigthana and Teresh, two of the king's officers who guard the doorway, to kill King Xerxes.

F. Mordecai exposes the plot to kill King Xerxes. The conspirators of the plot are executed.

G. Haman is given a prominent position in the kingdom. Therefore, it is required of everyone to pay respect to Haman by bowing down to him.

H. Mordecai refuses to bow down to Haman.

I. Mordecai tells the royal officials at the king's gate that he is a Jew.

J. Haman finds out that Mordecai is a Jew.

K. Haman devises an edict, which goes out to all of King Xerxes' kingdom, signed by the king himself, that all the Jews, young and old, male and female, are to be killed on a certain day and all their goods plundered.

L. Esther, herself a Jew, learns about this edict.

M. Mordecai urges Esther, through one of the king's eunuchs, to go to the king and plead for the lives of the Jews.

N. Esther has all the Jews in Susa and her maids fast and pray for her prior to her appearing before the king.

O. Esther courageously appears before King Xerxes, without being summoned by him.

P. The king graciously accepts Esther's unsolicited presence, rather than having her killed. According to the law, Xerxes could have had Esther killed for this presumptuous act.

Q. The king is so pleased with Esther that he is anxious to grant her any request that she has. He is prepared to give her up to half his kingdom.

R. The king complies with Esther's request to attend a banquet that she has arranged for Haman and him.

S. The king complies with Esther's request to attend a second banquet that she has arranged for Haman and him.

T. Haman becomes even more arrogant, thinking that he must be very special because he is the only one invited by Queen Esther to attend the banquets with the king.

U. After complaining to his wife and his friends about the Jew Mordecai, Haman follows their advice and has a pole erected on which he plans to ask the king to have Mordecai executed.

V. Because King Xerxes cannot sleep, he calls for the history book to be read to him. Through the reading of the book, the king remembers that Mordecai had exposed the plot to kill the king. He learns that Mordecai had not been recognized and honored for this.

W. Haman enters the king's court just as King Xerxes realizes that Mordecai had not been honored for exposing the plot to kill him. He asks Haman what should be done to the man that the king delights to honor. Thinking that the king must certainly be thinking of him, Haman devises a plan to publicly honor himself.

X. The king orders Haman to publicly honor Mordecai.

Y. Haman attends the second banquet given by Queen Esther for King Xerxes and Haman.

Z. The king is favorable toward Esther. He wants to grant her request.

AA. Esther courageously speaks up for herself and for her people.

BB. The king becomes angry at Haman for arranging to kill Esther and her people, the Jews.

CC. Haman is impaled on the pole he had erected for Mordecai.

DD. The king overrules his previous order to kill all Jews.

EE. The king gives Haman's estate to Esther.

FF. The king has Mordecai write another decree, this time in favor of the Jews, granting them rights, freedoms, and protection.

GG. Now, rather than mourning, there is joy. The Jews are celebrating!

HH. Many people of other nationalities become Jews.

II. The Jews stand up to those who sought their destruction, killing all of them.

JJ. Now the government officials (the nobles of the provinces, the satraps, the governors, and the king's administrators) help the Jews.

KK. Mordecai becomes second in rank to King Xerxes.

2. Because God is in control, He can turn circumstances around completely. Within a matter of weeks, Haman goes from being the king's noble in the highest position to being impaled on his own pole. Conversely, Mordecai goes from being threatened by death to becoming the second in rank to King Xerxes. **We are not at the mercy of blind fate, but a loving Father who knows all things and controls all things.**

3. Sometimes God may put us in a place where He wants us to take action against injustice and unrighteousness, and He gives us the resources to do this. A current example is praying for the end of abortion and supporting crisis pregnancy centers which help pregnant women who decide to allow their babies to be born rather than aborting them. Esther used her position as queen and the favor of the king to prevent all the Jews in the Persian empire from being killed! Esther chose to act rather than sitting around paralyzed by fear and depression about the circumstances. Mordecai advocated for the good of his people, the Jews.

4. God has placed each of us at this time and place in history – during the 21st century in the United States of America. What has He brought you to this time and place to do? Just as God put Esther in the powerful position as queen of a vast empire to accomplish the purpose of exposing Haman's plot to kill all the Jews, He has placed you in your position for a certain purpose. None of us is queen of a vast empire, but we all have spheres of influence. What stand has God called you to take "at such a time as this"? God has a unique purpose for your life. Do

not think it is insignificant just because He has not called you to be a queen who saves the lives of thousands of people. You have a position, even if it is just with family, friends, classmates, coworkers. God has placed you where you are so that you can help and influence others! Are you willing to sacrifice your own welfare for the good of others, like Mordecai and Esther did?

5. Consider how God provided for Esther:

   A. When she was orphaned, Mordecai adopted her.

   B. God allowed her to become queen. Though it probably had some pitfalls, still her basic needs were provided for, and she probably also enjoyed many luxuries. In addition, as queen, Esther was in a position to be able to help save her people, the Jews.

   C. God enabled her to find out about the plot against the Jews.

   D. God provided to Esther the courage and moral resolve to plead to the king for the lives of the Jews.

   E. God gave Esther favor in the eyes of the king.

   F. God saved Esther's life and the lives of her fellow Jews.

Mordecai and Esther's concern for their fellow Jews overrode their personal concerns. This is a sure way to dispel depression. When I serve God by helping others, my heart is lightened.

Do not sit around wringing your hands and becoming depressed when you see injustices and unrighteousness. Take action whenever possible! Remember, though, that **God calls you to always respond biblically.** God wants to work through you where He has placed you at this time. And take comfort in the fact that God is in control of all events at all times. He can use even adverse situations for His glory and for your good. Romans 8:28 says, "And we know that in all things God works for the good of those who love him, who have been called according to his purpose" (NIV).

Chapter Twenty-Four

The Study of Nehemiah

*"But out of reverence for God I did not act like that.
Instead, I devoted myself to the work on this wall."
Nehemiah 5:15 & 16 NIV*

One of the lessons in a previous chapter centered around the historical events just prior to the Babylonian Captivity. Another lesson centered around the historical events that took place shortly after the end of the exile of the Israelites.

We studied Jeremiah, who prophesied the coming destruction of Jerusalem if the people did not repent and turn from their sins. God brought about judgment because they refused to heed Jeremiah's warning to repent. The Babylonians plundered the city and set it on fire. The city walls were torn down, and most of the able-bodied people were taken into captivity to Babylon.

We also studied the book of Esther which chronicles the historical events of Esther, a young Jewish woman who became queen of the vast Persian empire and was used by God to save the Jewish people from obliteration. These events took place after some of the exiled Jews had returned to Israel after the captivity.

In this lesson, we will study some of the historical events that took place after the first people returned to Judah following their captivity in Babylon. Nehemiah, then the governor of Judah, led a group of people in rebuilding the walls of Jerusalem, despite much opposition. So, the historical events that the book of Nehemiah records took place after Jeremiah warned the people about the coming destruction and either shortly before or after the historical events that the book of Esther records. The book of Nehemiah was written around 430 BC, so the events it records took place prior to that.

Jeremiah – Jeremiah's prophetic ministry began in 626 BC and ended sometime after 586 BC.

Esther – The book of Esther was written sometime between 460 BC and 331 BC.

Nehemiah – The book of Nehemiah was written about 430 BC. Nehemiah went to Jerusalem in 445 BC and led the people in repairing the walls of Jerusalem.

Nehemiah 1:

1 The words of Nehemiah son of Hakaliah:

In the month of Kislev in the twentieth year, while I was in the citadel of Susa, **2** Hanani, one of my brothers, came from Judah with some other men, and I questioned them about the Jewish remnant that had survived the exile, and also about Jerusalem. **3** They said to me, "Those who survived the exile and are back in the province are in great trouble and disgrace. The wall of Jerusalem is broken down, and its gates have been burned with fire."

4 When I heard these things, I sat down and wept. For some days I mourned and fasted and prayed before the God of heaven. **5** Then I said:

"Lord, the God of heaven, the great and awesome God, who keeps his covenant of love with those who love him and keep his commandments, **6** let your ear be attentive and your eyes open to hear the prayer your servant is praying before you day and night for your servants, the people of Israel. I confess the sins we Israelites, including myself and my father's family, have committed against you. **7** We have acted very wickedly toward you. We have not obeyed the commands, decrees and laws you gave your servant Moses.

8 "Remember the instruction you gave your servant Moses, saying, 'If you are unfaithful, I will scatter you among the nations, **9** but if you return to me and obey my commands, then even if your exiled people are at the farthest horizon, I will gather them from there and bring them to the place I have chosen as a dwelling for my Name.'

10 "They are your servants and your people, whom you redeemed by your great strength and your mighty hand. **11** Lord, let your ear be attentive to the prayer of this your servant and to the prayer of your servants who delight in revering your name. Give your servant success today by granting him favor in the presence of this man."

I was cupbearer to the king.

Nehemiah 2:

1 In the month of Nisan in the twentieth year of King Artaxerxes, when wine was brought for him, I took the wine and gave it to the king. I had not been sad in his presence before, **2** so the king asked me, "Why does your face look so sad when you are not ill? This can be nothing but sadness of heart."

I was very much afraid, **3** but I said to the king, "May the king live forever! Why should my face not look sad when the city where my ancestors are buried lies in ruins, and its gates have been destroyed by fire?"

4 The king said to me, "What is it you want?"

Then I prayed to the God of heaven, **5** and I answered the king, "If it pleases the king and if your servant has found favor in his sight, let him send me to the city in Judah where my ancestors are buried so that I can rebuild it."

6 Then the king, with the queen sitting beside him, asked me, "How long will your journey take, and when will you get back?" It pleased the king to send me; so I set a time.

7 I also said to him, "If it pleases the king, may I have letters to the governors of Trans-Euphrates, so that they will provide me safe-conduct until I arrive in Judah? **8** And may I have a letter to Asaph, keeper of the royal park, so he will give me timber to make beams for the gates of the citadel by the temple and for the city wall and for the residence I will occupy?" And because the gracious hand of my God was on me, the king granted my requests. **9** So I went to the governors of Trans-Euphrates and gave them the king's letters. The king had also sent army officers and cavalry with me.

10 When Sanballat the Horonite and Tobiah the Ammonite official heard about this, they were very much disturbed that someone had come to promote the welfare of the Israelites.

11 I went to Jerusalem, and after staying there three days **12** I set out during the night with a few others. I had not told anyone what my God had put in my heart to do for Jerusalem. There were no mounts with me except the one I was riding on.

13 By night I went out through the Valley Gate toward the Jackal Well and the Dung Gate, examining the walls of Jerusalem, which had been broken down, and its gates, which had been destroyed by fire. **14** Then I moved on toward the Fountain Gate and the King's Pool, but there was not enough room for my mount to get through; **15** so I went up the valley by night, examining the wall. Finally, I turned back and reentered through the Valley Gate. **16** The officials did not know where I had gone or what I was doing, because as yet I had said nothing to the Jews or the priests or nobles or officials or any others who would be doing the work.

17 Then I said to them, "You see the trouble we are in: Jerusalem lies in ruins, and its gates have been burned with fire. Come, let us rebuild the wall of Jerusalem, and we will no longer be in disgrace." **18** I also told them about the gracious hand of my God on me and what the king had said to me.

They replied, "Let us start rebuilding." So they began this good work.

19 But when Sanballat the Horonite, Tobiah the Ammonite official and Geshem the Arab heard about it, they mocked and ridiculed us. "What is this you are doing?" they asked. "Are you rebelling against the king?"

20 I answered them by saying, "The God of heaven will give us success. We his servants will start rebuilding, but as for you, you have no share in Jerusalem or any claim or historic right to it" (NIV).

Nehemiah 3:

This chapter names those who helped with the rebuilding of the wall and which sections they repaired.

Nehemiah 4:

1 When Sanballat heard that we were rebuilding the wall, he became angry and was greatly incensed. He ridiculed the Jews, **2** and in the presence of his associates and the army of Samaria, he said, "What are those feeble Jews doing? Will they restore their wall? Will they offer sacrifices? Will they finish in a day? Can they bring the stones back to life from those heaps of rubble—burned as they are?"

3 Tobiah the Ammonite, who was at his side, said, "What they are building—even a fox climbing up on it would break down their wall of stones!"

4 Hear us, our God, for we are despised. Turn their insults back on their own heads. Give them over as plunder in a land of captivity. **5** Do not cover up their guilt or blot out their sins from your sight, for they have thrown insults in the face of the builders.

6 So we rebuilt the wall till all of it reached half its height, for the people worked with all their heart.

7 But when Sanballat, Tobiah, the Arabs, the Ammonites and the people of Ashdod heard that the repairs to Jerusalem's walls had gone ahead and that the gaps were being closed, they were very angry. **8** They all plotted together to come and fight against Jerusalem and stir up trouble against it. **9** But we prayed to our God and posted a guard day and night to meet this threat.

10 Meanwhile, the people in Judah said, "The strength of the laborers is giving out, and there is so much rubble that we cannot rebuild the wall."

11 Also our enemies said, "Before they know it or see us, we will be right there among them and will kill them and put an end to the work."

12 Then the Jews who lived near them came and told us ten times over, "Wherever you turn, they will attack us."

13 Therefore I stationed some of the people behind the lowest points of the wall at the exposed places, posting them by families, with their swords, spears and bows. **14** After I looked things over, I stood up and said to the nobles, the officials and the rest of the people, "Don't be afraid of them. Remember the Lord, who is great and awesome, and fight for your families, your sons and your daughters, your wives and your homes."

15 When our enemies heard that we were aware of their plot and that God had frustrated it, we all returned to the wall, each to our own work.

16 From that day on, half of my men did the work, while the other half were equipped with spears, shields, bows and armor. The officers posted themselves behind all the people of Judah **17** who were building the wall. Those who carried materials did their work with one hand and held a weapon in the other, **18** and each of the builders wore his sword at his side as he worked. But the man who sounded the trumpet stayed with me.

19 Then I said to the nobles, the officials and the rest of the people, "The work is extensive and spread out, and we are widely separated from each other along the wall. **20** Wherever you hear the sound of the trumpet, join us there. Our God will fight for us!"

21 So we continued the work with half the men holding spears, from the first light of dawn till the stars came out. **22** At that time I also said to the people, "Have every man and his helper stay inside Jerusalem at night, so they can serve us as guards by night and as workers by day." **23** Neither I nor my brothers nor my men nor the guards with me took off our clothes; each had his weapon, even when he went for water.

Nehemiah 5:

1 Now the men and their wives raised a great outcry against their fellow Jews. **2** Some were saying, "We and our sons and daughters are numerous; in order for us to eat and stay alive, we must get grain."

3 Others were saying, "We are mortgaging our fields, our vineyards and our homes to get grain during the famine."

4 Still others were saying, "We have had to borrow money to pay the king's tax on our fields and vineyards. **5** Although we are of the same flesh and blood as our fellow Jews and though our children are as good as theirs, yet we have to subject our sons and daughters to slavery. Some of our daughters have already been enslaved, but we are powerless, because our fields and our vineyards belong to others."

6 When I heard their outcry and these charges, I was very angry. **7** I pondered them in my mind and then accused the nobles and officials. I told them, "You are charging your own people interest!" So I called together a large meeting to deal with them **8** and said: "As far as possible, we have bought back our fellow Jews who were sold to the Gentiles. Now you are selling your own people, only for them to be sold back to us!" They kept quiet, because they could find nothing to say.

9 So I continued, "What you are doing is not right. Shouldn't you walk in the fear of our God to avoid the reproach of our Gentile enemies? **10** I and my brothers and my men are also lending the people money and grain. But let us stop charging interest! **11** Give back to them immediately their fields, vineyards, olive groves and houses, and also the interest you are charging them—one percent of the money, grain, new wine and olive oil."

12 "We will give it back," they said. "And we will not demand anything more from them. We will do as you say."

Then I summoned the priests and made the nobles and officials take an oath to do what they had promised. **13** I also shook out the folds of my robe and said, "In this way may God shake out of their house and possessions anyone who does not keep this promise. So may such a person be shaken out and emptied!"

At this the whole assembly said, "Amen," and praised the Lord. And the people did as they had promised.

14 Moreover, from the twentieth year of King Artaxerxes, when I was appointed to be their governor in the land of Judah, until his thirty-second year—twelve years—neither I nor my brothers ate the food allotted to the governor. **15** But the earlier governors—those preceding me—placed a heavy burden on the people and took forty shekels of silver from them in addition to food and wine. Their assistants also lorded it over the people. But out of reverence for God I did not act like that. **16** Instead, I devoted myself to the work on this wall. All my men were assembled there for the work; we did not acquire any land.

17 Furthermore, a hundred and fifty Jews and officials ate at my table, as well as those who came to us from the surrounding nations. **18** Each day one ox, six choice sheep and some poultry were prepared for me, and every ten days an abundant supply of wine of all kinds. In spite of all this, I never demanded the food allotted to the governor, because the demands were heavy on these people.

19 Remember me with favor, my God, for all I have done for these people.

Nehemiah 6:

1 When word came to Sanballat, Tobiah, Geshem the Arab and the rest of our enemies that I had rebuilt the wall and not a gap was left in it—though up to that time I had not set the doors in the gates— **2** Sanballat and Geshem sent me this message: "Come, let us meet together in one of the villages on the plain of Ono."

But they were scheming to harm me; **3** so I sent messengers to them with this reply: "I am carrying on a great project and cannot go down. Why should the work stop while I leave it and go down to you?" **4** Four times they sent me the same message, and each time I gave them the same answer.

5 Then, the fifth time, Sanballat sent his aide to me with the same message, and in his hand was an unsealed letter **6** in which was written:

"It is reported among the nations—and Geshem says it is true—that you and the Jews are plotting to revolt, and therefore you are building the wall. Moreover, according to these reports you are about to become their king **7** and have even appointed prophets to make this proclamation about you in Jerusalem: 'There is a king in Judah!' Now this report will get back to the king; so come, let us meet together."

8 I sent him this reply: "Nothing like what you are saying is happening; you are just making it up out of your head."

9 They were all trying to frighten us, thinking, "Their hands will get too weak for the work, and it will not be completed."

But I prayed, "Now strengthen my hands." [emphasis added]

10 One day I went to the house of Shemaiah son of Delaiah, the son of Mehetabel, who was shut in at his home. He said, "Let us meet in the house of God, inside the temple, and let us close the temple doors, because men are coming to kill you—by night they are coming to kill you."

11 But I said, "Should a man like me run away? Or should someone like me go into the temple to save his life? I will not go!" **12** I realized that God had not sent him, but that he had prophesied against me because Tobiah and Sanballat had hired him. **13** He had been hired to intimidate me so that I would commit a sin by doing this, and then they would give me a bad name to discredit me.

14 Remember Tobiah and Sanballat, my God, because of what they have done; remember also the prophet Noadiah and how she and the rest of the prophets have been trying to intimidate me. **15** So the wall was completed on the twenty-fifth of Elul, in fifty-two days.

16 When all our enemies heard about this, all the surrounding nations were afraid and lost their self-confidence, because they realized that this work had been done with the help of our God [emphasis added].

17 Also, in those days the nobles of Judah were sending many letters to Tobiah, and replies from Tobiah kept coming to them. **18** For many in Judah were under oath to him, since he was son-in-law to Shekaniah son of Arah, and his son Jehohanan had married the daughter of Meshullam son of Berekiah. **19** Moreover, they kept reporting to me his good deeds and then telling him what I said. And Tobiah sent letters to intimidate me" (NIV).

What lessons can we learn from the book of Nehemiah about how to handle disappointment, discouragement, defeat, depression, and despair?

Let's take each of these emotional conditions one at a time.

First, Nehemiah grieved over his beloved city, Jerusalem. He received this report about the city: "Those who survived the exile and are back in the province are in great trouble and disgrace. The wall of Jerusalem is broken down, and its gates have been burned with fire" (Nehemiah 1:3 NIV). This distressed Nehemiah so much that he sat down and wept. For several days, he mourned and fasted and prayed. I think that we can say that Nehemiah was greatly disappointed over the condition of Jerusalem.

I do not think he felt discouraged, though, or if he did, he overcame that discouragement very quickly. He mourned for several days but he also took positive action. And he fasted and prayed.

When he prayed, he confessed Israel's sin and his own sin of failing to follow God's commands. He also asked for God's favor in the presence of the king because he planned to seek permission of the king to go back to his homeland and repair the walls of the city of Jerusalem. He tells us in Nehemiah 2:12 that God had put it into his heart to do this.

Nehemiah did not experience defeat because he followed through with the plan that God had put into his heart. Despite severe opposition from others, he continued with the work. He kept his mind focused on what God had called him to do. He did not second-guess that call. He refused to dialogue with his opposition about what he was doing. He did not have time to do that because he was too busy "carrying on a great project." His enemies asked him four times to leave the work to go talk with them, but he always refused. He did not sway from his resolve to complete the task of rebuilding the wall. His enemies even accused him of being a traitor to the king, but still Nehemiah kept pursuing his calling.

He prayed for God's help over Israel's enemies. And when he learned that his enemies threatened to kill those working on the wall, he put into place a system of protection. Half of the workers were armed and ready to protect the others while they worked on the wall. Eventually, the wall was completely rebuilt – in fifty-two days! That is less than two months!

Nehemiah also took action when he realized that some of the Jews were taking advantage of their fellow Jews who were poor. He insisted that they stop doing this, and they did stop. Nehemiah stood up for what is right and thereby brought about change.

It does not seem that Nehemiah suffered from depression because he kept doing what he knew God wanted him to do, and he stood up for what was right. He did not waver in this. He continued to lead the people of Judah (the southern kingdom of the divided Israel) by encouraging them to repent and to promise the Lord that they would obey His commands. He trusted in God to help him do what God had put in his heart to do. And he experienced the completion of the job.

Even though Nehemiah saw and experienced some extremely depressing things – the destruction of the walls of Jerusalem, the captivity of his people by Gentiles, ridicule and death threats by his enemies, and the deplorable spiritual condition of the people – he had hope in God. He did not despair but prayed for God's help. And he got right to work and worked hard. He inspired the people to work hard. He saw the problems, and he implemented tactics to solve the problems. He did not let anything deter him.

Are you faithfully doing what God has called you to do? If you are a believer, God has something for you to do for His kingdom. Are you focused on that, or are you distracted by your opposition? Do you weep over the spiritual condition of God's people and their disgrace? Are you doing something to right the wrong or are you sitting by watching it happen?

The child of God who doggedly does what God has summoned him to do, who stands against injustice and unrighteousness, and who calls upon the true and living God for help, thereby takes the first steps to ward off disappointment, discouragement, defeat, depression, and despair!

Chapter Twenty-Five
The Study of Jehoshaphat

"As they began to sing and praise, the LORD set ambushes against the men of Ammon and Moab and Mount Seir who were invading Judah, and they were defeated."
2 Chronicles 20:22 NIV

We learned in an earlier lesson that one of the first things Job did when tragedy struck his life was to fall on his face and worship the true and living God.

Have you ever thought about the power of praise during times of danger, sadness, anxiety, loss, and grief?

In this lesson, you will read about how the enemies of Judah were defeated when the army of Judah shouted praises to God as they went to battle. Jehoshaphat had led the people of Judah in seeking help from the Lord because they knew that their army was not powerful enough to defeat the army which was attacking them. They did not know what to do, but they were looking to the Lord for deliverance. As they went to face their enemies, those at the head of the army shouted and sang praises to God.

Jehoshaphat was king of Judah after his father, Asa. A passage in 2 Chronicles says this about Jehoshaphat:

"The LORD was with Jehoshaphat because he followed the ways of his father David before him. He did not consult the Baal [false gods] but sought the God of his father and followed his commands rather than the practices of Israel. The LORD established the kingdom under his control; and all Judah brought gifts to Jehoshaphat, so that he had great wealth and honor. His heart was devoted to the ways of the LORD; furthermore, he removed the high places and the Asherah poles [poles dedicated to the goddess Asherah] from Judah" (2 Chronicles 17:3-6 NIV).

2 Chronicles 20:

1 After this, the Moabites and Ammonites with some of the Meunites came to wage war against Jehoshaphat.

2 Some people came and told Jehoshaphat, "A vast army is coming against you from Edom, from the other side of the Dead Sea. It is already in Hazezon Tamar" (that is, En Gedi). **3** Alarmed, Jehoshaphat resolved to inquire of the Lord, and he proclaimed a fast for all Judah. **4** The people of Judah came together to seek help from the Lord; indeed, they came from every town in Judah to seek him.

5 Then Jehoshaphat stood up in the assembly of Judah and Jerusalem at the temple of the Lord in the front of the new courtyard **6** and said:

"Lord, the God of our ancestors, are you not the God who is in heaven? You rule over all the kingdoms of the nations. Power and might are in your hand, and no one can withstand you. **7** Our God, did you not drive out the inhabitants of this land before your people Israel and give it forever to the descendants of Abraham your friend? **8** They have lived in it and have built in it a sanctuary for your Name, saying, **9** 'If calamity comes upon us, whether the sword of judgment, or plague or famine, we will stand in your presence before this temple that bears your Name and will cry out to you in our distress, and you will hear us and save us.'

10 "But now here are men from Ammon, Moab and Mount Seir, whose territory you would not allow Israel to invade when they came from Egypt; so they turned away from them and did not destroy them. **11** See how they are repaying us by coming to drive us out of the possession you gave us as an inheritance. **12** Our God, will you not judge them? For we have no power to face this vast army that is attacking us. We do not know what to do, but our eyes are on you."

13 All the men of Judah, with their wives and children and little ones, stood there before the Lord.

14 Then the Spirit of the Lord came on Jahaziel son of Zechariah, the son of Benaiah, the son of Jeiel, the son of Mattaniah, a Levite and descendant of Asaph, as he stood in the assembly.

15 He said: "Listen, King Jehoshaphat and all who live in Judah and Jerusalem! This is what the Lord says to you: 'Do not be afraid or discouraged because of this vast army. For the battle is not yours, but God's. **16** Tomorrow march down against them. They will be climbing up by the Pass of Ziz, and you will find them at the end of the gorge in the Desert of Jeruel. **17** You will not have to fight this battle. Take up your positions; stand firm and see the deliverance the Lord will give you, Judah and Jerusalem. Do not be afraid; do not be discouraged. Go out to face them tomorrow, and the Lord will be with you.'"

18 Jehoshaphat bowed down with his face to the ground, and all the people of Judah and Jerusalem fell down in worship before the Lord.

19 Then some Levites from the Kohathites and Korahites stood up and praised the Lord, the God of Israel, with a very loud voice.

20 Early in the morning they left for the Desert of Tekoa. As they set out, Jehoshaphat stood and said, "Listen to me, Judah and people of Jerusalem! Have faith in the Lord your God and you will be upheld; have faith in his prophets and you will be successful." **21** After consulting the people, Jehoshaphat appointed men to sing to the Lord and to praise him for the splendor of his holiness as they went out at the head of the army, saying:

"Give thanks to the Lord,
  for his love endures forever."

22 As they began to sing and praise, the Lord set ambushes against the men of Ammon and Moab and Mount Seir who were invading Judah, and they were defeated. 23 The Ammonites and Moabites rose up against the men from Mount Seir to destroy and annihilate them. After they finished slaughtering the men from Seir, they helped to destroy one another [emphasis added].

24 When the men of Judah came to the place that overlooks the desert and looked toward the vast army, they saw only dead bodies lying on the ground; no one had escaped. **25** So Jehoshaphat and his men went to carry off their plunder, and they found among them a great amount of equipment and clothing and also articles of value—more than they could take away. There was so much plunder that it took three days to collect it. **26** On the fourth day they assembled in the Valley of Berakah, where they praised the Lord. This is why it is called the Valley of Berakah to this day.

27 Then, led by Jehoshaphat, all the men of Judah and Jerusalem returned joyfully to Jerusalem, for the Lord had given them cause to rejoice over their enemies. **28** They entered Jerusalem and went to the temple of the Lord with harps and lyres and trumpets.

29 The fear of God came on all the surrounding kingdoms when they heard how the Lord had fought against the enemies of Israel. **30** And the kingdom of Jehoshaphat was at peace, for his God had given him rest on every side (NIV).

We are commanded to praise God. Psalm 150 says:

> **1** Praise the Lord!
> Praise God in his sanctuary;
> praise him in his mighty heavens!
> **2** Praise him for his mighty deeds;
> praise him according to his excellent greatness!
> **3** Praise him with trumpet sound;
> praise him with lute and harp!
> **4** Praise him with tambourine and dance;
> praise him with strings and pipe!
> **5** Praise him with sounding cymbals;
> praise him with loud clashing cymbals!
> **6** Let everything that has breath praise the Lord!

Praise the Lord! (ESV).

Praise exudes from this psalm! God does not **need** our praise. He is complete, perfect, and sufficient in and of Himself. He does not have an ego problem that causes Him to crave our praise to fill His need. But He certainly deserves our praise. Psalm 48:1 says:

> "Great is the LORD and greatly to be praised in the city of our God!" (ESV).

God would still be every bit almighty God if we ceased to praise Him, but our praise of Him does something for us! It changes our perspective because it causes us to gaze upon Him and trust Him more. Withholding praise only **magnifies** our circumstances in our eyes because, instead of looking to Him who is all-powerful, we look at our overwhelming circumstances and inward at our weakness and inadequacy. It is easy to praise God when things are going my way and I am delighting in my life, but praise is most urgent when things are not going my way and I feel like my life is falling apart. To withhold praise when I am feeling low only makes me feel worse. It sends me deeper and deeper into self-pity and despair.

Praising God means to meditate upon His great qualities and His great deeds and to give Him honor with our hearts and lips for these things. Some examples of God's qualities for which we can praise Him are His power and might, His sovereignty (His rule over all things), His justice, His holiness, His wisdom, His mercy, His love, His grace, and His help. Examples of His deeds are His acts of creation, His sustaining all things, His daily provisions, His provision of a Redeemer, His provision of the Holy Spirit to help us daily to live the Christian life, His keeping of our souls until we reach Heaven.

Notice how David praises God in Psalm 86:

> **1** Hear me, Lord, and answer me,
>   for I am poor and needy.
> **2** Guard my life, for I am faithful to you;
>   save your servant who trusts in you.
>   You are my God; **3** have mercy on me, Lord,
>   for I call to you all day long.
> **4** Bring joy to your servant, Lord,
>   for I put my trust in you.
> **5** You, Lord, are forgiving and good,

abounding in love to all who call to you.
6 Hear my prayer, Lord;
    listen to my cry for mercy.
7 When I am in distress, I call to you,
    because you answer me.
8 Among the gods there is none like you, Lord;
    no deeds can compare with yours.
9 All the nations you have made
    will come and worship before you, Lord;
    they will bring glory to your name.
10 For you are great and do marvelous deeds;
    you alone are God.
11 Teach me your way, Lord,
    that I may rely on your faithfulness;
    give me an undivided heart,
    that I may fear your name.
12 I will praise you, Lord my God, with all my heart;
    I will glorify your name forever.
13 For great is your love toward me;
    you have delivered me from the depths,
    from the realm of the dead.
14 Arrogant foes are attacking me, O God;
    ruthless people are trying to kill me—
    they have no regard for you.
15 But you, Lord, are a compassionate and gracious God,
    slow to anger, abounding in love and faithfulness.
16 Turn to me and have mercy on me;
    show your strength in behalf of your servant;
    save me, because I serve you
    just as my mother did.
17 Give me a sign of your goodness,
    that my enemies may see it and be put to shame,
    for you, Lord, have helped me and comforted me (NIV).

God's Qualities

He is forgiving.
He is good.
He abounds in love to all who call to Him.

There is no other god like Him.
He is great.
He alone is God.
His love is great towards me.
He is compassionate.
He is gracious.
He is slow to anger.
He abounds in love.
He abounds in faithfulness.

God's Deeds

No deeds can compare with His.
He made all the nations.
He does marvelous deeds.
He answers me.
He has delivered me from the depths of the grave.
He has helped me.
He has comforted me.

David's Requests

Hear and answer me.
Guard my life.
Save me.
Have mercy on me.
Bring joy to me.
Hear my prayer.
Listen to my cry for mercy.

Teach me Your ways.
Give me an undivided heart.
Turn to me.
Have mercy on me.

David's Condition

He is poor and needy.
He is devoted to God.
He claims God is his God.
He trusts in God.
He calls on God all day long.
He lifts up his soul to God.
He will call on God in the day of trouble.

He will walk in God's truth.
He wants to fear God's name.
He will praise God with all his heart.

David's Requests	David's Condition
Grant me Your strength.	He will glorify God's name forever.
Save me.	
Give me a sign of Your goodness so that my enemies may see it and be put to shame.	

Consider also what Paul says in Philippians 4:6 & 7:

> "Do not be anxious about anything, but in every situation, by prayer and petition, with thanksgiving, present your requests to God. And the peace of God, which transcends all understanding, will guard your hearts and your minds in Christ Jesus" (NIV).

Notice that God does not want us to be anxious about anything, no matter how severe our circumstances. Instead, He wants us to go to Him in prayer and pour out our requests to Him. But notice also that Paul mentions thanksgiving, which is praise. Our prayers of petition or request should include thanksgiving for who God is and what He has already done – just like David did in Psalm 86. Then God's unfathomable peace will guard our hearts and minds. Don't you love this picture of God's great peace guarding your heart and your mind? He will give peace to your weary, anxious heart and mind!

Praise God despite your problems. Praise will not necessarily eliminate your problems, but you will become hopeful about your circumstances and thankful for what you have, and your depression will eventually dissipate.

Chapter Twenty-Six

Word of Encouragement

> "Consider it pure joy, my brothers and sisters, whenever you face trials of many kinds, because you know that the testing of your faith produces perseverance. Let perseverance finish its work so that you may be mature and complete, not lacking anything."
> James 1:2-4 NIV

Has a painful situation in your life ever driven you to depression and despair? Have the severe circumstances that you face cast you down so low that you no longer enjoy life and you seek refuge through some means of escape?

If so, you must ask yourself if this is how God wants a child of His to live. If you are familiar at all with the biblical teaching on the abundant life that is available in Jesus Christ, then your answer will be no. In John 10:10, Jesus says, "The thief [Satan] comes only to steal and kill and destroy. I came that they may have life and have it abundantly" (ESV). God wants to fill you with His Spirit, and the fruit of the Spirit is love, joy, peace, patience, kindness, goodness, faithfulness, gentleness and self-control (Galatians 5:22 & 23). These things are supposed to be abundant in our lives, not depression and despair.

Of course, we will all have problems in life, and those problems are very real and sometimes very painful. However, we can be filled with genuine love, joy, and peace despite the trials.

Sometimes, God brings painful trials into our lives in order to fashion us to be like Jesus Christ. From the time we become Christians until the day we die, God is working in us to conform us more and more into the image of Christ. Even after we come into God's family from the dominion of Satan, we have a remnant of the sinful nature, and God seeks to put to death the control of the sinful nature (Romans 6:1-14). Often, God uses trials in the form of adverse circumstances to do His work of sanctification in our lives.

While we should welcome these trials as confirmation of our salvation and proof of God's love for us, we often recoil from trials and just want them to go away. We often view them as annoying irritations. Others are downright painful. God uses trials in the lives of His children in order to discipline them. "My son, do not despise the LORD'S discipline or be weary of his reproof, for the LORD reproves him whom he loves, as a father the son in whom he delights" (Proverbs 3:11 & 12 ESV).

The focus of this chapter is biblical instruction on the correct reactions to trials. **Remember that true followers of Jesus Christ are called to handle every situation in life in light of God's revelation in Scripture; therefore, we are to handle trials biblically.**

Hebrews 12:5-15:

5 And have you completely forgotten this word of encouragement that addresses you as a father addresses his son? It says,

"My son, do not make light of the Lord's discipline,

and do not lose heart when he rebukes you,
6 because the Lord disciplines the one he loves,and he
chastens everyone he accepts as his son." [Proverbs 3:11 & 12]

7 Endure hardship as discipline; God is treating you as his children. For what children are not disciplined by their father? **8** If you are not disciplined—and everyone undergoes discipline—then you are not legitimate, not true sons and daughters at all. **9** Moreover, we have all had human fathers who disciplined us and we respected them for it. How much more should we submit to the Father of spirits and live! **10** They disciplined us for a little while as they thought best; but God disciplines us for our good, in order that we may share in his holiness. **11** No discipline seems pleasant at the time, but painful. Later on, however, it produces a harvest of righteousness and peace for those who have been trained by it.

12 Therefore, strengthen your feeble arms and weak knees. **13** "Make level paths for your feet," so that the lame may not be disabled, but rather healed.

14 Make every effort to live in peace with everyone and to be holy; without holiness no one will see the Lord. **15** See to it that no one falls short of the grace of God and that no bitter root grows up to cause trouble and defile many (NIV).

Dictionary definitions:

discipline[15] – 1. training expected to produce a specific character or pattern of behavior, especially training that produces moral or mental improvement 2. punishment intended to correct or train

---

[15] The American Heritage Dictionary of the English Language (Boston: Houghton Mifflin Harcourt Publishing Company, 2016), p. 514.

chasten[16] – 1. to correct by punishment or reproof; take to task 2. to restrain; subdue 3. to rid of excess; refine or purify

We can think of discipline as God setting us straight or correcting us. It also means to train. God is training us to be mature, godly Christians.

He uses many different kinds of trials to perfect us. These trials sometimes come in the form of illness, financial difficulties, loss of something precious to us, relationship problems, disappointing circumstances, danger, accidents, and the like.

Wrong, sinful reactions to the Lord's discipline/chastening:

1. Making light of it (verse 5). (The King James Version says, "My son, despise not thou the chastening of the Lord…")

What would be an indication that I am making light of or despising the Lord's chastening? Some indications might be trying to ignore the trial and/or what God wants to accomplish within me, trying to minimize the trial, as if it is no big deal, not appreciating that this trial has come from God for my good, for example. Becoming angry and resentful is another sinful reaction to the trial.

2. Losing heart because of it (verse 5).

We probably all know very well what it means to lose heart when we are being disciplined by the Lord. I can get discouraged and depressed. I may want to give up. I feel sorry for myself. I become weary and bogged down by the trial. I feel that God must not love me or that His treatment is unfair and unwarranted. I feel like I just cannot handle this painful trial; it is more than I can take!

---

[16] Ibid., p. 314.

3. Not enduring it (verse 7).

To fail to endure the chastening would be to not patiently allow God to have His way with me and to not continue to look favorably upon the Lord's work in my life. It means to grow impatient with the trial and to decide that I do not want to cooperate with God in this trial. It might mean that I stop trying to grow spiritually because I am tired of the trial. Trying to escape the trial is another sinful reaction.

4. Not submitting to it (verse 9).

I can refrain from submitting to the Lord's discipline/chastening by not accepting the trial, not cooperating with the Lord, trying to get rid of the trial, refusing to allow the trial to reform me, resisting God's working through the trial, willfully sinning, and such. James 1:2-4 says, "Consider it pure joy, my brothers and sisters, whenever you face trials of many kinds, because you know that the testing of your faith produces perseverance. **Let perseverance finish its work so that you may be mature and complete, not lacking anything**" [emphasis added] (NIV). This makes it clear that I am supposed to allow the trial to work in me to bring about the changes that God desires – that I may become the person that He wants me to be.

5. Becoming bitter over it (verse 15).

Rather than thanking God for the trial that He has allowed to come into my life to cause me to become more like Christ, I can become angry at Him. I can resent the trials that He sends for this purpose. If I allow this attitude to fester, I will become very sour and think biting thoughts and perhaps speak biting words. This bitterness comes from not submitting to the Lord's will for this trial to discipline me.

There are several reasons why the above attitudes and behaviors are sinful:

1. God chastens all of His children. This is how He treats His children. Trials are a manifestation of God's love for His children.

2. God loves me. Trials are not meant to hurt me but to help me. He is for me, not against me. He is worthy of my trust, even when He is disciplining me.

3. God is in control of everyone and everything. He can bring about just the right amount of pressure to mold me but not break me.

4. God has infinite wisdom; He knows exactly what I need to grow in His likeness. He designs my trials carefully, purposefully, strategically, tactically, and lovingly.

5. God is good, and I can trust Him. He knows me better than I know myself, and no one loves me more than He does.

6. The trial has been designed by a loving God to bring something good (righteousness or holiness) into my life. The passage in Hebrews says that though discipline is painful, in time it will bring about good.

What is the consequence of not reacting biblically to the Lord's chastening?

If I do not look upon His chastening as a valuable lesson to be learned for my sanctification, I will go through the trial without gaining anything from the painful experience. The chastening will be a painful experience that benefits me nothing. Hebrews 5:11 says that discipline or chastening will bring about the good fruit of righteousness "for those who have been trained by it." If I have not been trained by God's discipline or chastening through the trial due to my bad attitude and uncooperative spirit, I will not acquire the good fruit that God intends for me to have.

Good fruit from the chastening is not automatic. In other words, we do not automatically grow or change simply because of the trial that God sends to us. We must cooperate with God as He chastens us, or we will not gain from the experience what God intends for us.

This cooperation entails trying to discern why God is sending the trial. What is He trying to teach me? Is there sin in my heart and life that I am cherishing? For example, have I become prideful? Independent of the Lord and self-sufficient? Are there idols in my heart? Have I become worldly in my outlook and practices? Is there resentment or hatred in my heart toward anyone? If so, it may be that He has sent this trial into my life to purify my heart and life of these sinful attitudes and practices. To cooperate with the Lord in His discipline of me, I must recognize that He has sent this trial to cause me to see my sin and to forsake it. This is part of the sanctification process. If I merely mindlessly endure the trial but have no idea what this trial has been designed to accomplish in my life, then I may not gain from the trial what He wants for me to learn.

There may be times, however, when I am not able to recognize the reason for the trial; yet, I still must cooperate with God in the trial and react with a godly attitude.

The following are other passages which indicate that God works through trials or sufferings to bring about our sanctification:

Romans 5:1-5:

"Therefore, since we have been justified through faith, we have peace with God through our Lord Jesus Christ, through whom we have gained access by faith into this grace in which we now stand. And we boast in the hope of the glory of God. **Not only so, but we also glory in our sufferings, because we know that suffering produces perseverance; perseverance, character; and character, hope. And hope does not put us to shame, because God's love has been poured out into our hearts through the Holy Spirit, who has been given to us**" [emphasis added] (NIV).

James 1:2-4:

"Consider it pure joy, my brothers and sisters, whenever you face trials of many kinds, because you know that the testing of your faith produces perseverance. Let perseverance finish its work so that you may be mature and complete, not lacking anything" (NIV).

"My brethren, count it all joy when ye fall into various trials; Knowing this, that the testing of your faith worketh patience. But let patience have her perfect work, that ye may be perfect and entire, lacking nothing" (KJV).

2 Corinthians 1:3-7:

"Praise be to the God and Father of our Lord Jesus Christ, the Father of compassion and the God of all comfort, who comforts us in all our troubles, so that we can comfort those in any trouble with the comfort we ourselves receive from God. For just as we share abundantly in the sufferings of Christ, so also our comfort abounds through Christ. If we are distressed, it is for your comfort and salvation; if we are comforted, it is for your comfort, which produces in you patient endurance of the same sufferings we suffer. And our hope for you is firm, because we know that just as you share in our sufferings, so also you share in our comfort" (NIV).

Are you cooperating with what God is attempting to do in your life? Do you view God's chastening favorably – as something good that He wants to accomplish in your life? Or do you whine and complain and grow bitter? Do you become weighed down and depressed when the Lord chastens you? Or worse, do you simply put God out of your mind and go on living the way that you have been living?

In an attempt to improve my health, I have been walking four or five times every week for thirty minutes. It is something I make myself do in order to reap many benefits to my body. I rarely feel like doing it. I go the same route every day, and I know about how many steps it takes to go the route and get back home. Many times on my walk, I think about how much longer it will be before I will reach home and I can go lie down, which is immensely more comfortable than walking!

One day on my walk as I was about half way home, in my weariness, a silly thought came into my head. (It must have been all that oxygen reviving my brain!) What a relief it would be, I thought, if God would just pick me up and place me at my doorstep! I dreaded walking the second half of the walk and wished I could be done. Immediately, I remembered that if I could be suddenly whisked home, which of course was not going to happen, I would miss out on fully gaining the results which were the very reason for my walk. One does not reap the benefits of walking without walking! And every time I finish my walk, I am so glad that I endured the discomfort of walking that half hour.

It is the same with trials. It is when we endure the discomfort until the end of the trial that we reap the full rewards.

I heard an interesting and somewhat humorous story from one of my pastors. Several years ago, he had on-going car problems. He frequently had to take his car to a mechanic to get it fixed. He became annoyed and frustrated because he viewed this as a waste of time. He kept thinking about all of the other things he needed to be doing – such as preparing for his weekly sermons, sharing the Gospel with others, and taking care of his family. Trips to the mechanic were eating up valuable time. Well, as time progressed, he witnessed to the mechanic about God's saving grace, and eventually, the mechanic came to faith in Christ! What the pastor initially viewed as a waste of time turned out to be a blessing in disguise! After the mechanic received Jesus Christ as his Lord and Savior, he became a valuable member of our church. It sure seems like God caused my pastor's car problems so that he would take the car to Eric, giving him the opportunity to share the Gospel with Eric and he would get saved. What at first seems like an irritating trial could actually be the opportunity to experience something great.

Allow your trials to accomplish in your life the good that God has designed. Don't resist His work because a trial is painful. God will not only see you through the trial if you trust Him; He will use the trial to help bring you to godly maturity.

This is one way to biblically handle disappointment, discouragement, defeat, depression and despair.

Chapter Twenty-Seven

Psalm 73 and Psalm 37

"Do not fret because of those who are evil or be envious of those
who do wrong; for like the grass they will soon wither,
like green plants they will soon die away."
Psalm 37:1 NIV

Contained in one of Jeremiah's prayers is a question he asked of God: "Why does the way of the wicked prosper?" This question has been asked by many people throughout the ages. In this lesson, we will look into Scripture where this concept of the wicked prospering is addressed.

Who has not at times observed that wicked people seemingly do very well in life while good people suffer? We all have probably watched corrupt politicians and unseemly actors and athletes on television or other media flaunting their wealth and status while advocating for and engaging in ungodly practices. If we dwell on this disparity for very long, we can really get depressed! If this observation has ever depressed you, you are not alone.

In this chapter, there are two psalms that deal with this topic. Correctly understanding God's message in these psalms should help to evaporate the frustration you might feel about the conflict between the welfare of the righteous compared to that of evil people in this world. Wrong thinking can cause depression. Right thinking should bring us joy. God's Word brings hope to His children who are striving to know and to please Him.

Psalm 73:

> **1** Surely God is good to Israel,
>   to those who are pure in heart.
> **2** But as for me, my feet had almost slipped;
>   I had nearly lost my foothold.
> **3** For I envied the arrogant
>   when I saw the prosperity of the wicked.
> **4** They have no struggles;
>   their bodies are healthy and strong.
> **5** They are free from common human burdens;
>   they are not plagued by human ills.
> **6** Therefore pride is their necklace;
>   they clothe themselves with violence.
> **7** From their callous hearts comes iniquity;
>   their evil imaginations have no limits.
> **8** They scoff, and speak with malice;
>   with arrogance they threaten oppression.
> **9** Their mouths lay claim to heaven,
>   and their tongues take possession of the earth.
> **10** Therefore their people turn to them
>   and drink up waters in abundance.
> **11** They say, 'How would God know?
>   Does the Most High know anything?'
> **12** This is what the wicked are like –
>   always free of care, they go on amassing wealth.
> **13** Surely in vain I have kept my heart pure
>   and have washed my hands in innocence.

14 All day long I have been afflicted,
   and every morning brings new punishments.
15 If I had spoken out like that,
   I would have betrayed your children.
16 When I tried to understand all this,
   it troubled me deeply
17 till I entered the sanctuary of God;
   then I understood their final destiny.
18 Surely you place them on slippery ground;
   you cast them down to ruin.
19 How suddenly are they destroyed,
   completely swept away by terrors!
20 They are like a dream when one awakes;
   when you arise, LORD,
   you will despise them as fantasies.
21 When my heart was grieved
   and my spirit embittered,
22 I was senseless and ignorant;
   I was a brute beast before you.
23 Yet I am always with you;
   you hold me by my right hand.
24 You guide me with your counsel,
   and afterward you will take me into glory.
25 Whom have I in heaven but you?
   And earth has nothing I desire besides you.
26 My flesh and my heart may fail,
   but God is the strength of my heart
   and my portion forever.
27 Those who are far from you will perish;
   you destroy all who are unfaithful to you.
28 But as for me, it is good to be near God.
   I have made the Sovereign LORD my refuge;

I will tell of all your deeds" (NIV).

What is the writer of this psalm, the worship leader Asaph, saying?

1. He is deeply troubled when he sees the prosperity of the wicked. It seems that they have lives of ease, free from care, and that everything goes their way.

2. He envies the arrogant because of their prosperity.

3. He feels that it was of no benefit to have lived righteously, for his life has been afflicted, and he does not enjoy a comfortable life like the wicked do.

4. Then he goes to the sanctuary and is exposed to the Word of God.

5. He realizes that he almost made a mistake by forsaking righteous living. He nearly lost his foothold – the thing that kept him grounded and secure.

What caused him to stumble?

1. He felt that his reward for being righteous was that he was plagued and punished every day.

2. He came to the conclusion that he had not gained anything good by keeping his heart pure and living righteously.

How did he view the wicked?

1. They have no struggles.

2. They are healthy and strong.

3. They are free from the burdens common to man.

4. They are not plagued by human ills.

5. Pride is their necklace.

6. They clothe themselves with violence.

7. Their hearts are callous.

8. They cause injury.

9. Their evil conceit is unlimited.

10. They scoff and speak with malice.

11. They are arrogant.

12. They threaten oppression.

13. They claim to have ownership of Heaven – to be going to Heaven.

14. They think they own the Earth.

15. They are honored by others, and others seek to get something from them.

16. They think they can get away with evil – that God does not know about their wickedness.

17. They are carefree.

18. They become more and more wealthy.

What changed the psalmist's mind about the futility of living righteously? He entered the sanctuary of God where he came in contact with the truth of God's Word.

What is actually the destiny of the wicked?

1. God has placed them on slippery ground.

2. God casts them down to ruin.

3. They will suddenly be destroyed.

4. They will be swept away by terrors.

5. God will look upon them, despise them as only a phantom, a dream – not real!

Before the psalmist came to his senses, his heart was grieved – it was weighed down and sorrowful – depressed! He had become bitter. He was not seeing things accurately; he had a crude understanding of how to live life. He had not yet come to see things as God sees them.

Then he went to the sanctuary of God and came to understand that while evil people may succeed for a time in their wicked ways, their doom is coming!

Asaph ends the psalm with praises to God for the benefits to the person who knows Him:

1. God holds him by his right hand.

2. God guides him with His counsel.

3. God will take him into glory.

4. God is the strength of his heart.

5. God is his portion forever.

6. God is his refuge.

Psalm 37:

> **1** Do not fret because of those who are evil
>   or be envious of those who do wrong;
> **2** for like the grass they will soon wither,
>   like green plants they will soon die away.
> **3** Trust in the LORD and do good;
>   dwell in the land and enjoy safe pasture.
> **4** Take delight in the LORD,
>   and he will give you the desires of your heart.
> **5** Commit your way to the LORD;
>   trust in him and he will do this:
> **6** He will make your righteous reward shine like the dawn,
>   your vindication like the noonday sun.
> **7** Be still before the LORD
>   and wait patiently for him;
>   do not fret when people succeed in their ways,
>   when they carry out their wicked schemes.
> **8** Refrain from anger and turn from wrath;
>   do not fret – it leads only to evil.
> **9** For those who are evil will be destroyed,
>   but those who hope in the LORD will inherit the land.
> **10** A little while, and the wicked will be no more;
>   though you look for them, they will not be found.
> **11** But the meek will inherit the land

and enjoy peace and prosperity.
12 The wicked plot against the righteous
    and gnash their teeth at them;
13 but the LORD laughs at the wicked,
    for he knows their day is coming.
14 The wicked draw the sword
    and bend the bow
    to bring down the poor and needy,
    to slay those whose ways are upright.
15 But their swords will pierce their own hearts,
    and their bows will be broken.
16 Better the little that the righteous have
    than the wealth of many wicked;
17 for the power of the wicked will be broken,
    but the LORD upholds the righteous.
18 The blameless spend their days under the LORD's care,
    and their inheritance will endure forever.
19 In times of disaster they will not wither;
    in days of famine they will enjoy plenty.
20 But the wicked will perish:
    Though the LORD's enemies are like the flowers of the field,
    they will be consumed, they will go up in smoke.
21 The wicked borrow and do not repay,
    but the righteous give generously;
22 those the LORD blesses will inherit the land,
    but those he curses will be destroyed.
23 The LORD makes firm the steps
    of the one who delights in him;
24 though he may stumble, he will not fall,
    for the LORD upholds him with his hand.
25 I was young and now I am old,
    yet I have never seen the righteous forsaken
    or their children begging bread.

26 They are always generous and lend freely;
   their children will be a blessing.
27 Turn from evil and do good;
   then you will dwell in the land forever.
28 For the LORD loves the just
   and will not forsake his faithful ones.
   Wrongdoers will be completely destroyed;
   the offspring of the wicked will perish.
29 the righteous will inherit the land
   and dwell in it forever.
30 The mouth of the righteous utter wisdom,
   and their tongues speak what is just.
31 The law of their God is in their hearts;
   their feet do not slip.
32 The wicked lie in wait for the righteous,
   intent on putting them to death;
33 but the LORD will not leave them in the power of the wicked
   or let them be condemned when brought to trial.
34 Hope in the LORD
   and keep his way.
   He will exalt you to inherit the land;
   when the wicked are destroyed, you will see it.
35 I have seen a wicked and ruthless man
   flourishing like a luxuriant native tree,
36 but he soon passed away and was no more;
   though I looked for him, he could not be found.
37 Consider the blameless, observe the upright;
   a future awaits those who seek peace.
38 But all sinners will be destroyed;
   there will be no future for the wicked.
39 The salvation of the righteous comes from the LORD;
   he is their stronghold in time of trouble.

40 The LORD helps them and delivers them;
he delivers them from the wicked and saves them,
because they take refuge in him (NIV).

What is the psalmist, David, saying in this psalm?

1. Do not fret because of evil people. To fret means to be constantly worried or anxious. God is telling us to not be concerned about the disparity of seeing the wicked getting away with evil and actually prospering while the righteous sometimes suffer.

2. Do not be envious of those who do wrong.

Why is He telling us these things?

1. The wicked will soon wither like the grass.

2. They will soon die away like green plants.

3. Evil men will be cut off.

4. Those who hope in the Lord will inherit the land.

5. The wicked last for only a short time.

6. The meek will inherit the land and enjoy great peace.

7. The Lord laughs at the wicked because He knows that their day is coming.

8. The wicked try to harm the poor and needy.

9. The wicked try to slay those who are upright, but God will cause their own devices to turn against them and do them harm.

10. The power of the wicked will be broken.

11. The Lord upholds the righteous.

12. The Lord knows how the blameless live their lives, and their inheritance will endure forever.

13. The blameless will not wither in times of disaster.

14. Even when famine strikes, the blameless will have plenty.

15. The wicked will perish; they will vanish like smoke.

16. The Lord blesses the blameless by allowing them to inherit the land.

17. The Lord curses the wicked, and He cuts them off.

18. The Lord delights in the blameless and makes his steps firm.

19. The Lord upholds the righteous with His hands.

20. The righteous have never been forsaken by the Lord.

21. God will bless the children of the righteous.

22. The Lord loves the just.

23. The Lord will not forsake the righteous.

24. The Lord will always protect the righteous.

25. The offspring of the wicked will be cut off by the Lord.

26. The righteous will inherit the land and will dwell in it forever.

What is David saying to do instead of fretting over the wicked?

1. Trust in the Lord.

2. Do good.

3. Take delight in the Lord.

4. Commit your way to the Lord.

5. Be still before the Lord.

6. Wait patiently for the Lord.

7. Refrain from anger and turn from wrath.

8. Turn from evil.

9. Hope in the Lord.

10. Keep His way.

It takes faith to implement these attitudes and practices. The attitude of the natural mind – one not instructed otherwise and renewed by God – is to do the opposite of what God is saying here. We think that the way to get ahead is to look out for ourselves and to cheat whenever necessary. It is natural to get angry when we do not get our way. We may even try to sabotage the success of anyone whom we regard to be outdoing us. Success is the goal, and some people are willing to do whatever it takes to succeed. But that is not God's formula for success. Are you willing to believe that God's ways are not only right but that they are what is best for you? Will you dare to trust God whom you cannot see? Will you commit to doing what God says in this psalm rather than relying on your own human understanding? Proverbs 3:5 & 6 is applicable here: "Trust in the LORD with all thine heart; and lean not unto thine own understanding. In all thy ways acknowledge him, and he shall direct thy paths" (KJV). Again, that takes faith, but without faith it is impossible to please God (Hebrews 11:6). We can either do things according to our own understanding, or we can do them according to God's revealed Word. Acting according to our own understanding displays a disbelief in God. We will suffer the natural consequences if we choose to trust our own instincts rather than God's law of cause and effect. If you are struggling with this, ask God to help you choose to obey His Word, even though you do not feel like doing so. Trust that He knows what is best.

What is David saying that God will do for the righteous (blameless, upright)?

1. They will dwell in the land and enjoy safe pasture (verse 3).

2. God will give them the desires of their hearts if they delight in Him (verse 4).

What does this mean? If we delight in Him, our desires will be in line with His. We approach the matter incorrectly if we seek to delight in Him merely to get whatever our hearts desire. Delighting in Him means to place a priority on our fellowship with Him – delighting in pleasing Him with our thoughts and conduct. It means to value what He values and to place as high a priority on eternal things as He does. He is not promising to give us the desires of our flesh. He wants to bless us in the spiritual realm while meeting our physical needs. Physical things are necessary as long as we live in this physical world, but they are only temporary. God wants to bless us with things that last – with eternal things.

3. He will make their righteous reward shine like the dawn, their vindication like the noonday sun (verse 6).

4. They will inherit the land if they hope in the Lord (verses 9 & 29).

5. They will inherit the land and enjoy peace and prosperity (verse 11).

6. God upholds the righteous (verse 17).

7. The blameless spend their days under the Lord's care, and their inheritance will endure forever (verse 18).

8. In times of disaster they will not wither; in days of famine they will enjoy plenty (verse 19).

9. God makes their steps firm if they delight in Him (verse 23).

10. God upholds them with His hand, and even if they stumble, they will not fall (verse 24).

11. God will not forsake them (verses 25 & 28).

12. God loves the just (verse 28).

13. God will not let their feet slip (verse 31).

14. God will not leave them in the power of the wicked or let them be condemned when brought to trial (verse 33).

15. God will exalt them to inherit the land; when the wicked are destroyed, they will see it (verse 34).

16. God will give a future to those who seek peace (verse 37).

17. God gives them salvation (verse 39).

18. God is their stronghold in times of trouble (verse 39).

19. God helps them and delivers them from the wicked and saves them (verse 40).

20. God is their refuge (verse 40).

Hopefully, we all understand the underlying message of both of these psalms: wickedness does not pay off in the long run, but righteousness does! Proverbs 10:25 confirms this: "When the tempest passes, the wicked is no more, but the righteous is established forever" (ESV).

Sometimes, depression is caused by faulty thinking. We can become depressed if our perceptions about life are not accurate. We can blow things out of proportion and become cast down if we perceive things inaccurately. This is one of Satan's strategies – to deceive us in our thinking so that we become depressed and ineffective. I think some of Asaph's observations about the wicked are correct; the wicked do seem to be able to prosper in their evil ways and live lives of ease. However, he was inaccurate when he thought that the wicked truly get away with their wickedness and that this kind of life pays off in the end. Of course, Asaph came to realize this after seeing things as God sees them.

Again, the solution to incorrect thinking is to start thinking correctly – to get educated about the truth. We can always look to God, who is consistently truthful to the fullest extent, to help us see life clearly

– as it truly is. God has given us the Scriptures so that we can understand these things.

God is telling us in these psalms to be focused on trusting Him and doing good rather than fretting, or being troubled, anxious, and envious about how well evil people are faring. Fretting over this is such a waste of precious time! Our attention should be upon our own pursuit of righteous living and not upon the prosperity of the wicked, confident that God sees the behavior of all people and will reward us all accordingly. The prosperity of the wicked is just an illusion. They are headed for calamity, but the righteous will reap good things when all is said and done. Again, the key is focus. Staying focused on the right things is a cure for discouragement, depression, and despair.

When our focus is on fretting over the wicked of this world seeming to enjoy lives of prosperity and ease while we may be suffering, not only do we lack joy, which can lead to depression; we also lose out on opportunities to do the good which pleases God and the good which will reap eternal rewards. Do not give Satan the opportunity to steal these things from you!

Chapter Twenty-Eight

The Study of Peter

"The Lord turned and looked straight at Peter. Then Peter remembered the word the Lord had spoken to him: 'Before the rooster crows today, you will disown me three times.' And he went outside and wept bitterly."
Luke 22:61 & 62 NIV

Have you ever felt totally defeated? Perhaps you failed a class at school, failed in your marriage, lost your job, lost your home, declared bankruptcy, mistreated your children, or made some serious sinful choices in the past. Maybe you even committed a crime and are or were in prison. There are many circumstances in life that can leave us feeling defeated. Some of these circumstances may not even be of our own doing.

Peter, a close follower of Jesus Christ and one of the twelve apostles, failed a number of times. And his failures were big ones! Many of his failures came from an earthly, natural, merely human mind; he was thinking on a temporal, physical level rather than a spiritual level. 1 Corinthians 2:14: "The natural person does not accept the things of the Spirit of God, for they are folly to him, and he is not able to understand them because they are spiritually discerned" (ESV). In time, of course, Peter came to learn about spiritual things, and his thinking and behavior changed.

What were some of Peter's failures?

1. Peter tried to argue with Jesus Christ when Jesus revealed to His disciples that He would suffer and die and would be raised to life on the third day. Peter thought that this should never happen to Jesus (Matthew 16:21-23). At that time Peter had apparently not yet come to understand that without Jesus dying a sacrificial death on the cross and rising from the dead, we would all still be dead in our sins and under condemnation by a holy, just God. The only reason Jesus left Heaven to come to Earth was to live a perfect life in fulfillment of God's moral law so that He could die in our place in payment for our sin.

2. Peter cut off the ear of the official who had come to arrest Jesus (John 18:1-11). Jesus rebuked Peter for this action. Jesus touched Malchus' ear and healed him.

3. Peter denied three times that he even knew Jesus. My guess is that he did this out of fear. If so, he allowed his feelings rather than truth to dictate his actions.

Luke 22:54-62:

> "Then seizing him [Jesus], they led him away and took him into the house of the high priest. Peter followed at a distance. And when some there had kindled a fire in the middle of the courtyard and had sat down together, Peter sat down with them. A servant girl saw him seated there in the firelight. She looked closely at him and said, 'This man was with him.' But he denied it. 'Woman, I don't know him,' he said. A little later someone else saw him and said, 'You also are one of them.' 'Man,

I am not!' Peter replied. About an hour later another asserted, 'Certainly this fellow was with him, for he is a Galilean.' Peter replied, 'Man, I don't know what you're talking about!' Just as he was speaking, the rooster crowed. The Lord turned and looked straight at Peter. Then Peter remembered the word the Lord had spoken to him: 'Before the rooster crows today, you will disown me three times.' And he went outside and wept bitterly" (NIV).

4. The Apostle Paul rebuked Peter face to face over an issue which was troubling the church in Antioch (Galatians 2:11-14). Due to the influence of some Jews from Judea (Judaizers) — false teachers who insisted that Gentiles must be circumcised and follow Jewish law in order to be considered righteous in God's eyes — Peter began to withdraw from associating with the Gentile believers in the church. These Gentile believers had not been circumcised, according to Mosaic Law, as the Jewish believers had been before coming to Christ. The Apostle Paul had clearly taught the correct doctrine of salvation through faith in Jesus Christ, apart from the law. The matter of whether Gentiles must be circumcised in order to be saved had already been settled at a council in Jerusalem years earlier (Acts15:7-11). Peter had agreed at the council that Gentiles did not need to be circumcised in order to be saved. Now, due to the false teaching of the Judaizers who infiltrated the church, Peter began to withdraw from fellowship with the Gentile believers. This caused some of the other Jewish believers to do the same. **The correct teaching of salvation through faith in Jesus Christ apart from the law was being threatened in the church in Galatia**. Paul had to step in and correct the Galatian church about this doctrine because they were being led astray by the false doctrine. Paul corrected Peter because Peter was to be blamed.

So, after such bitter defeat, did Peter give up and cease to live for Christ because of his disastrous failures? Did he allow his failures to set the direction of his life? Did he take his own life, thinking that all was lost?

No, Peter did none of these things. Despite Peter's failures, he went on to become a very dedicated Christian who accomplished much for the kingdom of God! These are some of the good, godly things for which Peter can be commended. (Some happened before and some happened after his failures cited above.)

1. Peter's confession that Jesus is the Christ forms the foundation of the church today (Matthew 16:13-19).

2. Jesus chose Peter as well as James and John to accompany Him to the mountain where Jesus was transfigured (Matthew 17:1-13). Though not really an accomplishment as such, it shows that Jesus valued Peter as one of His disciples.

3. Through God's power, Peter healed a crippled beggar (Acts 3:1-10).

4. He instructed other believers about various doctrines:

   a. that those speaking in tongues at Pentecost were not drunk but filled with the Holy Spirit (Acts 2:14-21).

   b. that God intends to save Gentiles as well as Jews and that He makes no distinction between them as far as salvation is concerned (Acts 10:27-48).

5. He gave a sermon that caused many to repent and turn to Christ (Act 2:22-41).

6. He laid his hands on believers in Samaria so that they received the Holy Spirit (Acts 8:9-25).

7. Through the inspiration of the Holy Spirit, he wrote the books of 1 and 2 Peter.

What about you? Do you allow failures to keep you defeated and sidelined, or do you move on and attempt to do great things for God? Do you shuffle through life feeling like a failure because of some defeat you experienced years earlier? Do your current defeats keep you from being all that God wants you to be? Do you feel that there is no use in trying hard to live for Christ?

I am reminded of the words of the Apostle Paul about not allowing the past to keep him from accomplishing something for Christ in the present:

> "...forgetting those things which are behind, and reaching forth unto those things which are before, I press toward the mark for the prize of the high calling of God in Christ Jesus" (Philippians 3:13 & 14 KJV).

Everyone experiences defeat at some point in life. If you are a child of God, because you have accepted the gift of salvation through the death, burial, and resurrection of Jesus Christ, then you **can** move on! Confess to God any sin you have committed in the process of your defeat, and know that He will gladly forgive your sin. Ask for His help to keep moving forward for His glory and for His kingdom, and trust that what happened in the past was under His control. Ask God to help you learn from the past. Is there something He wants to teach you? Learn from your past and move on, making the most of the opportunities He has given you today! **The key is to stay focused on what is ahead and not what is behind you. _Strain_ toward the goal to win the prize of being faithful to God's calling on your life.** Even if you are feeling totally overwhelmed by the amount and severity of your problems, God can help you move forward – one step at a time.

The following passage offers a very encouraging message from God to a group of people who had miserably failed. It is an excerpt from the letter that the prophet Jeremiah sent from Jerusalem to the "surviving elders among the exiles and to the priests, the prophets and all the other people King Nebuchadnezzar had carried into exile from Jerusalem to Babylon." They had been held in captivity by Nebuchadnezzar for seventy years because God was chastising them and teaching them lessons about Himself. Though they sinned greatly, they were still God's chosen people, and He had a plan and future for them.

Jeremiah 29:10 & 11:

"For thus says the LORD: When seventy years are completed for Babylon, I will visit you, and I will fulfill to you my promise and bring you back to this place. For I know the plans I have for you, declares the LORD, plans for welfare and not for evil, to give you a future and hope" (ESV).

God has a plan and future for you as well. Do not give up after you have been defeated! Get up and live your life for His glory, one step at a time. Don't minimize one little step; one step will set the foundation for other steps. Many little steps will add up to some visible, valuable progress!

Chapter Twenty-Nine

The Study of Paul

"So to keep me from becoming conceited because of the surpassing greatness of the revelations, a thorn was given me in the flesh, a messenger of Satan, to harass me, to keep me from becoming conceited. Three times I pleaded with the Lord about this, that it should leave me. But he said to me, 'My grace is sufficient for you, for my power is made perfect in weakness.' Therefore I will boast all the more gladly of my weaknesses, so that the power of Christ may rest on me."
2 Corinthians 12:7-9 ESV

Have you ever had an afflicting burden in your life that you asked God to remove? Maybe it was an illness or financial difficulties or an unpleasant job or some other difficult circumstance. You asked God to take it out of your life, but He has not done so – not yet anyway.

There could be a lot of reasons for this, but maybe it is because God wants this troublesome burden to remain in your life to serve some good purpose. I know! Nobody likes burdens! Ugh!

The Apostle Paul, who wrote many of the books in the New Testament, had a burden in his life that he asked God three times to remove. We are not really certain what this burden was; he called it "a thorn in my flesh, a messenger of Satan, to harass me." Some think it may have been poor eyesight since he was blinded by light on the road to Damascus where Christ spoke to him and he was converted (Acts 9:1-9). Whatever it was, he wanted it out of his life, and he appealed to God to take it away.

Paul tells us the reason God had given him this thorn in the flesh. In the first part of 2 Corinthians 12, he says that he was caught up to heaven, and he heard things that "cannot be told, which man may not utter." He experienced an extremely rare, privileged revelation that could cause him to become prideful.

God did not take away Paul's thorn in the flesh, even though he pleaded with the Lord three times to remove it. This must have been disappointing to Paul – at first anyway. Let's see how Paul reacted to this big disappointment.

2 Corinthians 12:7-10:

> "So to keep me from becoming conceited because of the surpassing greatness of the revelations, a thorn was given me in the flesh, a messenger of Satan, to harass me, to keep me from becoming conceited. Three times I pleaded with the Lord about this, that it should leave me. But he said to me, 'My grace is sufficient for you, for my power is made perfect in weakness.' Therefore I will boast all the more gladly of my weaknesses, so that the power of Christ may rest on me. For the sake of Christ, then, I am content with weaknesses, insults, hardships, persecutions, and calamities. For when I am weak, then I am strong" (2 Corinthians 12:7-10 ESV).

Paul accepted God's plan for his life. Though he pleaded with God three times to take away his "thorn in the flesh," God refused to do so. God could have easily taken away this thorn in the flesh, whatever it was. God is almighty and in control of all things! But God had bigger, better plans for Paul, and they involved these things:

- weaknesses
- insults
- hardships
- persecutions
- calamities

Really? How could Paul accept these things so readily? Was Paul crazy? How could he say that he delights in these things? Don't we despise these things and avoid them whenever possible? Paul tells us in verse 9 how he could rejoice in these things: "so that the power of Christ may rest on me." Paul explains that God's power is made perfect in the midst of weakness. God shines when He works through vessels that are weak!

The following is another passage explaining Paul's problems in ministry:

2 Corinthians 11:23-28:

> "I have worked much harder, been in prison more frequently, been flogged more severely, and been exposed to death again and again. Five times I received from the Jews the forty lashes minus one. Three times I was beaten with rods, once I was pelted with stones, three times I was shipwrecked, I spent a night and a day in the open sea, I have been constantly on the move. I have been in danger from rivers, in danger from bandits, in danger from my fellow Jews, in danger from Gentiles; in danger in the city, in danger in the country, in danger at sea; and in danger from false believers. I have labored and toiled and have often gone without sleep; I have known hunger and thirst

and have often gone without food; I have been cold and naked. Besides everything else, I face daily the pressure of my concern for all the churches" (NIV).

This is what Paul's ministry brought him:

- imprisonment
- floggings
- exposure to death
- beatings of thirty-nine lashes
- beatings with rods
- stoning
- shipwrecks
- inability to stay in one place very long
- danger from rivers
- danger from bandits
- danger from the Jews and from the Gentiles
- danger in the city
- danger in the country
- danger at sea
- danger from false brothers
- labor and toil
- sleeplessness
- hunger and thirst
- cold and nakedness
- pressure of his concern for all the churches

What a list! Just a few of these things would send some of us into a state of depression. But was Paul depressed about his hardships? It does not appear that he was. He kept right on doing what God had called him to do.

Another passage gives us more insight into Paul's perspective.

Marti Scott

2 Corinthians 4:

1 Therefore, since through God's mercy we have this ministry, we do not lose heart. **2** Rather, we have renounced secret and shameful ways; we do not use deception, nor do we distort the word of God. On the contrary, by setting forth the truth plainly we commend ourselves to everyone's conscience in the sight of God. **3** And even if our gospel is veiled, it is veiled to those who are perishing. **4** The god of this age has blinded the minds of unbelievers, so that they cannot see the light of the gospel that displays the glory of Christ, who is the image of God. **5** For what we preach is not ourselves, but Jesus Christ as Lord, and ourselves as your servants for Jesus' sake. **6** For God, who said, 'Let light shine out of darkness,' made his light shine in our hearts to give us the light of the knowledge of God's glory displayed in the face of Christ.

7 But we have this treasure in jars of clay to show that this all-surpassing power is from God and not from us. **8** We are hard pressed on every side, but not crushed; perplexed, but not in despair; **9** persecuted, but not abandoned; struck down, but not destroyed. **10** We always carry around in our body the death of Jesus, so that the life of Jesus may also be revealed in our body. **11** For we who are alive are always being given over to death for Jesus' sake, so that his life may also be revealed in our mortal body. **12** So then, death is at work in us, but life is at work in you.

13 It is written: 'I believed; therefore I have spoken.' Since we have that same spirit of faith, we also believe and therefore speak, **14** because we know that the one who raised the Lord Jesus from the dead will also raise us with Jesus and present us with you to himself. **15** All this is for your benefit, so that the grace that is reaching more and more people may cause thanksgiving to overflow to the glory of God.

16 Therefore we do not lose heart. Though outwardly we are wasting away, yet inwardly we are being renewed day by day. **17** For our light and momentary troubles are achieving for us an eternal glory that far outweighs them all. **18** So we fix our eyes not on what is seen, but on what is unseen, since what is seen is temporary, but what is unseen is eternal (NIV).

Observe what Paul says about the effect that these hardships had upon him:

hard pressed on every side	**but not**	crushed
perplexed	**but not**	in despair
persecuted	**but not**	abandoned
struck down	**but not**	destroyed
carries around in his body the death of Jesus	**so that**	the life of Jesus may also be revealed in his body
outwardly wasting away	**but**	inwardly being renewed day by day
his light and momentary troubles	**are achieving**	an eternal glory that far outweighs them all

Though he experienced many hardships, those things did not overwhelm or defeat or depress him. Nor did they immobilize him.

None of us is called to do what the Apostle Paul did. However, God does want to use every believer for ministry purposes, and sometimes He brings hardships into our lives to prepare us for those ministries. What is your reaction to the hardships that He brings into your life? Do you accept them as a means to display the power of God in your life, or do you gripe and complain about them? Or perhaps you withdraw and become despondent, overwhelmed by the weight of them. None of the hardships that Paul faced was pleasant. However, were the results of his ministry worth these hardships? Paul would say, "Yes! Absolutely!"

Why was Paul's ministry worth it despite the hardships? He called his hardships "light and momentary" (2 Corinthians 4:17). These light and momentary troubles were achieving something great for Paul – something that far outweighs his hardships, which compared to eternity, were "light and momentary." Eternal glory far outweighs these troubles which are, comparatively speaking, minor disturbances which last for such a short time. Paul chose to focus on the things of eternal value – the eternal glory which he would realize in full only after he finished, by God's grace, the battle here on Earth.

Besides this, Paul explains that the death of Jesus that he experienced was bringing about life to the Corinthian believers. Look at verse 12:

"So death is at work in us, but life in you" (NIV).

He could endure all the ministry troubles because what his labor was producing was worth it. To see these believers in Corinth grow in Christ because of his ministry to them was worth the "death of Jesus" that he carried around in his body.

Please catch the big picture of Paul's life. Though God refused to take away the torment of his thorn in the flesh, Paul went on to glory in that weakness so that God's power could be manifested in his life. He did not quit the ministry because of this and other hardships. He was faithful to his calling, all the way to his death. He accomplished what God had called him to do – all despite weaknesses, insults, hardships, persecutions, difficulties. Instead of getting depressed about his hardships, he was thankful for them, and he went on to do great things for God's kingdom by the power that God provided.

Paul had a choice, and so does each of us. We can either let go of our plans, hopes, and desires when God does not allow us to fulfill them, or we can try to cling to them and resent God's plan for our lives. We can submit ourselves to God's **better** plan for us, or we can allow disappointments to overwhelm us and rule our lives, which could cause us to accomplish little of eternal value. The truth is, often we would prefer to have comfort and ease rather than God's grace providing the wherewithal to endure the problems. But that is settling for a life of mediocrity. More is accomplished for God's glory by allowing His grace to sustain us than living a life of comfort and ease.

It takes faith to believe that God's plans are better than what we seek for ourselves. Humanly speaking, we all want comfort and pleasure; we attempt to avoid discomfort and want. It takes faith in a loving, all-knowing God to praise Him for the difficulties He allows in our lives and to believe that He has our best interest in mind. It takes an eternal perspective to follow Jesus Christ through the trials, knowing that having a righteous attitude and behavior now will pay off later in this life and in the life to come.

Will you choose to trust in God's wisdom in the midst of your difficulties?

1 Peter 4:19:

"Therefore let those who suffer according to God's will entrust their souls to a faithful Creator while doing good" (ESV).

Chapter Thirty

The Study of Jesus

"'Father, if you are willing, remove this cup from me. Nevertheless, not my will, but yours, be done.' And there appeared to him an angel from heaven, strengthening him. And being in agony he prayed more earnestly; and his sweat became like great drops of blood falling to the ground."
Luke 22:42-44 ESV

"Jesus said to them, 'My food is to do the will of him who sent me and to accomplish his work.'"
John 4:34 ESV

Throughout these lessons on how to biblically handle disappointment, discouragement, defeat, depression and despair, we have studied some bad examples – people who sometimes did not handle their emotions in a biblical way, and we have studied some good examples of people who did handle their emotions in a biblical way. In this lesson, we are going to study the very best example of all – the Lord Jesus Christ, whose thoughts, speech, and behavior always conformed to the righteous standards of God the Father. Therefore, He always handled His emotions biblically, and is the perfect example!

There is a lot we can learn from Jesus Christ who was "a man of sorrows, and familiar with suffering" (Isaiah 53:3 NIV). Just because Jesus was fully God does not mean that He never experienced sorrow, grief, anguish, suffering, and other negative emotions. He was also fully man, and He experienced the same emotions we do, except without sinning (Hebrews 4:15).

Let's look at some passages that show us how Jesus handled His emotions and how He was able to do so.

John 4:1-38:

1 Now Jesus learned that the Pharisees had heard that he was gaining and baptizing more disciples than John— **2** although in fact it was not Jesus who baptized, but his disciples. **3** So he left Judea and went back once more to Galilee.

4 Now he had to go through Samaria. **5** So he came to a town in Samaria called Sychar, near the plot of ground Jacob had given to his son Joseph. **6** Jacob's well was there, and Jesus, tired as he was from the journey, sat down by the well. It was about noon.

7 When a Samaritan woman came to draw water, Jesus said to her, "Will you give me a drink?" **8** (His disciples had gone into the town to buy food.)

9 The Samaritan woman said to him, "You are a Jew and I am a Samaritan woman. How can you ask me for a drink?" (For Jews do not associate with Samaritans.)

10 Jesus answered her, "If you knew the gift of God and who it is that asks you for a drink, you would have asked him and he would have given you living water."

11 "Sir," the woman said, "you have nothing to draw with and the well is deep. Where can you get this living water? **12** Are you greater than our father Jacob, who gave us the well and drank from it himself, as did also his sons and his livestock?"

13 Jesus answered, "Everyone who drinks this water will be thirsty again, **14** but whoever drinks the water I give them will never thirst. Indeed, the water I give them will become in them a spring of water welling up to eternal life."

15 The woman said to him, "Sir, give me this water so that I won't get thirsty and have to keep coming here to draw water."

16 He told her, "Go, call your husband and come back."

17 "I have no husband," she replied.

Jesus said to her, "You are right when you say you have no husband. **18** The fact is, you have had five husbands, and the man you now have is not your husband. What you have just said is quite true."

19 "Sir," the woman said, "I can see that you are a prophet. **20** Our ancestors worshiped on this mountain, but you Jews claim that the place where we must worship is in Jerusalem."

21 "Woman," Jesus replied, "believe me, a time is coming when you will worship the Father neither on this mountain nor in Jerusalem. **22** You Samaritans worship what you do not know; we worship what we do know, for salvation is from the Jews. **23** Yet a time is coming and has now come when the true worshipers will worship the Father in the Spirit and in truth, for they are the kind of worshipers the Father seeks. **24** God is spirit, and his worshipers must worship in the Spirit and in truth."

25 The woman said, "I know that Messiah" (called Christ) "is coming. When he comes, he will explain everything to us."

26 Then Jesus declared, "I, the one speaking to you—I am he.

27 Just then his disciples returned and were surprised to find him talking with a woman. But no one asked, "What do you want?" or "Why are you talking with her?"

28 Then, leaving her water jar, the woman went back to the town and said to the people, **29** "Come, see a man who told me everything I ever did. Could this be the Messiah?" **30** They came out of the town and made their way toward him.

31 Meanwhile his disciples urged him, "Rabbi, eat something."

32 But he said to them, "I have food to eat that you know nothing about."

33 Then his disciples said to each other, "Could someone have brought him food?"

34 "My food," said Jesus, "is to do the will of him who sent me and to finish his work. **35** Don't you have a saying, 'It's still four months until harvest'? I tell you, open your eyes and look at the fields! They are ripe for harvest. **36** Even now the one who reaps draws a wage and harvests a crop for eternal life, so that the sower and the reaper may be glad together. **37** Thus the saying 'One sows and another reaps' is true. **38** I sent you to reap what you have not worked for. Others have done the hard work, and you have reaped the benefits of their labor" (NIV).

Philippians 2:1-11:

1 Therefore if you have any encouragement from being united with Christ, if any comfort from his love, if any common sharing in the Spirit, if any tenderness and compassion, 2 then make my joy complete by being like-minded, having the same love, being one in spirit and of one mind. **3 Do nothing out of selfish ambition or vain conceit. Rather, in humility value others above yourselves, 4 not looking to your own interests but each of you to the interests of the others.**

> 5 In your relationships with one another,
>   have the same mindset as Christ Jesus:
> 6 Who, being in very nature God,
>   did not consider equality with God something
>   to be used to his own advantage;
> 7 rather, he made himself nothing
>   by taking the very nature of a servant,
>   being made in human likeness.
> 8 And being found in appearance as a man,
>   **he humbled himself**
>   **by becoming obedient to death—**
>   **even death on a cross** [emphasis added]!
> 9 Therefore God exalted him to the highest place
>   and gave him the name that is above every name,
> 10 that at the name of Jesus every knee should bow,
>   in heaven and on earth and under the earth,
> 11 and every tongue acknowledge that Jesus Christ is Lord,
>   to the glory of God the Father (NIV).

John 17:1-26:

1 After Jesus said this, he looked toward heaven and prayed:

"Father, the hour has come. Glorify your Son, that your Son may glorify you. 2 For you granted him authority over all people that he might give eternal life to all those you have given him. **3** Now this is eternal life: that they know you, the only true God, and Jesus Christ, whom you have sent. **4** I have brought you glory on earth by finishing the work you gave me to do. **5** And now, Father, glorify me in your presence with the glory I had with you before the world began.

6 "I have revealed you to those whom you gave me out of the world. They were yours; you gave them to me and they have obeyed your word. **7** Now they know that everything you have given me comes from you. **8** For I gave them the words you gave me and they accepted them. They knew with certainty that I came from you, and they believed that you sent me. **9** I pray for them. I am not praying for the world, but for those you have given me, for they are yours. **10** All I have is yours, and all you have is mine. And glory has come to me through them. **11** I will remain in the world no longer, but they are still in the world, and I am coming to you. Holy Father, protect them by the power of your name, the name you gave me, so that they may be one as we are one. **12** While I was with them, I protected them and kept them safe by that name you gave me. None has been lost except the one doomed to destruction so that Scripture would be fulfilled.

13 "I am coming to you now, but I say these things while I am still in the world, so that they may have the full measure of my joy within them. **14** I have given them your word and the world has hated them, for they are not of the world any more than I am of the world. **15** My prayer is not that you take them out of the world but that you protect them from the evil one. **16** They are not of the world, even as I am not of it. **17** Sanctify them by the truth; your word is truth. **18** As you sent me into the world, I have sent them into the world. **19** For them I sanctify myself, that they too may be truly sanctified.

20 "My prayer is not for them alone. I pray also for those who will believe in me through their message, **21** that all of them may be one,

Father, just as you are in me and I am in you. May they also be in us so that the world may believe that you have sent me. **22** I have given them the glory that you gave me, that they may be one as we are one— **23** I in them and you in me—so that they may be brought to complete unity. Then the world will know that you sent me and have loved them even as you have loved me.

24 "Father, I want those you have given me to be with me where I am, and to see my glory, the glory you have given me because you loved me before the creation of the world.

25 "Righteous Father, though the world does not know you, I know you, and they know that you have sent me. **26** I have made you known to them, and will continue to make you known in order that the love you have for me may be in them and that I myself may be in them" (NIV).

Luke 22:39-46:

39 Jesus went out as usual to the Mount of Olives, and his disciples followed him. **40** On reaching the place, he said to them, "Pray that you will not fall into temptation." **41** He withdrew about a stone's throw beyond them, knelt down and prayed, **42** "Father, if you are willing, take this cup from me; yet not my will, but yours be done." **43** An angel from heaven appeared to him and strengthened him. **44** And being in anguish, he prayed more earnestly, and his sweat was like drops of blood falling to the ground.

45 When he rose from prayer and went back to the disciples, he found them asleep, exhausted from sorrow. **46** "Why are you sleeping?" he asked them. "Get up and pray so that you will not fall into temptation" (NIV).

1 Peter 2:21-25:

21 To this [suffering] you were called, because Christ suffered for you, leaving you an example, that you should follow in his steps.

22 "He committed no sin, and no deceit was found in his mouth."

23 When they hurled their insults at him, he did not retaliate; when he suffered, he made no threats. Instead, he entrusted himself to him who judges justly. **24** "He himself bore our sins" in his body on the cross, so that we might die to sins and live for righteousness; "by his wounds you have been healed." **25** For "you were like sheep going astray," but now you have returned to the Shepherd and Overseer of your souls (NIV).

From these passages, we see how Jesus handled His emotions and how He was able to do so.

1. Jesus knew who He was and where He was going. He had a strong, unwavering sense of purpose. That purpose was the driving force of His life. His purpose was "to do the will of him who sent me and to finish his work" (John 4:34 & 6:38 NIV). It was always His goal to completely fulfill the purpose for which He came to Earth – to do the will of God the Father who had sent Him here. In the passage in John 4, Jesus tells His disciples that what drives Him is "food" that they know nothing about. Jesus is not talking about physical food. Of course, Jesus got hungry because He was human. Jesus needed to eat food and drink water, just like every other human being. But there was something more important and more urgent than physical things that drove Him. He was dealing with the soul of a woman who needed eternal life, and at that moment, that was His focus. He could eat physical food later. While the disciples were thinking about physical food, Jesus was thinking about spiritual food.

I sometimes watch a program about morbidly obese people who are on a quest to lose weight. Many of them say that the only thing that brings them joy is food and that food has been the only reliable thing in their lives. Eating also brings love, comfort, peace, and safety, they think. Many confess that while they are eating breakfast, they are already savoring the thought of lunch. Some have said that what they live for is food. Most reveal that they suffered neglect, abuse, or rejection as children or teens. They have been looking to food their whole lives as a salve to calm their aching hearts. It is obvious that many of these people worship food; it is their idol!

We can all sympathize greatly with people who have been abused and mistreated to this extent. Most people condemn such abuse. The stories of the people featured on this program are truly heartbreaking. However, using food to comfort one's soul, as these morbidly obese people have done, only causes more injury. Most of them are so overweight that they cannot work. Some can hardly get out of bed and are dependent upon others for their daily needs. Further, they have done so much damage to their bodies that, barring immediate treatment and drastic changes in lifestyle, most of them will die soon, according to their doctors.

Excessive use of alcohol and the use of recreational drugs are other means some people use to numb the pain they are feeling. It is sobering (no pun intended) to think about how many people have wasted precious time and money on mere temporary solutions that have ultimately cost them their health, their freedom, their families, and sometimes their own lives.

Though most of us can understand the temptation to overeat or to drink too much, it is not a workable solution to the heartbreak of abuse. Jeremiah 2:13 says, "My people have committed two sins: They have forsaken me, the spring of living water, and have dug their own cisterns, broken cisterns that cannot hold water" (NIV). Most people look to many things other than God to satisfy their soul's needs. Instead of going to the source of living water, figuratively speaking, they dig their own wells that cannot hold the living water that they crave and need. How foolish and needless! And we can witness the futility of that pursuit.

I do not say this to bring shame to anyone, for we have all looked to hollow things rather than God to satisfy our needs at some point in our lives. Rather, I say this to invite you to partake of the free, abundant, reliable, unshakable, satisfying, never-ending source for all your needs – God Himself! Why settle for a temporary solution to your needs which will ultimately turn into a life-threatening curse?

Jesus' "food" was to please God the Father and do His will. Is that your food? Or do you seek to satisfy the longings of your soul with things that can never truly satisfy? Again, food is necessary as long as we live in these earthly bodies, and God has provided a variety of delicious food for us to enjoy. But overindulging in food or anything else to satisfy the longings of one's heart instead of going to God, the Giver of all good things, is idolatry and a futile pursuit.

Jesus took time to set aside His own physical needs to meet the needs of others. Have you ever been so caught up in the temporal, physical world that you were blind to the physical and spiritual needs of people around you? Maybe you were in a situation where opportunities for ministering to other people were right in front of you, but you did not realize it because you were so focused on your own world. I am sure that I have missed opportunities for ministry because I was scurrying around, focusing on my tasks for that day and was not looking for people to whom I could exemplify the qualities of Jesus Christ. Am I willing, if necessary, to postpone or skip a meal in order to take time to minister to the spiritual needs of another human being? Am I willing to set aside my plans and go out of my way to help someone else?

In preparing for a short-term mission trip to Brasilia, Brazil, the mission organization encouraged our team to look at the whole trip as an opportunity to minister to people, not just at our final destination. For example, in the airport waiting for our flight, there may be people with whom we could share the Gospel. Enroute to our assignment destination, an English camp where Brazilian teens could learn English and hear the Gospel, we would also be around people on the airplane and in the taxi. We were encouraged to look for opportunities there to minister to people. Wherever we are, there may be opportunities around us to share the love of Christ.

2. Jesus was fully surrendered to the will of the Father. Jesus knew He was going to die a horrible death on the cross and that His Father would forsake Him because all the sins of the world would be laid upon Him. He agonized over going to the cross and asked God the Father to spare Him from that experience. Still, at the end of the prayer, Jesus told His Father that regardless of these feelings about going to the cross, He wanted to do the will of the Father, not His own will.

Are you fully surrendered to God's will, or does your own agenda supersede His? Do you fulfill God's will only when it is convenient, or are you willing to sacrifice your own will to fulfill His?

3. Despite His sufferings, Jesus did not feel sorry for Himself. Rather than being absorbed in self-pity, He focused on the needs of others. In the John 17 passage, Jesus prayed that believers would be protected from the evil one (Satan), that they would have joy, and that God the Father would sanctify them (set apart as holy). He prayed that unbelievers would come to believe. Jesus prayed this prayer just hours before He would be arrested and crucified. Being God, He knew that His time

was short. He knew the exact hour when He would die a ghastly death by crucifixion and worse, that He would experience separation from the Father. But He stayed focused on accomplishing His purpose and looked forward to the glory that would follow His accomplishment of that purpose.

Are you willing to focus on the needs of others, even though you are hurting? Do you help others while you are waiting on God to meet your own needs, or do you withhold helping others until you feel that your needs are fully met?

4. Jesus cared deeply about the spiritual welfare of people. This is evident in the way He dealt with the Samaritan woman recorded in John 4 and His prayer for believers recorded in John 17. He was not wrapped up in His own deity, though He knew very well that He was fully God. Even though He was God, He humbled Himself and became a servant so that guilty sinners might be saved from the wrath of God and be adopted into His family.

We see His humility and servanthood (Philippians 2:7 & 8) in many ways as He dealt with the Samaritan woman. Talking with a woman in itself was a cultural taboo. Women at that time were not nearly as valued by society in general as they are today. In fact, they were far less valued than men. Secondly, His approach was unconventional because this woman was not a full Jew. Anyone not fully Jewish – either a halfbreed or a Gentile – was considered by Jews to be a dog, an unclean, loathsome animal. Lastly, the Samaritan woman was morally loose; she had had several husbands, and the man she was with at that time was not even her husband. Here was Jesus, every bit as righteous as God the Father, talking with a deeply sinful non-Jewish woman. He took time to talk to her and offer her what she needed – a relationship with Himself. Jesus said that He came not to seek righteous people (there are none, only people who are self-righteous) but sick sinners (all of us!). It is the sick who need the doctor, and Jesus is the doctor (Matthew 9:12; Mark 2:17; Luke 5:31)!

Jesus did not allow the woman's spiritual ignorance and darkness to deter Him from ministering to her. Rather than allowing spiritual snobbery to cause Him to be repulsed by her, to be impatient with her, and to give up on her, He dealt with her needs. This is the ultimate example of selflessness!

Romans 15:2 & 3:

> "Let every one of us please his neighbor for his good to edification. For even Christ pleased not himself…" (KJV).

5. Jesus turned to God the Father in prayer when He was in agony. Can you imagine His anguish, knowing that the cross awaited Him? Jesus knew that God would soon pour out His wrath upon Him because He became sin for us. In Matthew 26:38, Jesus describes His agony this way: "My soul is overwhelmed with sorrow to the point of death" (NIV). Remember, Jesus was fully human! He asked God the Father to spare Him from "this cup" (death on the cross).

Do you take advantage of the wonderful privilege you have as a child of God to go directly to His heavenly throne room in prayer? Or do you instead allow your mind to be controlled by the fruitless and destructive habits of worry, fear, and anxiety? Do you realize that God invites you to come to Him with your worries, fears, and anxieties? 1 Peter 5:7 says, "Cast all your anxiety on him because he cares for you" (NIV). Do you believe that God is bigger than your problems? Do you believe that He has all the power to solve your problems? He is worthy of your trust! He is our Great High Priest who understands and sympathizes with what you are going through. "For we do not have a high priest who is unable to sympathize with our weaknesses, but we have one who has been tempted in every way, just as we are – yet was without sin. Let us then approach the throne of grace with confidence, so that we may receive mercy and find grace to help us in our time of need" (Hebrews 4:15 & 16 NIV).

6. Jesus entrusted Himself to God the Father, confident that He would judge justly. When Jesus suffered at the hands of sinful men, He trusted His Father. 1 Peter 2:23 says, "When they hurled their insults at him, he did not retaliate; when he suffered, he made no threats. Instead, he entrusted himself to him who judges justly" (NIV). Do you trust God to take care of your mistreatment by others, or do you lash out at those who insult you?

7. Jesus endured what He despised (the shame of the cross) in anticipation of future reward. Hebrews 12:2 & 3 says, "Looking unto Jesus the author and finisher of our faith; who for the joy that was set before him endured the cross, despising the shame, and is set down at the right hand of the throne of God. For consider him that endured such contradiction of sinners against himself, lest ye be wearied and faint in your minds" (KJV). Jesus looked forward to the future joy of having completed His task, of accomplishing the greatest goal in history, and giving the greatest gift ever given. He knew that His suffering on the cross would bring Him the future reward of the joy of this great accomplishment, and so He was willing to endure the shame of the cross for a short time. This is not to minimize the shame and agony of the cross. Though relatively speaking, it was a short time in human history, Jesus' grief and agony were very real and extremely painful. He suffered more than any other human being. But He endured that grief, agony, and pain for the joy of pleasing His Father by rescuing guilty sinners from their just, eternal punishment!

In this life, we too will suffer, though of course not to the extent that Jesus did. Look to Jesus, the One who began your faith and will complete your faith (Philippians 1:6). Look at what He endured to procure your salvation – to redeem you from sin, death, the wrath of God, and the devil! Think about the opposition that He endured from sinful human beings. He was opposed by the religious leaders of His day who constantly tried to trip Him up and to kill Him. He was betrayed by one of His disciples. Another disciple denied even knowing Jesus. He was sneered at and mocked by soldiers as He hung naked on the cross for His claims to be God. Look to Jesus for the strength and resolve to endure hardship. What can give us the incentive to endure? The promise of future reward caused Jesus to endure the hardship, and it can help us to do the same. What reward? Our reward is Christ Himself – fellowship with God! Our reward is living a life that is truly worth living – one that glorifies God – the Creator and Sustainer of the universe! Our reward is also one that is even further in the future, when we see Christ face to face and we hear Him say, "Well done, good and faithful servant!" (Matthew 25:21 NIV).

Look to Jesus Christ for the perfect example of how to biblically handle disappointment, discouragement, defeat, depression, and despair. While none of us will ever fully be like Christ until we see Him face to face, we should all be striving to be more like Him every day. He is the Christian's role model. When we focus on meeting the needs of others, as Jesus did, we accomplish something great. When we accomplish the purposes for which God has created us rather than living selfishly, we find that feelings of disappointment, discouragement, defeat, depression, and despair are replaced with feelings of fulfillment, peace, and joy.

Chapter Thirty-One

The Study of Psalm 42 & 43

"Why art thou cast down, O my soul? And why art thou disquieted in me? Hope thou in God; for I shall yet praise him for the help of his countenance."
Psalm 42:5 KJV

If you have ever been depressed, you will be able to understand the cries of the psalmist in Psalms 42 and 43. Though translated in 1611 as what we know as the King James Version, I think you will be able to understand what he is saying. These psalms can teach us how to biblically handle depression.

Psalm 42:

1 As the hart [deer] panteth after the water brooks, so panteth my soul after thee, O God.

2 My soul thirsteth for God, for the living God: when shall I come and appear before God?

3 My tears have been my meat day and night, while they continually say unto me, Where is thy God?

4 When I remember these things, I pour out my soul in me: for I had gone with the multitude, I went with them to the house of God, with the voice of joy and praise, with a multitude that kept holyday.

5 Why art thou cast down, O my soul? and why art thou disquieted in me? hope thou in God: for I shall yet praise him for the help of his countenance [emphasis added].

6 O my God, my soul is cast down within me: therefore will I remember thee from the land of Jordan, and of the Hermonites, from the hill Mizar.

7 Deep calleth unto deep at the noise of thy waterspouts: all thy waves and thy billows are gone over me.

8 Yet the Lord will command his lovingkindness in the day time, and in the night his song shall be with me, and my prayer unto the God of my life.

9 I will say unto God my rock, Why hast thou forgotten me? why go I mourning because of the oppression of the enemy?

10 As with a sword in my bones, mine enemies reproach me; while they say daily unto me, Where is thy God?

11 Why art thou cast down, O my soul? and why art thou disquieted within me? hope thou in God: for I shall yet praise him, who is the health of my countenance, and my God [emphasis added] (KJV).

Psalm 43:

1 Judge me, O God, and plead my cause against an ungodly nation: O deliver me from the deceitful and unjust man.

2 For thou art the God of my strength: why dost thou cast me off? why go I mourning because of the oppression of the enemy?

3 O send out thy light and thy truth: let them lead me; let them bring me unto thy holy hill, and to thy tabernacles.

4 Then will I go unto the altar of God, unto God my exceeding joy: yea, upon the harp will I praise thee, O God my God.

5 Why art thou cast down, O my soul? and why art thou disquieted within me? hope in God: for I shall yet praise him, who is the health of my countenance, and my God [emphasis added] (KJV).

These two psalms are asking the same question: "Why is my soul depressed?"

They also have the same solution: "Hope in God and praise Him! He is my health!"

Regardless of my problems, my soul should not be cast down or depressed. Rather, I should hope in God and praise Him!

Chapter Thirty-Two

Truths about the True and Living God and the Christian Life

1. God sees everything. He sees me. He sees me in my distress and is able to help me. (Hagar, Ruth, Jonah) Genesis 16:7-13; Genesis 21:14-19; 2 Chronicles 16:9; Psalm 12:5; Psalm 10:13 & 14; Proverbs 15:3; Jonah 2:1-10; 1 Peter 3:12

2. God gives, and He sometimes takes away. Since He owns all things, He has the right to give and take away anything that He wants anytime He wants. (Job) Job 1:20 & 21; Job 41:11; 1 Samuel 2:7

3. God sometimes allows Satan to do things to me that He will ultimately use for my good and His glory. (Job) Romans 8:28

4. God is sovereign, which means that He rules over everything in the universe. (Job, Jeremiah) Psalm 103:19

> God is sovereign over the events of history. (Ruth, Esther, Jehoshaphat, Joseph) 2 Chronicles 36:22 & 23

> God rules over all the kingdoms of the nations. (Jehoshaphat) 2 Chronicles 20:5 & 6; Daniel 4:17; Psalm 47:8 says, "God reigns over the nations; God is seated on his holy throne" (NIV).

5. God is worthy to be praised, even if He takes everything away from me. (Job) Job 1:20 & 21; 1 Chronicles 16:7-36; Psalm 48:1; Psalm 150:2

6. God is just. (Job) Job 40:6-8; Deuteronomy 32:4; Psalm 111:7; Romans 3:5 & 6, 25 & 26

7. God has a reason for the trials that He allows into my life. He has a greater purpose in mind than I do for myself. Sometimes, He brings trials into my life to purify my faith, much like gold is purified by being put into the fire. (Job) "But he knows the way that I take; when he has tested me, I will come forth as gold" Job 23:10 (NIV).

8. God knows how to bring good from a bad situation. He can take any situation and turn it around. (Job, Ruth, Esther, Joseph). He can bring beauty from ashes (Isaiah 61:3) and restore the years that the locusts have eaten! (Joel 2:25)

9. Sometimes, God refuses my requests. It is not because He cannot grant me what I request or because He does not care about my feelings. It is because He has something better planned for me. (Paul) 2 Corinthians 12:7-10

10. Christ's strength is made perfect in my weakness. (Paul) 2 Corinthians 12:7-10

11. God's grace is sufficient for me. (Paul) 2 Corinthians 12:7-10

12. He is a God of redemption. He loves to redeem people and situations. He is our Kinsman Redeemer! (Ruth) Psalm 40:1-3; Ephesians 1:7-10

13. God orchestrates situations for my welfare and the welfare of others. (Ruth, Joseph) Romans 8:28

14. God knows how to provide for me, even when my circumstances are dire. (Hagar, Ruth, Esther, Nehemiah, Joseph) 1 Timothy 6:17; Philippians 4:19

15. God loves and wants to save Gentiles as well as Jews. (Hagar, Ruth, Jonah) Isaiah 42:6 & 7; Romans 3:22-24; Romans 1:16; Romans 11:13; Acts 20:21

16. Jesus, our Great High Priest, sympathizes with our weaknesses. Hebrews 4:14-16

17. Jesus was tempted in every way, just as we are – yet without sin. Hebrews 4:14-16

18. Jesus gives mercy and grace to help in time of need when true believers boldly approach the throne of grace with confidence. Hebrews 4:14-16

19. God has given us everything we need to live the Christian life as He calls us to live it. 2 Peter 1:3

20. God will not allow me to be tempted beyond what I can bear. He will always provide a way out so that I can stand up under it. 1 Corinthians 10:13

21. God forgives all my sins and heals all my diseases (spiritual, not necessarily physical). Psalm 103:3

22. God redeems my life from the pit. Psalm 103:4

23. God crowns me with love and compassion. Psalm 103:4

24. God satisfies my desires with good things so that my youth is renewed like the eagle's. Psalm 103:5

25. God works righteousness and justice for all the oppressed. Psalm 103:6

26. God made known His ways to Moses and the people of Israel. Psalm 103:7

27. God is compassionate and gracious. Psalm 103:8

28. God is slow to anger. Psalm 103:8

29. God is abounding in love. Psalm 103:8

30. God will not always accuse, nor will He harbor His anger forever. Psalm 103:9

31. God does not treat me as my sins deserve or repay me according to my iniquities. Psalm 103:10

32. God's love to those who fear Him is as high as the Heavens are above the Earth. Psalm 103:11

33. God has removed my transgressions from me as far away as the east is from the west. Psalm 103:12

34. God has compassion on those who fear Him just like a father has compassion on his children. Psalm 103:13

35. God remembers that I am formed from dust. Psalm 103:14

36. God's love is with those who fear Him from everlasting to everlasting, and His righteousness is with their children's children. Psalm 103:17

37. God has established His throne in Heaven, and His kingdom rules over all. God is sovereign over all things! Psalm 103:19

38. The Spirit of God can come upon me in power. (Saul, Jehoshaphat) 1 Samuel 11:1-13; 2 Chronicles 20:14

39. God puts one man in position of power and takes another man out of position of power. (Saul) Daniel 2:21; Romans 13:1

40. God expects obedience. (Saul, Jeremiah) Deuteronomy 13:4; John 14:23; 1 John 5:3; 2 John 6

41. God prohibits the practice of divination, sorcery, or witchcraft and prohibits the consulting of mediums, spirits, or the dead. (Saul) Exodus 22:18; Leviticus 19:26; Leviticus 20:6; Leviticus 20:27; Deuteronomy 18:9-12; 1 Samuel 15:22 & 23; 2 Kings 17:16 & 17; 2 Chronicles 33:6; Galatians 5:19 & 20

42. God is aware of the wickedness of nations, and He calls those nations to repentance, or His judgment will fall upon them. (Jonah, Jeremiah) Jonah 1:1 & 2; Jonah 3:1-4; Jeremiah 18:5-10; Joel 3:12

43. God cares about wicked people and wants them to repent and turn to Him. (Jonah) Jonah 4:10 & 11; Luke 13:3; Acts 17:30; Acts 20:21

44. God may sometimes call me to do something that is unpleasant and distasteful to me, but He will give me the grace to do it. (Jonah, Jeremiah, Esther, Nehemiah, Paul) 2 Corinthians 9:8; 2 Corinthians 12:9

45. God controls the weather and nature, and He sometimes uses these to accomplish His purpose. (Jonah) Jonah 1:4,17; 2:10, 4:6, Matthew 8:23-27

46. God is not limited by any circumstance. He can use any means He wants to accomplish His will. (Hagar, Joseph, Jonah, Elijah, Esther) Genesis 18:14; Jeremiah 32:17

47. God hears and responds to my cry for help. (Jonah) Jonah 2:1 & 2; Psalm 118:5; Jeremiah 33:3

48. God is patient with me when I try to run away from what He wants me to do. (Jonah) Jonah 3:1 & 2

49. God sees what I do in secret. (David) Matthew 6:4; 2 Samuel 12:12; Mark 4:22; Luke 8:17

50. God confronts sin. (David) 2 Samuel 12:1-14

51. God's favor is upon those who obey Him. (David) Psalm 5:12; Proverbs 12:2; Isaiah 66:2

52. God searches my heart. (David) Psalm 139:1

53. God knows when I sit and when I rise. His eyes are always observing everything I do. (David) Psalm 139:2 & 3

54. God knows what I am going to say even before I say it. (David) Psalm 139:4

55. God is all around me and has laid His hand upon me. (David) Psalm 139:5

56. God is everywhere; therefore, I cannot really flee from His presence! (Jonah, David) Psalm 139:7-10

57. To God, darkness is as light. (David) Psalm 139:12

58. God knit me together in my mother's womb, and I am fearfully and wonderfully made. (David, Jeremiah) Psalm 139:13-16; Jeremiah 1:5

59. God knew all about everything in my life even before I was born. (David) Psalm 139:16

60. God's thoughts about me are precious and numerous. (David) Psalm 139:17 & 18

61. God can accomplish His will for me through the actions of people who seek my harm. (Esther, Nehemiah, Joseph) Genesis 50:19 & 20

62. God can give me favor in the eyes of others. (Joseph) Genesis 39:1-4 (Esther) Esther 2:9; 5:1 & 2 (Nehemiah) Nehemiah 2:1-8; 2:18

63. God works behind the scenes and through the actions of others to accomplish His will. (Joseph) Genesis 50:20 & 21

64. When God says something is going to happen, it happens. He knows all things and is always truthful. (Jeremiah, Joseph) Numbers 23:19; 2 Samuel 22:31; 1 Kings 8:20 & 24; John 17:17

65. God's plans for me are better than my own plans for myself. (Joseph) Isaiah 55:9

66. God has given us the Bible, and all Scripture is useful for teaching, rebuking, correcting, and training in righteousness so that we will be thoroughly equipped for every good work. 2 Timothy 3:16

67. He has given us His Word to teach us so that through endurance and the encouragement of the Scriptures, we might have hope. God wants us to have hope! Romans 15:4

68. God is active and is actively working in our universe. He is responsive. (Elijah) Psalm 135:6

69. God is powerful. (Elijah, Jeremiah) 1 Kings 18:36-38; Psalm 24:8; Jeremiah 32:18

70. God knows about my physical needs and knows how to meet those needs. (Hagar, Ruth, Elijah) Philippians 4:19

71. God rescues the life of the needy. (Hagar, Ruth, Jeremiah, Esther, Jehoshaphat, Joseph) Psalm 12:5; Psalm 113:7

72. God made the Heavens and Earth by His great power and outstretched arm. (Jeremiah) Jeremiah 32:17

73. Nothing is too hard for God. (Jeremiah) Jeremiah 32:17

74. God shows love to thousands but brings the punishment for the parents' sins into the laps of their children after them. (Jeremiah) Jeremiah 32:18

75. God's purposes are great and His deeds are mighty. (Jeremiah) Jeremiah 32:19

76. God's eyes observe all the ways of men. (Jeremiah) Jeremiah 32:19

77. God rewards everyone according to his conduct and to what his deeds deserve. (Jeremiah) Jeremiah 32:19

78. God performed miraculous signs and wonders in Egypt and continued them in Jeremiah's day. (Jeremiah) Jeremiah 32:20

79. God brought His people Israel out of Egypt with signs and wonders, by a mighty hand and an outstretched arm and with great terror. (Jeremiah) Jeremiah 32:21

80. God gave His people Israel the land of Canaan – a land flowing with milk and honey. (Jeremiah) Jeremiah 32:22

81. Jesus is the pioneer (author) and perfecter (finisher) of our faith. (Jeremiah) Hebrews 12:2 & 3

82. God is long suffering, and patient, compassionate, gracious, and forgiving. (Jonah, Jeremiah) Exodus 34:6; Numbers 14:18; Psalm 86:15; Nehemiah 9:30 & 31; Romans 2:4; Romans 9:22

83. God will eventually deal with the wicked. Psalm 73, Psalm 37

84. God holds me by my right hand. Psalm 73:23

85. God guides me with His counsel. Psalm 73:24

86. God will take me into glory. Psalm 73:24

87. God is the strength of my heart. Psalm 73:26

88. God is my portion forever. Psalm 73:26

89. God is my refuge. Psalm 73:28

90. God laughs at the wicked because He knows that their day is coming. Psalm 37:13

91. God upholds with His hand anyone who delights in Him. Psalm 37:17 & 24

92. God makes firm the steps of anyone who delights in Him. Psalm 37:23

93. God will never forsake the righteous. Psalm 37:25 & 28

94. God will bless the children of the righteous. Psalm 37:25

95. God loves the just. Psalm 37:28

96. God will not forsake His faithful ones. Psalm 37:28

97. God will give me the desires of my heart as I delight in Him. Psalm 37:4

98. God will make my righteousness shine like the dawn. Psalm 37:6

99. God will help and deliver the righteous from the wicked. Psalm 37:33 & 40

100. God is my stronghold in the time of trouble. Psalm 37:39

101. God disciplines those He loves. Hebrews 12:6

102. God punishes (or "scourgeth") everyone He accepts as a son. Hebrews 12:6

103. God disciplines us for our good, so that we may share in His holiness. Hebrews 12:10

104. God has poured out His love into my heart by the Holy Spirit whom He has given me. Romans 5:5

105. God is the Father of compassion and the God of all comfort who comforts us in all our troubles so that we can comfort those in any

trouble with the comfort we ourselves have received from God. 2 Corinthians 1:3 & 4

106. God has protected His chosen people, the Jews, from extinction. (Hagar, Esther, Nehemiah) Exodus 3:7-10; Esther 9:1-5

107. Just as God placed Esther in her position at a particular time in history to accomplish a particular purpose, God has placed each of us at this time and in this place in history for some purpose. (Esther) Esther 4:14

108. God keeps His covenant of love with those who love Him and obey His commands. (Nehemiah) Nehemiah 1:5

109. God promised Moses, "If you [Israel] are unfaithful, I will scatter you among the peoples, but if you return to me and keep my commandments and do them, though your outcasts are in the uttermost parts of heaven, from there I will gather them and bring them to the place that I have chosen, to make my name dwell there." (Nehemiah) Nehemiah 1:8 & 9 ESV

110. Power and might are in God's hand, and no one can withstand Him. (Jehoshaphat) 2 Chronicles 20:6

111. God drove out the inhabitants of the land before His people Israel and gave it forever to the descendants of Abraham. (Jehoshaphat) 2 Chronicles 20:7

112. The battle is not mine but God's! (Jehoshaphat) 2 Chronicles 20:15

113. God's love endures forever. (Jehoshaphat) 2 Chronicles 20:21

114. Though God does not need our praise, He is deserving of our praise. (Jehoshaphat) Psalm 86:8-10; Revelation 4:11; Psalm 96:4; 2 Samuel 22:4

115. God is forgiving and good. (Jehoshaphat) Psalm 86:5; Ephesians 1:7; 1 John 1:9; Psalm 34:8; Psalm 107:8

116. God abounds in love to all who call upon Him. (Jehoshaphat) Psalm 86:5

117. Among the gods, there is none like the true and living God, and no deeds can compare with His. (Jehoshaphat) Psalm 86:8

118. God has delivered me from the depths of the grave. (Jehoshaphat) Psalm 86:13

119. God is compassionate and gracious. (Jehoshaphat) Psalm 86:15; Psalm 103:8

120. God is slow to anger. (Jehoshaphat) Psalm 86:15; Psalm 103:8

121. God is abounding in love and faithfulness. (Jehoshaphat) Exodus 34:6; Psalm 86:15; Psalm 103:8

122. God can help me and comfort me. (Jehoshaphat) Psalm 46:1; Psalm 86:17; 2 Corinthians 1:3-4

123. God's peace will guard my heart and mind when I present my requests to God with thanksgiving. (Jehoshaphat) Philippians 4:6 & 7

124. Jesus prayed that "this cup" (His death on the cross) would pass from Him, but He submitted to the will of God the Father. Luke 22:42

125. Jesus committed no sin and no deceit was found in His mouth. 1 Peter 2:22

126. Jesus did not retaliate or make threats when His enemies hurled their insults at Him. 1 Peter 2:23

127. Jesus entrusted Himself to God the Father who judges justly. 1 Peter 2:23

128. Jesus bore our sins in His body. 1 Peter 2:24

129. It was always Jesus' goal to completely fulfill the purpose for which He came to Earth and to do the will of God the Father. John 4:34

130. Jesus was fully surrendered to God's will. Matthew 26:39

131. Jesus did not feel sorry for Himself but focused instead on the needs of others. Matthew 20:28

132. Jesus cared about the spiritual welfare of people. John 4:10; John 17:12, 15, & 24; Matthew 9:11-13; Luke 22:31 & 32

133. Jesus was not wrapped up in His own deity, which He fully acknowledged, but humbled Himself and became a servant. Philippians 2:6-8

134. Jesus turned to God the Father in prayer when He was in agony. Luke 22:39-44

Chapter Thirty-Three

Final Conclusion

Though it may seem like taking your own life is the answer to your problems, it is not. Nowhere in Scripture is it condoned. Indeed, there are several reasons why suicide is unbiblical. God has better remedies for dealing with your problems than taking your own life.

We all face challenges and trials of many kinds in life. For believers, trials are carefully and strategically designed by a loving, all-knowing God to change us into the image of Jesus Christ, our model.

We live in trying and uncertain times. Food shortages, high cost of living, loss of our assets, civil unrest, crime, disease, government corruption, the erosion of our rights, moral degradation and hatred for God, and war are constant threats. It is imperative that we focus on Christ and our inheritance in Him rather than the chaos around us. In the last days, perilous times will come, according to 2 Timothy 3:1. But we are told to not fear, that God is with us – even to the end of time (Matthew 28:20). Our hearts should not be troubled and burdened with worry and fear.

One bad choice affects other things: overeating because you are frustrated about your weight can lead to spending too much money on food and then not being able to pay rent, so you get evicted. Then you feel depressed so you eat too much in an effort to comfort yourself. The vicious cycle continues. You have to stop the cycle by accomplishing one good thing, which can help you accomplish something else. Take one step at a time. Many of those who are battling morbid obesity say that they never thought their lives would turn out like this – with carrying so much bodily weight that they can hardly get around. But seemingly, little choices done day after day and year after year add up and take their toll. This is true not just with weight control; it applies to every area of our lives.

Instead of lying around being depressed, accomplish a small, worthwhile goal which will make you happy, such as cleaning out a drawer, working on a craft project, writing a thank you note, watering your plants, going for a walk, or making a meal for someone in need. The good feeling that will result from that one accomplishment will probably spur you on to complete another task. And that is a lot healthier than eating a bag of chips and a gallon of ice cream!

Abuse can cause depression which can cause overeating which can cause weight gain which can cause depression. Stop focusing on the abuse. Stop feeling sorry for yourself. Work on a project. Accomplish some worthwhile goals every day.

Engage in the spiritual disciplines: reading the Bible, praying, going to church and fellowshipping with other believers; serving in the church and elsewhere; witnessing to others; giving to the church and others.

God sees you in your distress and cares about your welfare. He can use any means He desires to help you. He is in control of all things.

God gives, and He takes away, and He has the right to do so because He created and owns all things. We should bless His name when disaster strikes as readily as when things are going well for us. Any other attitude displays an idol in our hearts. Do not cling to anything tightly but God and His Word.

Satan must get God's permission to bring disaster into our lives.

God is a God of redemption. He can redeem a hopeless situation and turn it into a joyful one.

God can completely turn around any situation. He is in control of all things. Many things are happening behind the scenes of which we are not aware. God is always working for our good, and Satan is always working for our destruction. There is a real, spiritual battle constantly going on between good and evil. Ultimately, however, God is in control! God can even take the evil that others do to us and turn it into good.

Confess your sins frequently to God. Do not allow sinful attitudes to fester in your heart. It will only lead to depression and more sin.

Have nothing to do with witchcraft or other forbidden forms of the demonic spirit world.

Guard your heart and your eyes from adultery. This sin could ruin your life.

Do not cover your sin, but confess and forsake it.

Refuse to repay evil for evil. Instead, return good for evil.

Fear God and keep His commandments, for this is the whole duty of man.

Take care of your physical body as much as possible. Poor physical health can contribute to depression.

Trust God in times of danger. He can take care of you. Take all necessary precautions to protect yourself and others, but trust in His promises instead of despairing.

Do not try to run away from God. God is everywhere, so you cannot really run away from His presence. Submit your will and your way to Him and do what He has called you to do. He will give you all that you need to follow His lead.

Take great joy in fulfilling God's call on your life, and do not let adverse circumstances keep you from that joy.

God has placed you at this time in history for a reason. What social issues is He calling you to address and/or help to solve?

Keep working to fulfill the purpose for which God has created you, using your spiritual gifts, natural talents, and resources with which He has blessed you. Let nothing distract you from it. Refuse to even dialogue with those who are trying to derail you.

Let praises to God continually flow in your mind and from your mouth. Praising Him can ward off the enemy and depression.

God tells us that He designs trials to refine Christians and make them more and more like Jesus Christ. Cooperate with God in your trials. Consider trials as positive things, not negative.

Do not be envious of evil people. Their prosperity is temporary and their destruction is looming.

After you have failed spiritually or otherwise, do not wallow in defeat. It will only lead to depression. Put your past behind you and start today to do the right things. God is not finished with you because you have failed spiritually. He can still use you if you confess your sin and resolve to do the right things. He will always joyfully receive your genuine repentance. Get going doing what God wants you to do today!

Do not let anything keep you from running the race and winning the prize!

Accept God's will for your life. Submit your will and your ways to God. Remember that God's grace is sufficient for anything and everything He allows you to encounter in your life. Think about future joys in knowing that you have done God's will.

Pray to God in times of great anxiety.

Hope in God and praise Him.

If you have not repented of your sins and placed your faith in Jesus Christ, who alone can forgive sin, do that today! Without that relationship with Christ, you are an enemy of God, and His wrath is being stored up against you. One day, you will face that wrath, if you are not in Christ. Trusting in Christ alone takes away the wrath and condemnation of God.

If you have placed your faith in Jesus Christ to save you from the penalty of your sin, find a Bible-believing church and start attending. Let the pastor there know that you are a new believer and need the help of the church to begin to grow as a Christian and to live a life that honors God. That is one of the God-given roles of the church!

Of course, Satan is going to do everything he can to keep the message of this book from getting into the hands of the people who need to hear it. He will also do what he can to try to discredit the message of this book.

As I am close to finishing the writing of the book, my belief in the principles I have exposited herein are being put to the test. I have experienced disappointment and discouragement. As I think about Job, Jeremiah, and Elijah, I can sympathize more deeply with their struggles with these emotions. They were trying hard to live righteously, but they had negative feelings that could have defeated them had they not confronted these feelings in a way that pleases God.

Some of the ways Satan is tempting me (or maybe it is my flesh), is to prompt me to feel sorry for myself, to grow resentful and bitter, to become despondent and grumpy, and to withhold good from others because of my self-absorption. Satan wants me to be discouraged because I don't see a solution to my circumstances. I have had to battle with my emotions and resolve that I will respond to the disappointing circumstances biblically – in a way that honors God and denies my flesh. I recall the verse that says that when we sow to the flesh, we reap corruption (Galatians 6:8). Further, if I respond in any way unbiblically, I give honor to Satan, and I dishonor the Lover of my soul – the One who gave His life for mine. Despite my desire to ease the hurt, I resolve to handle my emotions biblically. I am being called to "put my money where my mouth is," so to speak. I remember my admonition that others can see God's power working in us as we handle our trials biblically. Okay, this is a time to authenticate my point by reacting biblically to my circumstances.

One of the ways I am striving to do this is by reaching out to others in their need. The people I have in mind do not need my financial assistance. Some need a phone call to let them know somebody is thinking about them and cares about their difficulties. Others need a word of encouragement. I can sit around and wallow in self-pity, or I can get up and do something for others, even if I do not feel like doing so. Neither choice is likely to change my immediate discouraging circumstances. However, in choosing to do the godly thing – the biblical thing – I honor God and can rely on His help. I know that I will be glad when I see Jesus face to face that I made this choice. That day is coming, and then I will have no more trials and suffering. Now is the time to live so as to make an impact for eternity. As I write this in 2022, I am already feeling better. Maybe the verse that says, "Submit yourselves, then, to God. Resist the devil, and he will flee from you" (James 4:7 NIV) is coming to life right before my spiritual eyes.

Two weeks after writing about the above trial, I was confronted with an even more pesky situation. I had cracked a tooth as I was eating some homemade chicken noodle soup. I guess I failed to remove one of the little chicken bones. The dentist had to do a root canal and insert a crown in place of the cracked tooth to resolve the situation. My dental work was done the day after the 2022 midterm elections, which ended in some disappointing results, so I was already feeling a little disheartened.

I sat in the dental chair for nearly three hours getting the work done, which included five x-rays. The dentist and his assistant would work on the tooth for several minutes and then exit the room to do some prep work, leaving me in the chair with only my own thoughts and some piped-in music to occupy me. Determined not to resort to the flesh in any way, I was praising God in my mind, thinking of applicable Bible verses, singing "Doxology" to myself in spite of the pain in my mouth, the inconvenience of spending three hours of my day doing something so unpleasant (though necessary), and trying to resign myself to paying the $3,535 bill that was waiting for me! I was working hard on my attitude, praising God and acknowledging that my money was really His money, and the tooth was part of the body that belongs to Him. "I choose to praise You right now, Jesus! You do everything well. You never make a mistake. I know I can trust You. Everything I have is Yours. You will always take care of me."

Then the piped-in music started to mock me and lure me away from concentrating on Jesus! John Lennon's song, "Imagine"[17] vied for my attention. I struggled to stay focused on the Lord and His provisions, but the humanistic words to that song demanded my attention, distracting me from my praise. In an effort to stop hearing the music, I covered my ears with my hands. The song is so distasteful to me because it carries the opposite message from the one I wanted and needed to hear. It is antithetical to the truths of Scripture.

As a musician, I admire the dreamy, soothing musical composition of this song. However, I reject its misleading message. Not only does the song propose that the world would be a better place if we did away with religion and thoughts of Heaven and Hell; it also seems to promote Socialism. We would all be able to live at peace with one another, the song implies, if we had no possessions and we did not divide ourselves into various countries. These are disturbing, unbiblical ideas.

John Lennon was murdered nearly forty-three years ago, just nine years after he wrote the song. Of course, his shooting was a wicked act. No one has the right to take the life of someone else like that. It is grievous that we live in a world where hate dwells in the hearts of some of our fellow human beings, and that hate compels them to harm others. I suppose that Lennon wrote his song in part due to remorse over man's inhumanity to man. He just posited some unworkable, ungodly solutions to that problem.

He now knows that there is indeed a Heaven and a Hell. I wonder how many people have been deceived over the years by others who mock the reality of Heaven and Hell. What a regrettable, unprofitable legacy! I choose to build a different legacy – one on God's side.

---

[17] John Lennon (1971). The song belongs to Ascot Sound. It is in the public domain in the United States.

Satan was taunting me as I sat waiting in the dental chair striving to focus on the goodness of God.

However, I continue to choose to praise God, despite my circumstances. I stand with Job, with Habakkuk, with Shadrach, Meshach, and Abednego in saying that even if I lose everything, I will go down praising God. I will live my life to glorify Him, thereby being loyal to the sovereign Lord of the universe – the One who loves my soul and gave His life to save me. May He forever be praised!

Acknowledgements

Several people helped me to get this book ready to be published. I am indebted to their generosity.

Joan Hendee, a long-time faithful friend and retired teacher, did some editing for me. Joan was in one of my Sunday school classes where I taught my lessons on how to biblically handle disappointment, discouragement, defeat, depression, and despair.

My cousin, Carrol Roark, edited the long Scripture passages. Carrol recently lost her husband and had been asking God to direct her how to use her newfound time. When I realized that Carrol was looking for projects of eternal value, I knew she was right for the job. Her response to my request for help was, "I am so blessed to be part of this project that will have such eternal consequences. May God grant you every resource you need to complete this important work." She has certainly been one of the resources that God provided!

My daughter, Rachel Barsch, helped me with computer support.

My son, Stephen Scott, and one of my granddaughters, Audrey Barsch, helped me edit some Scripture passages.

Lynnie Klingler, my sister, tracked down some information I needed to cite a reference.

One of my former pastors, Dr. Wesley Rowe, encouraged me to write this book. He also edited the manuscript on matters of theology and doctrine.

The photo on the book cover, my desk, was taken by Jodi Bullinger.

Throughout our relationship, my husband, Jeff, has encouraged me to pursue my gifts and talents inside and outside of the church. He has supported all of my endeavors. Without his consistent financial and emotional support throughout our marriage, I probably would not have been able to write this book.

Many people prayed for me as I worked through the challenging requirements to get this book ready for production. I thank specifically the prayer chain of my home church, Milan Baptist, for their faithful prayer support.

What a blessing to have such encouraging people support me!

Printed in the USA
CPSIA information can be obtained
at www.ICGtesting.com
LVHW091313161123
763810LV00092B/590